THE GREAT TRAVELLING ADVENTURE

Christopher Portway

 The Oxford Illustrated Press

© Christopher Portway
Printed in Great Britain by J.H.Haynes & Co Limited
ISBN 0 946609 06 3
The Oxford Illustrated Press, Sparkford, Yeovil, Somerset, England
Distributed in North America by Interbook Inc.,
14895 E. 14th Street, Suite 370, San Leandro, CA 94577 USA

British Library Cataloguing in Publication Data

Portway, Christopher
  The great travelling adventure
  1. Voyages and travels — 1951-
  I. Title
  910.4   G465

ISBN 0-946609-06-3

Contents

Acknowledgement

The author wishes to thank Richard Matthews, Polytechnic of Central London Tana River Expedition 1976, for permission to use his photographs of the expedition.

Introduction

My favourite method of travel will, I think, always be walking. It was my original intention to write a book to be called *The Great Walking Adventure*, chronicling my wanderings about the world on foot, but, upon assembling my experiences of travel over sixty years of a lifetime I discovered that undiluted walking covered but a fraction of them. Travel with a horse, a camel, a mule, a bicycle; journeying by train, bus, lorry, raft, dinghy, elephant, covered wagon, dog-sledge, car, felucca, steamer and more opened up the subject considerably and put extra colour into the realm of travel and travel writing.

Being a tidy-minded person I then attempted to arrange the order of chapters into journeys made using a particular mode of vehicle. This has worked for the first two, covering a phantom highway in Canada's North-West Territories (walking), and hacking in America's Badlands (horseriding) and also for a third (chapter six) where I take a train ride in India's Rajasthan, but thereafter I discerned that my further journeyings became muddled with a mass of vehicles and methods of conveyance. So I turned the theme to one of geographical environments. Thus chapter three covers a multitude of 4-legged, 4-wheeled and floating conveyances that carried me around the Saharan lands. Chapter four features the same line of presentation but with mountains as the connecting link, though here I have stretched a point and taken ranges as far apart as the Atlas and the Himalayas. The point is stretched still further in chapter five in which I chronicle my journeys — mainly by car and bus — along famed highways in Asia and North America. And if the trains got short measure in chapter six then I make up for it in chapter seven where I narrate an experience of clandestine travel taken from the desperate days of World War Two.

1

And so to chapter eight which details a host of methods — few to be recommended if you prefer a peaceful life — of moving along or alongside an East African river under the theme-heading of expeditionary travel. It is the longest chapter by far, perhaps because the three months I was on it were the most fruitful and momentous of all my journeyings.

My main problem arising from writing this book is that of choosing which travelling adventures to include and which to leave out. In my years I have ridden elephants in Thailand jungles, driven Landrovers around North Yemen, gone dog-sledging in Greenland, tried camping on glaciers in Iceland, crewed tall ships amongst the Canaries, ridden horses in Inner Mongolia, climbed mountains in Macedonia and Ecuador, been imprisoned in Uganda, driven trains in Jordan, sampled parasailing in Wales, flown co-pilot in Alaska, been arrested in Russia, crawled over Iron Curtain mine-fields, hitch-hiked in Colombia, cycled in Albania and more. But these were incidents, not adventures, though it is hard to differentiate since one man's incident can be another's adventure. So I made my criterion the degree of satisfaction gained, and my memory — plus a few notes — released each adventure accordingly and insomuch as it fitted into the framework of my self-imposed themes of travel.

I am often being asked *why* I am such a travel fanatic and it is a very difficult question to answer. I know I'm not the only person born with this wanderlust; many have it to a greater or lesser degree and few indeed are those who positively detest it. Witness the great holiday high season exodus when those that can get away to pastures new do so with a vengeance — even if many are basically in search of no more than warm seas and a tanning sun. However an increasing number of us are becoming curious about our fellow *homo-sapiens* about the globe; particularly in the more inaccessible, remote or politically 'awkward' corners of it. Newspapers and television are responsible for both the pros and the cons of this interest. The more discerning tourist or traveller wants to see with his and her own eyes a territory 'in the news' even though the media is all too often tending to dismiss such territory in the eyes of the less curious as beyond the pale. A regime, however hateful, does not reflect the populace who have to live under it. Nor do the politics of a nation affect the beauty, character and way of life of a country.

2

I find an easier answer to the supplementary question put to me: why do I like travelling so *uncomfortably?* My wife says I'm a masochist but this is not entirely the case. To me, the most interesting portions of this earth are so often those where life is primitive and to see it requires a certain degree of ruggedness of existence and movement. Likewise to feel how a country ticks it is necessary to live in approximately similar conditions as do the inhabitants. I remember my first visit to India more than twelve years ago when I spent some weeks existing in a manner as do the vast majority of Indians. This meant sleeping on railway station platforms, eating from curry stalls in the more humble end of town, living in accommodations that can only be described as doss houses and travelling lowest class on horrifically overcrowded trains. I returned home with my ribs sticking through my skin and considerable relief but the ordeal taught me more about India than have all my many subsequent and more tourist-orientated visits put together. And there you have what to me is a vital *raison d'être* of world travel.

It is a strange addiction, this travel lust and it is made stranger still for those travellers who have seen or experienced the very worst the world can fling at them. Mishap or disaster never turns them off travel; on the contrary it only increases the fanaticism. So what is it, this magic, that demands so much from its devotees? Surely it must spring from more than simple curiosity. At worst it is boredom, at best a restless searching, however brief, for a personal truth. We take so much for granted here in our comfortable, secure little island and grumble mightily when the slightest ruffle disturbs the tranquility. At such times it can put such seemingly important matters into their proper perspective, reducing them to trivia when one can switch to a memory of some distant land where people find contentment with far far less worldly goods and 'necessities' than we accumulate around us. Humility and the ability to feel humble is an emotion all too rare in our society.

The Great Travelling Adventure has no aspirations to be a guide or 'how to do it' book. Adventuring and exploring are personal matters and cannot be taught like algebra. Some of the sections are written in a slightly instructional vein, however, and contain more facts than a welter of purple prose: the sections on trekking in the Himalayas and driving the Alaska Highway for instance. I

3

am so often questioned about both propositions that I thought some practicalities and figures amongst the descriptive material might be helpful.

And also for the benefit of those readers who may feel inclined to follow my example or footsteps I have, where relevant, added a short appendix listing guide or text books, firms, and methods that could provide a basis for doing so.

My dictionary defines 'adventure' as 'a chance', 'a remarkable incidence', 'a risk', 'an exciting experience', 'the spirit of enterprise'. 'Travel' it expounds as, 'to move along a course', 'to go with impetus'. Put all these aspirations together, raise the will to do something about them and you hold the key to the elixir of a full and satisfying life.

1

Pear Brown Betty on the Canol Road

TREKKING A GHOST HIGHWAY IN CANADA'S NORTHWEST TERRITORY

Walking, they say, is good for the soul. It is, assuredly, the best way of getting acquainted with a country or the countryside. A walker is in touch with the land; not insulated from it by glass or perspex. He or she trudges the landscape, sees it slowly unfold and will come to understand something of its rhythm, its harshness or softness of texture, its sense of space. Walking is a human's natural pace, a normal speed of progress, a tempo giving time to think, to reflect and cogitate upon life in general and the passing world. On a less euphoric note, walking is also a cheap method of transportation.

Not every walker might feel bound to follow the crazed but inspired footsteps of explorer Sebastian Snow (whose observations on the subject these are though they match my own), tripping the light fantastic lengthways up the coast of South and Central America to very nearly walk himself to death. But such accomplishments as his can light a flame of determination in a traveller's heart.

They do in mine, though in comparison to his mighty efforts my walks, hikes and treks about the world are but modest affairs. I have trekked considerable portions of it but cannot, hand on heart, say I obtained more satisfaction out of stumbling endlessly across remote and dramatic territory than I did from simple trail-finding hikes in homely Britain. However, for sheer adventure I shall never forget the trudges I made in the Andes of South America and the desolate Northwest Territories of Canada where the elements conspire to bring a walker to his knees; even his death.

When I came to write this initial chapter I pondered long upon the choice of hike. A week's saunter I once made, free of any encumbrance upon my shoulders, along the delicious 115-

kilometre King Ludwig's Way in Germany's Bavaria, I remember for the contentment it offered. I was alone but the exquisite countryside and villages through which the route led offered adequate companionship supplemented by raucous nights in the friendliest of *gasthäuser*. A small group of walkers I led along the 210-kilometre Robert Louis Stevenson Trail in the French Cevenne was another pedestrian highlight in my life. We chose to follow the master's footsteps — minus donkey — on the centenary of his death spending our nights in the same villages; even the same lodgings as he. Again the magic environment lightened my footsteps if not my rucksack. I also recollect with a certain degree of pleasure a somewhat more arduous trek I made in company with half a dozen others amongst the wild Pindus Mountains of northern Greece, staying in the simplest tavernas of the primitive villages of Epirus. But, in the end, I selected the Canadian marathon simply on account of its quality of high adventure and ingredient of having taken place in a part of the world seldom visited by man. Also, perhaps, for the gut feeling of *accomplishment* it offered in reward.

It was in spring 1981 that I was invited to northern Canada to take part in a reconnaissance of a route across the Mackenzie Mountains linking the remote oil-bearing township of Norman Wells on the great Mackenzie river to the state of Yukon. Here I was to join up with three others to traverse the lonely, rugged miles of this forgotten artery with the object of ascertaining whether any sections of it were suitable for the running of small group trekking forays on a commercial basis.

The assignment intrigued me. It had that ring of the pioneering spirit about it and I'd had enough of following well-trodden, if idyllic, footpaths. Perhaps the way would not be *entirely* devoid of the tracks of man however for once it had been a road, an old (though not quite old enough to qualify as historic) highway driven through the wilderness. But now it was dead or dying and only its decaying bones would offer a banister.

The water was perceptibly rising. A bright-tinted stone clear of the stream an hour ago, was now submerged. The island upon which we were standing was shrinking fast; there was no doubt about it. The previous night we had waded to the elongated neck of land with the water level no higher than our thighs. Today this backwater had become impassable. The main stream made even more of a formidable obstacle and was frightening to behold. The Twitya river is no placid brook at the best of times and now it was swollen and angry from days of rain channelled into it from the mountains.

Though midnight when we had pitched the tents on the sodden island there had been no darkness. But the June sun was lost behind heavy drapes of surly clouds vomitting cascades of rain. We slept uneasily as each of us pondered our situation. How were we going to negotiate the Twitya together with our heavy rucksacks? Previous rivers along the route had been fordable affairs even though the bitter cold water and strong currents made the task risky and unpleasant. The Twitya, however, was in a different category. To swim it, fighting a vicious current that would all too soon sweep one helpless to the rapids below the site of the old road bridge, was out of the question, and anyway what of our baggage? No, the river would have to be crossed by raft. There were trees on the island; young saplings too fresh for raft-building and others that lay beached and waterlogged among the flotsam all around. Only some of these were suitable but, here another problem had arisen. Amongst our combined stores and provisions we could locate only one small axe and a saw blade. The saw frame itself had been lost. Calculations produced the sum of twenty-six trees, topped and tailed, as a minimum requirement for a raft capable of carrying the four of us and our loads. On the credit side we could raise two dozen six-inch nails and plenty of cord while one of our number possessed knowledge of raft construction. The odds against us reaching safety were uncomfortably high but what was the alternative? We had arrived at the point of no return on our journey, our retreat was cut off and our refuge was reducing by the hour.

We lay nursing our thoughts, hearing the rain beating on the canvas; aware that our refuge might be submerged before we could leave it. David, our leader, was the most worried, the yoke of decision-making on his shoulders. An Englishman, residing in the Yukon town of Dawson City, this project had been his idea. A fellow-citizen but of Canadian birth was Byrun, a fractious character but extremely knowledgeable when it came to survival in the outback. The youngest member of the quartet was Reinhard from Germany; grotesquely fit and never displaying the slightest sign of exhaustion following the most gruelling exertion. I was the oldest and weakest, a walker but no backpacker and my concern at our predicament must have been equal to David's — though I fear it was mostly concern for my own skin.

Across the Twitya the opposite bank was another world, an unattainable world flaunting our onward path, a broken banister of a ghost road leading yet another hundred miles to salvation...

The Canol Road; a thin red line on the empty map of northwest Canada that winds from Johnson's Crossing, some thirty-five miles north of Yukon's Teslin astride the Alaska Highway, to the Northwest Territories border. A summer-only route, north Canadians know it as a wilderness road running 300 tortuous miles into the Mackenzie Mountains to MacMillan Pass, with a lead-zinc mine and an airstrip as its terminus. The road's history is known only by a generation of older Canadians who will remember the circumstances of its construction over forty years ago when, during World War Two, the United States Army undertook the building of a pipeline from Norman Wells on the broad Mackenzie river to Yukon's capital, Whitehorse. The object was to supply fuel to Alaska and the military traffic en route from the United States at a time when its far northern state and, more particularly, the Aleutian Islands, were under threat from a Japanese enemy. The project was a fiasco from the start and the price tag of $134,000,000 a fruitless waste that was eventually to undermine the credibility of the United States War Department. Additional to the pipeline was its servicing road but, with the subsequent receding of the threat, very little oil was ever to find its way into the storage tanks of Whitehorse. The pipeline and its road were quietly abandoned.

With renewed oil and gas exploration in recent years being carried out at Norman Wells and the remoter regions of the Northwest Territories, the spectre of a further pipeline following the course of the old has arisen; the present-day fear of energy shortage compares ominously with the 1942 invasion threat. But though technology has changed, the savage environment of the Mackenzie Mountains remains constant and has had to be taken into account. Thus the lessons learnt by American engineers have been given serious appraisal by the new generation of, this time, Canadian pipeline builders.

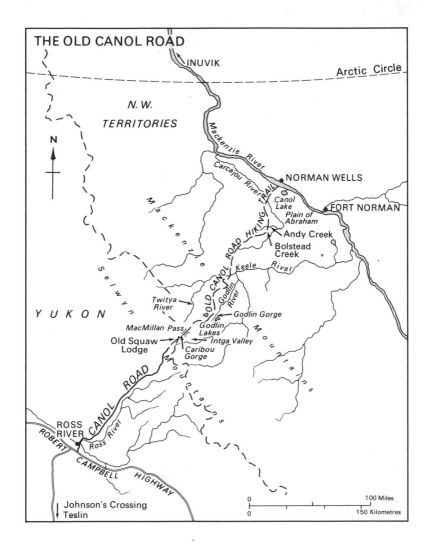

THE OLD CANOL ROAD

INUVIK

Arctic Circle

N.W. TERRITORIES

N

Mackenzie River

Carcajou River

NORMAN WELLS

Canol Lake

FORT NORMAN

Plain of Abraham

Andy Creek

Bolstead Creek

OLD CANOL ROAD HIKING TRAIL

Keele River

Mackenzie

Selwyn

Twitya River

Godlin River

Godlin Gorge

YUKON

MacMillan Pass

Godlin Lakes

Intga Valley

Old Squaw Lodge

Caribou Gorge

Mountains

CANOL ROAD

Mountains

ROSS RIVER

Ross River

ROBERT

CAMPBELL HIGHWAY

Johnson's Crossing
Teslin

0   100 Miles
0   150 Kilometres

All this, of course, is for the specialists and those who guide the destinies of the regions in which we live. However, for all Canadians the idea of a possible repeat of history and the recollection of a road to nowhere are surely of more than passing interest to those who live north of the sixtieth parallel. The Canol Road may not have the allure and romance of the other, Northwest-Territories-bound, Dempster Highway, but a rekindled thirst for

9

knowledge of the forgotten road may indeed have arisen. Anyone with a sturdy vehicle can drive to Mac Pass (as it is called) to satisfy this curiosity but the Canol Road does not end there. The route continues as the Old Canol Road Hiking Trail through the multiple barrier of the Mackenzie Mountains for another two hundred and forty desolate yet inspiring miles to Norman Wells bearing, along the way, the mouldering relics of an army's passing.

Although some maps cautiously label the route the 'Old Canol Road Hiking Trail' let me warn anyone considering following it that this is an understatement supreme. Rivers have washed away the bridges, landslides have obliterated the road, and rainstorms, cold winds and grizzly bears make the going arduous and dangerous in the extreme. We thought we knew the score and guessed the path would be hard and hazardous, the elements hostile and the terrain relentless, but none of us was prepared for the physical adversities that nature was accumulating along the way.

This then was the path I had set myself to walk carrying sixty pounds of victuals and vital equipment upon my back and in the company of three companions I had never met.

Two weeks previously I had driven the Alaska Highway, but the walking challenge arises following accomplishment of the rebuilt sections of the Canol Road. This is divided into two sections: that from the Alaska Highway to Ross River (139 miles) is referred to as the South Canol Road; the other from Ross River to the Northwest Territories border (160 miles) as the North Canol Road. Thereafter you are on the phantom Hiking Trail.

David's plan was to undertake the walking of it in reverse — starting at Norman Wells and so travelling back to MacMillan Pass and the Northwest Territories border. To reach our starting point we first had to drive the 451-mile Dempster Highway to remote Inuvik and from there fly to Norman Wells out in the great void of the vast million-and-a-quarter square-mile state. That bridge-less rivers would have to be crossed was a factor we had taken into account but only one, wider, deeper and bigger than the rest, offered the slightest stirrings of concern amongst us as we unpacked our provisions and gear from the vehicle at Inuvik.

10

Inuvik is the second town of the Northwest Territories by virtue of the fact that, with Yellowknife the capital, it is the only other town in the state. Even so, Inuvik's population today is not much over three thousand souls. The place has to be seen to be believed. It consists of rows of brightly-painted buildings standing on stilts, of a church shaped like a monstrous igloo, of bloated metal conduits running in and out of houses and all over town. Yet Inuvik is one of the most scientifically-planned places in Canada; it is a government-created community designed to overcome the frightful building problems caused by an unstable ground surface and the bitter cold of a long dark winter.

The piles on which the buildings of Inuvik stand ensure stability. They are driven through the muskeg overlay into the gravel stratum twenty feet down and there frozen solidly into the gravel. The buildings sit on the piles several feet above ground level, this to prevent their interior heat from melting the ground surface and turning it into a mucky sludge. And since underground pipes cannot be laid in permafrost, all utilities, including steam heat, running water, and sewage disposal, are carried through these metal tunnels.

I must admit to finding Inuvik a most depressing town. The only way in and out, besides by an unreliable air service, is via the daunting miles of the tyre-lacerating, oft-blocked Dempster Highway which was how the four of us had reached it. A sensation of being entirely cut off from even the vestiges of civilisation assailed me. Here the phrase 'dead end' has literal meaning.

We spent a restless night under canvas in the town's campsite, a notorious meeting place of Inuvik's criminal fraternity, and next day thankfully flew to Norman Wells.

Norman Wells is more a community than a township, by which I mean that everyone who lives in the expanded collection of dwellings is employed, directly or indirectly, by the oil companies who are the only reason for its existence. Though even more remote than Inuvik and not connected by road to anywhere, I found it a cheerful spot. Again every house was brightly, even garishly, painted as if in defiance of the staggering loneliness of its situation but the populace was an everchanging one; their main topic of conversation being what they were going to do when they returned home on leave or expiry of their contract. In Inuvik the people *lived* there; chained to desolation by fate.

Those of Norman Wells were paid considerable sums to exist and work in the outback for a limited period, serving out their sentence based in a house that wasn't home.

I had never flown in a seaplane (or floatplane as they call them in North America) but I enjoyed the short flight, hopping across the mighty Mackenzie river, by which Norman Wells stands, to the Canol Lake, hardly more than an overgrown pond, to where we put down. The sides were of soft mud which meant a damp and slimy landing as, one by one with our rucksacks and accoutrements, we jumped from the aircraft's float to what we fondly hoped would be *terra firma*. Up to our knees in clinging black slime we watched the floatplane heave itself into the air and disappear. We were alone — and rarely have I felt so excruciatingly alone.

The old road lay some miles west of the lake and, shouldering our loads, we staggered across the marshy scrub — a combination of tufts of thicket grass and bog — towards it intent upon raising our first camp astride the artery. Besides our bulging rucksacks, festooned with cooking implements, we carried coils of rope, a .303 rifle, fishing gear, an axe and a radio-transmitter. Straightaway the notion arose in me that I had bitten off more than I could chew as my load turned the act of walking into a drunken slouch.

The Trail, when we came to it, was plain to see, a track, not yet overgrown to extinction, etched into the landscape by tree saplings and alder growth seemingly addicted to its stony surface. As if to emphasize its presence the flattened remains of some wooden buildings lay untidily about a stream crossing. Much of the timber was rotten but made convenient fuel for a fire we soon had blazing merrily, and on this we heated up our first day's supper. Above, the faint outlines of the road could be discerned gently spiralling up hill on its way back to its starting point at the Mackenzie river, just outside our range of vision. The stream offered fresh cool and safe drinking water, a forerunner of many such sources that precluded any concern over supply of at least *one* vital commodity. We slept, that first night, adequately but uneasily, David, Reinhard and I occupying the main tent with Byron, at his own request, in a small bivouac. 'I've been known to snore', he told us. It was the understatement of the year.

Next morning, breakfasted on porridge, toast and marmalade with a choice of tea, coffee or cocoa, we set off down the road, a great deal more confident than we had felt the previous day when we had floundered through the bog. We had re-arranged our loads, adjusted rucksacks so they rode higher on our shoulders and better-distributed the loose items amongst us. And 'down' did go the road — but not for long. In the first of many 'wash-outs' (a morass of rock carried down by a sometimes raging torrent that was now no more than a humble stream), it disappeared though our maps showed it to have once followed this watercourse. Thereafter the route became an uphill one, made hard going and uncertain by the fact of its disappearance. However, the occasional leaning or broken telegraph pole and attendant coils of cable, making grim entanglement traps for unwary animals, pointed out the general direction.

Halfway up the hill we came upon traces of the road again and, at the same time, a cloud of mosquitoes to give us a sample of what these insects had in store. Having liberally covered all exposed skin with an evil-smelling but effective repellent we spent an energetic half-hour with arms flailing like windmills in an effort to ward them off. In spite of the mosquito menace I wore shorts as I do on most treks since where a soaking by river, rain or sweat is to be a recurring theme I find bare legs an advantage. In this instance so did the mosquitoes.

The road re-established, it then proceeded to bifurcate though no such junction showed on the map. We chose, on principle, to follow the lower route and consumed a picnic lunch in another stony river-bed cleaved by a playful brook in which we found ourselves. As we ate the sun sank behind a mass of grey clouds and it began to rain. If this was meant as a warning, none of us got the message. Rain, if prolonged, has an awkward habit of turning playful brooks into seething rapids as we were to learn.

The rain on this occasion was no more than a shower in company with an icy breeze and this pattern of sunshine and cold showers remained constant for the rest of the day as we toiled through the Little Keele Valley, finally raising camp close to a deep section of the Little Keele river. In an initial and misguided sense of bravado we immersed ourselves extremely briefly in its paralysing waters to be savaged, as we emerged, by mosquitoes of Stuka-like fanaticism and intent. In future hygiene was to go by

13

the board with only our feet benefitting from immersion — and this on an involuntary basis when forced to wade unbridged rivers.

With each meal consumed our packs became that much lighter, a condition that tempted us to make over-enthusiastic inroads into our food supplies. But against this had to be borne in mind the fact we would receive no further rations for a fortnight when an aircraft was scheduled to deliver provisions at one of the Godlin Lakes at least 170 miles ahead. David's resourceful Swedish wife, back in Dawson City, had packaged individually-prepared meals — main courses and puddings — to last over that period of time and each plastic-wrapped and labelled pack was to be used strictly on the dates indicated. The fact that we carried a gun — vital for protection against unprovoked attack by grizzly bear — and fishing tackle meant that anything we might obtain for the pot could be looked upon as a bonus.

The night's slumber was interrupted when the tent collapsed; the rocky ground had defied all our efforts to insert metal tent pegs and they bent like hairpins. Thus we had had to rely upon boulders as anchors for holding up the canvas and these proved unsuitable for the role. It rained in the night too but fortunately the two events did not coincide.

Our continued progress in the morning was governed by the obstacles in the path rather than by the fading course of the road. The highway itself had long been ravaged by a river that was forever intent upon widening its banks and was nowhere to be seen. So we walked along the centre of the wide valley still partly covered by thick platforms of dirty snow, crossing and re-crossing the Little Keele at its shallowest points. Again fallen telegraph poles and, now, lengths of rusting four-inch pipe (incredible as it may seem the Canol oil pipeline was of no more than four inches in diameter) affirmed we were on the correct route.

Already the journey was becoming a simple march during which the highlights of each day were to be meal stops. Regular as clockwork was the solemn proclamation of our good intentions of rising with the dawn and making early starts but, alas, my companions displayed a disturbing inclination to morning lie-ins which boded ill for our schedule. Thus we usually failed to get away until after ten with a hefty chunk of the day already lost. On the other hand we were in a land and a season of eternal daylight so perhaps our laziness was of no consequence. Our meals too were taken at the insistence of stomachs rather than the clock.

Lunch, the third day out, was served amongst the depressing wreckage of a one-time oil storage depot overlooking a graveyard of dead military vehicles neatly lined up as though for inspection by the keeper of some ethereal garage. Old machinery — oil pumps, generators and the like — stood directly under the skies, their once-enveloping buildings having fallen away to match-wood. Here and there a shed still stood; a Nissen hut complete with springless beds or garage without a roof. Strangely a water-closet continued to flush but the graffiti on the wall was of a generation past. While sipping our tea bunched around an oily fire an airliner crawled across the sky. Its passing not only accentuated the loneliness but, in a limbo where time means nothing, a link with a world out of reach.

The vehicle parade marked the spot where we turned into a side valley to begin the ascent towards the Plain of Abraham. A relentless sun in a suddenly azure-blue sky beat down upon us as we slowly zig-zagged our way up a minor canyon liberally sprink-led with the debris of landslides and rain-inspired flood-water. Each obstruction had to be negotiated or detoured, a fiendish test of stamina and avoidance of broken ankles; even legs, for the appalling loads on our backs continued to upset the normal human sense of balance as we skipped from rock to rock. Hardy mountain Dall sheep grazed, uncaring, on the higher ridges and small herds of caribou stared quizzically, even moving towards us to satisfy their curiosity, as, bathed in sweat, we grimly narrowed the distance to the summit.

Sections of pipe together with the ubiquitous telegraph poles became our constant companions as did, later, occasional traffic notices and mileposts that had survived the years and the elements. The pipes were invariably occupied by families of ground squirrels who made their homes in them to escape the attentions of bears and other predators. Their squawks had a curious hollow ring as we passed by. Otherwise a great silence pervaded the air; frightening in its intensity.

But there was beauty too. Whenever sections of the road broke to the surface, recovering from obliteration by avalanche and landslide, the surface became mottled with colour by reason of a display of wild flowers that was spellbinding. Their delicate blossoms and fragrance amongst the grey dust and in defiance of a fruitless soil lightened our hearts a little. Close to the final ridge at the top of the valley the telegraph poles drew themselves erect in military fashion as if to challenge us to a race to the summit, then keeled over as if the effort was too much.

Ahead and all around the scenery opened up to reveal the plain stretching away into glorious flatness to offer last-ditch encouragement to totter the last mile of a now clearly-discernible road. Only one of a number of wooden buildings of the camp at milepost 80 was habitable but it was enough. Behind our backs a range of distant mountains shimmered in the heat haze while the crimson blooms in the road winked at us as, wiping the stinging perspiration from our eyes, we made it to the night's haven, thankful we did not have to find the additional energy to raise the tents.

The night was cold but bright as day. We lit the little cast iron stove and were glad of its warmth though our beds were no more than the hard dirty floor. Ground squirrels and porcupines scratched beneath the rotting foundations and other noises caught our listening ears. With the Plain of Abraham we had reached grizzly country. A large specimen had, it was alleged, attempted to dislodge this very cabin occupied by a group of surveyors a month or so before, a threat that was not lost upon us. Thus we went to bed with the loaded rifle to hand, half listening for sounds that were more than the scufflings of squirrel and porcupine. 'A Night on a Bare Mountain' could well have been the theme of this vigil — and on two counts.

The morning remained cold but dry as we moved away along a road tailing into the distance. It continued to climb, but gently, for three miles offering, at each bend, a false crest to be attained. The final crest rewarded us with a staggering view of yet another range of snow-dappled mountains though our admiration was tempered by the knowledge that our path led through them. From the viewpoint, however, it was a downhill course with the road cork-screwing into a new valley, this one marked as Andy Creek. We short-circuited some of the hairpins and, risking the grizzlies prone to inhabiting such terrain, cut through a belt of spruce pines alive with mosquitoes to reach the river at the bottom.

16

Progress down inevitably has to be countered by subsequent progress up but the fresh climb offered fine close-up observation of caribou herds with one handsome bull repeatedly returning to investigate us after the main herd had departed. Immensely attractive animals are caribou and how people can bring themselves to shoot them for no reason except 'prestige' is beyond me. Still-warm dung and pug-marks indicated that a large grizzly was close and we proceeded with the utmost caution, the rifle loaded and cocked. Handfulls of bear-fur and porcupine quills showed where the beast had made its last attempt at a meal but nothing appeared. We camped close to milepost 94 in the snow-streaked Carcajou valley with a view one could describe as alpine. Our dinner was mysteriously labelled 'Beef & Fusilli with tomato paste & parmezan cheese' which was followed by a sweet called 'Pear Brown Betty', and it went down a treat.

Footfalls in the night had us nervously peering out of the tent in the small hours but the visitor was only a moose. A rain shower had turned to snow on the mountain flanks to display a whiter world to the one we had previously looked upon. The morning's walk was marred by an erroneous decision to take a short cut across the valley for which we were punished by an excruciating one-and-a-half-mile crossing of lunar-like rock and a wet negotiation of the Carcajou river. The saving was less than a mile of easy road walking and the crossing of a river by a bridge that still held. From this moment on short cuts became strictly taboo.

Whilst massaging sore feet and throbbing ankles David saw a large porcupine which we pursued with the aim of having it for supper. Difficult to catch for obvious reasons we attempted to shoot it but, with ammunition in short supply our marksman, Byron, had to ensure he got it with the first shot. Unfortunately he failed to do so and the animal got away — to my secret relief though they say porcupine meat is quite tasty.

A while later a brief siting of a grizzly had us eyeing the scrub that closed in on the road with deep suspicion but the only animals we met that afternoon were a family of wolverines and more waddling porcupines as we toiled along Bolstead Creek with the warm sun fighting a losing battle with a bitter wind. But the grizzly menace remained. The danger with these beasts is not so much in themselves as of us getting between parents and off-

17

spring, a situation that arouses the deepest fury in the former. To fell a full-grown grizzly on the attack is no easy matter even with a high-calibre rifle. A .303 bullet will kill a man with no trouble at all but can be deflected by a bear's thick hide and immense frame. There are few spots on the animal where a single shot is likely to bring it down — and you only have time for one shot. The worry too, so far as we were concerned, was that none of us were all that sure where the weak spot was. On the assumption that prevention was better than cure we made as much noise as possible while continuing on our way the idea being to frighten the danger away.

Our immediate destination was the long-disused military camp at the head of the valley where we hoped there would be at least one cabin suitable for an overnight stay. Long before we reached it we could see the camp buildings rotting on their timber-strewn site like discarded toys and as we approached we came to the skeletal remains of some mouldering Chevrolet lorries, one with its Goodrich tyres in near-perfect condition plus Schroder valves that still held the air in them. A dirty and decaying cabin makes a poor substitute for a tent but the one we found at least contained some serviceable spring beds though water for the evening meal had to be brought from a considerable distance away.

Up and over Bolstead Creek and into Trout Creek to stumble through a series of 'washouts' where rivers of boulders had obliterated the road. The weather turned hostile again to unleash repeated hailstorms from a sky that made the day into as near night as I had seen. The quantity of rivers that had to be forded multiplied, the one-time bridges either no more than driftwood on the shingle or entirely vanished.

There is a technique for wading a river. First, the shallowest section within half a mile or so of one's arrival point has to be located. This is usually where the river is widest. The entry and exit point selected, one can either advance with care into the water wearing boots or these can be removed and replaced with plimsolls but attempting the crossing in bare feet is foolhardy as the riverbed will be treacherous and very slippery. On the Canol Road Trail the rivers were fast-running and exceedingly cold so that, at the halfway mark, one's legs lost their feeling and ceased to function properly. And with a heavy load — plus boots swinging round the neck — falling is all too easy, particularly as the movement of the water adds an optical illusion to increase the likelihood of overbalancing. And a stumble in such circumstances can result in drowning since the weight of the rucksack can hold its carrier beneath a water-level that may be no higher than two feet.

As the trek proceeded — and the weather worsened — so the rivers became more and more of an obstacle. At first they were laughable affairs that could be bounded across with the help of a few well-placed stones but, with the Carcajou and other more formidable water-courses, the problems increased. We helped one another as best we could and the three English-speaking members of our group will not forget the agility shown and firm hand offered by the young Reinhard. It is a strange feature of life that, given a little hardship and danger, a man's character is so often enhanced. David, Byron and myself initially found it impossible to see anything likeable in the rather arrogant German who made up the quartet. Always he was ahead of the rest of us marching determinedly across the countryside pausing only to express exasperation at our more leisurely progress. But the frightening crossings of those rivers and his unstinting aid had us ashamed and humbled. I like to think that, by the time the trek ended, either Reinhard had become a very credible human being, or we had become more tolerant ones.

Byron, on the other hand, showed a fiery temperament that belied my initial judgement of his character. But his occasional unprovoked bursts of fury, never did more than temporarily dent a sustained friendship. We all admired his outdoor living capabilities, knowing that in the company of such a man, we had, in the last resort, little to fear when it came to survival. David, for his part, steadfastly remained calm, reassuring, kind and tolerant. When Reinhard forged ahead and had to be rebuked, when Byron blew his top and had to be pacified, or when I funked a nearly-vertical cliff of scree it was David's action that brought encouragement, understanding and peace. He was the perfect leader; leading without being seen to do so.

We could hear the sullen roar of the major obstacle of the route long before we reached the Twitya river. Prior to plunging into a hillside canopy of trees we even glimpsed it from afar and could make out the white flecks of madness upon its surface. Everyone became unnaturally silent as we descended by a bounding *agger*

19

of a road to its edge. Our future depended upon the state of this river; our plans and expectations were now entirely based upon 'once we're across the Twitya'. All at once it lay before us.

The previous night's camp had been close to the Trout river, a friendly stream but one already swollen by melting snow and rain in the mountains. We had crossed it with no great difficulty on at least three occasions because the road kept being deflected to the opposite side by sheer towers of granite crowned by trees. But the road, where its route lay alongside the river, had, again, been washed away forcing us to make a nightmare progress along its treacherous course or by clawing a way along the scree-lined buttresses of the granite walls. Rain fell incessantly adding to the misery so that when at last we had emerged upon a shelf overlooking the valley of the Twitya we evoked a feeling that the worst was over. Even fresh grizzly dung and pug-marks in the sandy soil failed to subdue our sense of optimism.

Arrival at the northern shore of the Twitya, however, drained our hopes, like water down a plug-hole. There before us lay a wide, raging torrent of uncontrolled water, its surface a cauldron of threshing waves. The road marched straight up to this horrifying impasse and disappeared. Of the bridge or its remains that once carried the road to the other bank there was no sign. A short way downstream lay the rapids where the great surge of near-freezing water came hard up against a solid wall of rock forcing a change of direction. We gazed, aghast, at what lay before us, lit a small fire and brewed a pot of tea. It was all we could think of to do.

David's information from those who had been this way before included the advice to proceed upstream some two miles and attain an island formed between the mainstream and a backwater. From the island a raft would have a chance of making it to the opposite shore before disaster overtook it in the rapids. This intelligence was, of course, based upon *normal* river conditions and the availability of plentiful supplies of timber. For better or for worse there seemed no alternative but to make for this alleged island and then assess the situation from there.

Accordingly began a particularly unpleasant side-trek made, in plimsolls, along the river's edge, rock-infested, slippery, wet and under heavy rain. It was long past midnight when, having waded up to our thighs the wide but only gently-moving backwater, we pitched camp on the sodden soil of a fast-disappearing island.

None of us slept a wink that night as we listened to the rain beating down upon the canvas. Our sleeping bags became soaked from the water-logged ground, and for once, we rose early for there was work to be done. Our council of war had swiftly decided the only action we *could* take. With our retreat cut off we could but go forward and the only method of going forward was by raft.

Under Byron's expert guidance we set to work. Felling with our ludicrously inadequate axe those growing saplings not already deep in water, and sawing, with a saw-blade alone, those not already waterlogged that formed the flotsam on the island, we heaved each trunk with a brute force born of desperation to the water's edge. Four layers of logs Byron had calculated as the minimum necessary to carry the four of us and our baggage across the raging Twitya though the only way of discovering whether, in fact, this *was* enough, would be when we cast off. And by then it would be too late to do anything about it.

All day we toiled in the torrential downpour meekly administering to Byron's barked instructions, and gradually the craft on which everything depended began to take shape though our island fastness reduced by the hour. By evening, soaked and shivering with cold, I experienced the first paroxysms of hypothermia as exhaustion sapped my ability to maintain a blood-circulation by means of log-hauling while my younger companions were not in a much better condition.

In all it took fifteen hours to complete the craft with but one brief pause for a hot meal deemed vital if we were to retain our strength. Another hour and the wierd vessel, its timbers lashed together with yellow cord, had been loaded and stood ready at the top of its 'slipway' of smoothed-down saplings. The last job was to cut ourselves long punting poles for guiding and pushing the raft to a designated landing point on the opposite bank. Then we took a last look-round, sent a private prayer to the Almighty, named the craft 'Pearl' after Byron's girlfriend, clambered aboard and cut the retaining rope.

We hit the water with a great splash, sank to our midriffs, then swirled, out of control, in the scurry of water. Desperately we heaved with our clumsy poles against the river bed, attempting to propel ourselves out of the main stream and towards the far bank but the current held us firmly in its grip, whirling us at high speed towards those terrifying rapids.

Our designated landing point swept by and was gone. 'Make for that outcrop!' screamed Byron, indicating a small beach that protruded a little way into the water and, again, we threshed and wrestled with the poles but to no avail. The new beaching point whirled past leaving one last hope, a patch of quieter water the far side of the main stream intimating the presence of shallower water where the river made a slight curve. The cold water was fast sapping our reserves of strength; the foaming waves smashing over us drenching the rucksacks and rocking the raft in angry little motions that threatened to loosen the bindings. Gyrating madly we spun out of the main stream and, inexplicably, ground to a halt on the shallows. Leaping into the water we hastily removed the rucksacks before the tugging current could release the beached craft. Shaking but jubilant we never even saw 'Pearl' slide away into oblivion; only triumph registered in minds that were aware we had attained the promised land, that *other* bank of the Twitya.

But the nightmare had not quite ended. It was long after midnight and we had a considerable distance to go to reach a Canol Road encampment which offered the only hope of a dry refuge from the rain, cold and the very real likelihood of exposure. Judging the direction we plunged into the dense undergrowth, making our way through forest and bog with the deluging rain hissing against the foliage. It took our last remaining ounces of strength to relocate the road and track it back to the broken-down cabin — the only one of several still habitable — a mile inshore from where the river bridge had once been.

Shakily we set about fuelling and lighting the rusty oil-drum stove and soon our efforts were rewarded as we became enveloped in a clammy haze of steam rising from our dripping clothes and bedding spread around the dirty little room. Not even sojourns I have made in some of the world's finest hotels have given me greater pleasure than did that simple cabin in the wilderness.

We rose late since it was well into morning when we had climbed into steaming damp sleeping bags. The new day was a brilliant one with a sun lighting up the landscape to make the previous day but a bad dream. Snow covered the tops of the surrounding mountains turning the countryside into a scene of ethereal beauty and child-like innocence. Following a substantial brunch we laid out our belongings to air and ourselves to bask anew in our deliverence.

But we had lost time and were behind schedule — and we had a tryst to keep with an aeroplane at the Godlin Lakes. In the afternoon, therefore, we reluctantly repacked the rucksacks, girded our loins and set out to put ten miles of distance between the Twitya and ourselves. The road was a gradual incline, the sun was hot, but to be warm was a pleasure. Byron expended another bullet on a spruce grouse, hitting the target this time but half blowing the wretched bird to pieces. We grilled it for supper to supplement the evening's fare and by the time we had squirmed into our bags it was raining again.

It rained all night but politely dried up before we stirred our stumps next morning. A flooded road and flooded terrain made the going tricky, involving jumping from tuft to tuft of thicket grass 'islands' marooned in a marshy sea. It was a time-consuming progress too and none of us escaped wet feet. But the reward was a luncheon of ham in sherry sauce and banana cream pudding taken by the side of a delightful stream pushing its way through a new valley. Alas, full enjoyment of the banana pud was curtailed by another downpour which at least provided reason for hastening us on our way. With the appearance of the Godlin river, here set in its picturesque Godlin gorge, movement became really tough. The road had long since ceased to exist, having been washed away by malignant flood waters, and in its place was a two-hour stumble high above the river along a near-perpendicular scree-slope of knife-sharp slate where one slip could send one, in a welter of this odious material, straight to the bottom. It would have been difficult enough to move empty-handed but with sixty pounds of dead-weight on tired shoulders it was positively hell.

We were fast approaching the prettiest section of the Canol Road and our camp site that night reflected this change of landscape. Byron missed another spruce grouse but, luckier with his rod, caught a trout to add to our rations which were showing ominous signs of running out. A belligerent porcupine produced some light relief from the sombre task of surveying and attending to blisters, cold sores, dirty bodies and wet socks with which we were all afflicted. Abed but not asleep we became aware of sounds all too reminiscent of stalking grizzlies but nobody felt inclined to investigate.

Any worries David may have harboured concerning food supplies were dispelled next day when, during the lunch-stop, Byron began pulling arctic thar and greyling out of the Godlin river at a ludicrous rate. We could see them in big shoals in the clear water and, getting down on hands and knees, were able to entice individual fish to a finger and, sometimes, flick them to the shore without benefit of line and hook. In a moment we had a twig fire going and were gorging ourselves silly on the most delicious grilled fish I have ever tasted.

Our route was leading us along a tranquil section of the road which ambled, with no broken bridges, cave-ins or washouts, along a valley of sheer loveliness. White-capped peaks made the perfect setting for a river-scene spliced with dark green sentinel pines and moss-covered hillocks. It was all too idyllic to last of course and very soon the river intruded rudely to cross our path, forcing another wading operation. This one however was aided and abetted by old bridge supports that stuck incongruously out of the water.

Another encampment, this one in better state of repair, became home for our twelfth night out. The reason for the higher standard of accommodation was that its buildings were in support of an airstrip. We had arrived at the Godlin Lakes, and with but two hours to spare. But the aircraft was late and it was not until well into the small hours that we heard the unaccustomed sound of an aero engine. We rushed out of the cabin to welcome the little floatplane as it appeared out of the subdued pre-dawn sky, circled the camp and put down with scarcely a splash on the most northerly of the small lakes past which the road had led. To reach it we had to run a mile over marshy ground but the longing to talk to fellow-humans — besides ourselves — was strong. Until it has actually been experienced, the emotion of enforced loneliness; the results of being shut away in a vast desolation of unimagined remoteness, cannot be understood. Nor can such a visitation by strangers from the other world arouse the new emotion of intense excitement until the first has been experienced.

Like children we waved and shouted, pumped the hands of the pilot and his mate, unloaded the boxes from the aircraft's hold and, with a sickening pain, watched the little machine take off again and lift into a sky that, in a moment, became no less empty than our hearts and minds drained of further feeling.

But among the packages was a bottle of whisky and two of wine. 'Why do we have to add weight to our loads?' we asked ourselves, drank the lot and felt better. We were even able to sleep through what remained of the night and, in the morning, we redistributed the stores and, by midday, were once more on the way.

Three miles brought us to the banks of the Ekwi river to enforce the first of a selection of river crossings that had us in and out of fast-flowing icy water for days on end. The valley was steep, the choice of crossing point restricted and hardly had we fought our way across when we had to repeat the performance as the river coiled about our lame highway. Only for the final crossing of that day was luck on our side. Here the bridge was down but not out and by clinging to rusty spars and splintered timbers we managed a dry passage.

The Ekwi remained with us for three days, its tributaries catching us when the main river failed to do so. Once we became so confused we twice waded it when we didn't have to. If nothing else got washed our legs did and the marvel is we did not end up with webbed feet. In this delta-like environment we were back in grizzly country and sightings became quite common. Whenever we espied these great beasts we gave them a wide berth — even if it involved added mileage. Our ammunition stock was down to five rounds and none of us were too sure how many would be required to drop such a hefty animal if the crunch came.

Entry into the Caribou gorge provided dramatic scenery, a prickly detour over it and through thorn scrub since the road through the canyon had vanished, and a sun and showers combination of weather that turned to constant shower. At mile 208 we came upon another dump of derelict military vehicles and, with the Intga valley, we were in sight of the Selwyn Mountains standing straightbacked out of an extensive plain. Excitement swelled once more in our breasts as we pitched camp by a rock-encased narrows of the Intga river. Just behind those Selwyns lay the Mackenzie Pass and the end of the trek. While chopping wood in a surge of anticipation I cut my hand with the axe and bled like a pig.

The previous night we had camped at five thousand feet at the head of the Caribou Pass amongst last vestiges of snow and ice. It had rained all night and the long trudge up the valley had almost defeated me. But on this new morning, a morning that afforded sight of the Selwyns, the sun joined us in silent thanksgiving, splashing their jagged summits an impossible hue of pink.

Plains walking had its points. The terrain was flat, the road surface composed of springy turf and the rivers were little more than trickles that could be jumped across with little inconvenience. But the Canol is an obtuse road and manages to find gradients in the most horizontal of territory, meandering mindlessly in its effort to locate and climb them. Plains, however, soon become monotonous tramping grounds; there are no surprises — cruel or kindly — to anticipate over the next crest, or the next, or the next, for the route being walked can be seen going on forever. And this plain — the Barrens — went on forever, its little rises no more than an aggravation. But the grass verges of the road; indeed the whole endless plateau, sparkled with wild flowers though the pace did not allow for dawdling. Had I sat down I would never have got up since there was not a boulder in sight against which I could lever myself into an upright position again.

Suddenly we were in sight of Sam's place. It was like a mirage. Atop a slightly bigger hill, bypassed by the road, appeared a collection of chalets that were very different from the remnants of a military camp. A handsome, even sophisticated, timber residence stood, solid and square, amongst half a dozen smaller chalets glass-fronted and fresh-painted. With one accord we swung off the road and staggered up the steep incline, taking it the short way — straight up — in our eagerness.

We had arrived at Old Squaw Lodge, a naturalist's paradise built by wildlife biologist Sam Miller and his associates, an away-from-it-all guesthouse attainable by specialist-driven, high-clearance, four-wheel drive vehicles from Mac Pass. And with Old Squaw Lodge we had reached the outer fringes of civilisation.

Sam was not at home but two of his colleagues were and they invited us to spend our last night on the Canol Road beneath a solid roof. In the evening Sam arrived in his jeep-like automobile we had watched approaching in a balloon of dust from the base of a still-distant Selwyn range as radiant in the evening sun as they had been that morning. In new-found company we talked well into the night watching a sunset of an unbelievable majesty.

What a paradise for the nature-seeker is this lodge named after the melodiously talkative oldsquaw duck that breeds on the arctic coast and the barrenlands of the Northwest Territories. Here among a patchwork of silver ponds, alpine meadows and mossy green tussocks is a heaven on earth. Here it would be easy to ignore the outside world — and yet not *quite* be out of touch with it — and roam for a magic week or two encountering caribou herds, listening to the soft chirp of bank swallows and langspurs, and glimpsing the flash of white from willow ptarmigan. And roaming amongst a foliage of dwarf birches turning an intense orange in the autumn, and of blue carpets of forget-me-nots and cushions of lichen curled like starched lace. Not all is cruel along the ghost road of the Canol. Here I can record a tranquil spot upon its gruelling course to which I will return one day unencumbered by a load upon my shoulders.

The last day's march to the Mackenzie Pass was one that was dictated by the rule of the motorcar. Vehicle tracks scarred the muddy surface of the old road and the serrated channels trapped our feet in a vice that held them in their grip the last dozen miles. There were people at the airstrip too but they took not the slightest notice of us. And why should they? For at this point the Canol becomes a highway of today. Just back down the road we had waded the considerable Intga river, a tributary of the larger Keele, and the last obstacle. But that too was behind us and none of us were to look back. It was as if the past had never been.

2

Horsing about in the Badlands

TRAVELLING BY HORSE IN THE DAKOTAS OF THE USA

My days as a fledgeling horserider are but a half-forgotten
memory of restrictions at Pony Club gymkhanas and occasional
meets of the East Essex Hunt. I was never a horseman by ambi-
tion; come to think of it I was never a horseman at all, but my
parents were of the opinion that I should go through the motions
since they gained a certain social standing from the fact that their
son could sit correctly in the saddle. Today every child seems to
be equestrian-orientated but in the late 1930s this was not the
case. And it could have been no later than the year 1941 that I
last galloped my uncontrollable little Arab pony across the Essex
landscape. Thirty eight years later — in early 1979 — had come
the invitation to renew this tenuous bond with the horse and to
ride one across the wild territory of North and South Dakota in
the American Mid-West.

It was not, however, so much my anxiety to renew this
acquaintanceship as the chance to assuage a curiosity that
prompted my acceptance. The United States is full of 'trails'
and, though the word there has more literal connotations than it
does in Europe, the idea of tracing such historic trails as that of
the Santa Fé, the Oregon and the Butterfield was irresistible. I
was hooked from the very outset. Already I could hear the creaking of stagecoach and wagon wheels, the crack of whips and the
strain of harness in my romantic soul and the fact that the trail on
offer was no more than an obscure stagecoach line of some 215
miles founded by a little-known French marquis in 1884 mat-
tered not at all.

I had been in Alaska and Canada's Yukon on other assignments all of May 1979 and, at its end, I journeyed south by train
to Fargo, North Dakota. Here, at 3 o'clock on a raw morning my
host, Mike Martin, met me at the station to drive me to his farm-

28

stead home at remote Enderlin, some three hours south across a dead flat empty countryside that is part of the granary and meat larder of the United States. The land of the cowboys was an appropriate one for a 215-mile hack.

With the peace that followed the war of 1812, the tide of migration moved the American frontier steadily westward. The 'movers' came by foot, on horseback, in wagons and by river. But it was land as well as gold (not simply adventure) that lured most migrants to the great Mississippi and Missouri rivers and beyond. Canals, stagelines and, later, railways quickened the pace, and, within a generation, industrial cities were thriving — Cincinnati, Detroit, Milwaukee, Chicago — where not so long before Indians had hunted and fished.

For those in the American cattle business the years of the late 1870s and early 1880s were a heady, wildly optimistic time. The profits that could be made raising livestock on the grasslands seemed unlimited; if anything, the money multiplied at a faster rate than the animals themselves. Ranches in the West, some of which covered areas as large as whole states, were the feeding grounds for hundreds of cows, steers, heifers and bulls and if most of the millions of acres on which these animals grazed were the public domain, which would eventually be carved up into homestead plots, few people at first contested the ranchers' claims to the land.

During these brief halcyon years, when shares in vast spreads were selling like stock in diamond mines, the ranchers benefitted from a rising market. Year in and year out, the steers brought higher and higher prices, for there seemed to be no limit to the world's appetite for American beef.

Reports of sudden riches circulated throughout the West, spread to travellers heading east, and found their way into the clubrooms of London, Edinburgh and Paris. It was hardly surprising that financiers from both Wall Street and Europe (particularly Britain) were eager to pump an unprecedented infusion of capital into the Great Plains. They formed joint stock companies to buy out and combine ranches, bring in new breeds of cattle, and recruit managers and cowboys to run their projects. Grizzled old ranchers with the smell of cow dung embedded in their skins suddenly found themselves near-celebrities, as eastern dudes and

European dandies hung on their every word and marvelled at their business acumen.

Many foreign investment syndicates sent representatives of their own to oversee their vast American properties, but some Europeans came over in person. Most spent money with incredible prodigality to establish themselves as cattle barons, while at the same time reproducing as near as possible the luxurious lifestyles they had left behind. Among these was a titled Frenchman, the Marquis de Mores, who settled on the Dakota Badlands with twenty servants to staff the mansion he had built in the town of Medora (founded by the marquis himself and named after his wife, New York heiress Medora von Hoffman). The ambitious Frenchman's interests included beef and sheep ranches, a stagecoach line, a refrigeration company, a slaughterhouse, and a firm that specialized in shipping Columbia river salmon to the dining tables of New York's wealthy.

The discovery of gold in the Black Hills increased the pressure of the migrants to occupy the region, notwithstanding a treaty obligation guaranteeing the hunting rights of the occupying Sioux Indians. There were no established trails; much less roads, leading to the Black Hills and Deadwood, the centre of the new and frenzied excitement, was more than two hundred miles from the nearest railway or water route.

With the tracks of the Northern Pacific Railroad now crossing the Missouri river, people naturally sought a shorter route from the goldfields to the railhead and government surveying and reconnaissance parties were sent out to determine the shortest and most feasible route from the Black Hills to some town on the Northern Pacific extension west of Bismark. Thus several townships were soon bidding for the very worthwhile freight and passenger service to the hills and it was within this aura of frenetic development that the Medora—Deadwood Stage Line came into being. Since the marquis's meat packing and refrigeration plant was already established in Medora, North Dakota, his opening of the stage line to Deadwood was but a logical extension of his enterprise.

Throughout the route stage stations were erected approximately every ten to fifteen miles. The line out of Medora led south, then east up Sully Creek, thence south again to Rocky Ridge. From this point the trail continued southward by Robert

Springs and Cedar Creek, thence to Cold Turkey Creek and onto Crooked Creek near the North Dakota—South Dakota state border. With the station at O'Dell, the route carried on to Bull Creek, Macey's, South Moreau, Belle Fourche, Spearfish and Deadwood, again with stations as convenient intermediate points. Four coaches were put into service and were christened respectively, 'Kittie', 'Dakota', 'Medora' and 'Deadwood'.

The modern individual can have little conception of the strength and durability of the old Concord stagecoach. The driver sat at the top with tight reins, his feet braced against the dash board in the front boot, usually with a fellow passenger by his side. Mail, express and light baggage were carried on top held in position by an iron-railing adapted to the purpose. Heavier items and express packages were carried in the rear boot and sometimes inside, if passengers were few. When crowded, those who could not be contained inside rode on top holding on as best they could to avoid being thrown overboard. The leather compensating rocker springs produced a motion not unlike the swell of the sea. These coaches often carried a two-ton load and stood up under the weight while moving at a good six to ten miles an hour over the roughest of trails.

The company's stock included about 150 horses while each of the stations had a tender whose duty it was to take care of the incoming teams and have the outgoing ones harnessed and ready to hitch with the least delay. The time allowed for changing teams was ten minutes.

A coach left Medora every day of the week, the 215 miles being covered in 36 hours. Departure was scheduled for the early morning arriving at Deadwood the following evening. On the more level portions of the route four horses were used on each coach and, over the rougher portions, six. A passenger ticket for the full journey cost $21.50 or about ten cents a mile and the cargo fee was ten cents a pound with, on occasions, the coach carrying as much as 2,500 pounds of express freight.

Competition was intense. Medora's location was not such as to give the company a monopoly of the business of carrying freight. Gradually a combination comprising the heavy grades in Badlands territory, loss of freight, a slump in the express business, and a sharp reduction in passenger traffic signified the beginning of the end of the Medora—Deadwood stage line. Economies

31

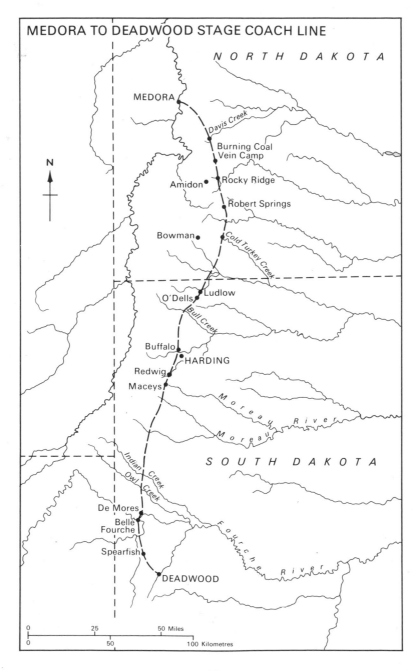

MEDORA TO DEADWOOD STAGE COACH LINE

N O R T H   D A K O T A

N

MEDORA

Davis Creek

Burning Coal
Vein Camp

Amidon

Rocky Ridge

Robert Springs

Bowman

Cold Turkey Creek

Ludlow

O'Dells

Bull Creek

Buffalo

HARDING

Redwig

Maceys

M o r e a u   R i v e r

M o r e a u

S O U T H   D A K O T A

Indian Creek

Owl Creek

De Mores

Belle
Fourche

Spearfish

B e l l e   F o u r c h e   R i v e r

DEADWOOD

0   25   50 Miles

0   50   100 Kilometres

which cut down the horses' feed and the paying off of employees failed to sustain the company. The end was in sight.

Operations ceased sometime in the winter of 1885-6. The stock was sold for what it would bring, and was scattered across the territory. One of the coaches is now at Miles City; another at Mandan, both museum specimens of the days that were. The remaining two coaches have been retired to Karlsbad, Minnesota. If any could speak, they would find no audience to take time to listen to their garrulous tales. The Marquis de Mores, his other business ventures collapsed around his ears, moved away to invest his remaining money and initiative to finally depart American shores for the friendlier climes of his native France. Medora declined to what it originally had been and today few people even know the approximate route of the one-time stage trail I was proposing to follow.

All this I learnt from Mike as we drove across the featureless plains of North Dakota, a land of a green, brown and yellow ochre chessboard laid out in numberless rectangular sections. The pattern overwhelms its details, even such recurrent motifs as the silver silos and dark red barns. But it is the pattern of the old America, of the Protestant English farming stock that defeated the Indians, cleared the forests, broke the prairies with the plough, defeated the British Empire and won a civil war.

The story and Mike's obvious pride in his Dakotan upbringing brought the impending ride of ours into sharp focus. It was he who, backed by a master's degree in American history, had undertaken most of the research of the stage line and its route. The previous year he had attempted the journey alone but his horse had fallen lame after 50 miles and he'd had to give up. I had simply drifted into the project, accepting an offer to join Mike in his fresh attempt. A young farmer of 25 with a satirical sense of humour that hid his generous heart I felt no concern over the disparity of our ages though I wasn't, perhaps, so happy about being reunited with a horse. A third member of the team however extended the age differential. During our brief stay at Enderlin I met Steve Traynor, a gruff hard-smoking, hard-drinking ex-soldier and railway worker of 58 years, some three years my senior.

Everyone in the small town of Enderlin knew of our project

and were not slow in offering advice and opinions. Many thought we were crazy and, since Englishmen in Enderlin were hardly two a penny, these opinions were expressed loud and clear in the local newspaper. Not the slightest discouraged we departed the third morning in two cars trailing horseboxes containing four horses — Duke, Bill, Trixie and Beauty — the fourth being the pack carrier. Our destination: Medora.

Medora has refused to die completely and it stands, vaguely defiant, at the gateway to the Theodore Roosevelt National Memorial Park. The town's other famous son had a ranch there and the legacy of his hunting lodge competes for tourist patronage with that of the de Mores' chateau and the remaining chimney stack of the meat packing factory. With a day to spare we had toured the township now slightly self-conscious of its cowboy image and the strange import from France that sits, as a museum, high on a nearby hill. I had also successfully managed to remain aloft during a few circuits on Trixie's back though I foresaw trouble from the excruciating cavalry saddle I'd been given that made riding akin to sitting astride a bucking railway line.

The venture opened with a minor disaster when Beauty, designated as packhorse, took fright at her substantial load. She bolted while I was leading her and my desperate hold was simply on account of the lead being wrapped around my leg. She repeated the performance with Mike as ringmaster, nearly running him down in her frenzy and strewing our provisions over a wide area. Damage amounted to a plethora of broken eggs, a fractured bottle of syrup, scattered packets of noodles and a dented pannier. Aware that Beauty was not destined to become the packhorse of the year the honours were transferred to the more stolid Bill.

The Badlands of North Dakota are a geographical phenomenon. Straddling the final 200 miles of the Little Missouri river they were formed from the ancient, pre-glacial plains. Moving waters carried eroded materials eastwards from the Rocky Mountains depositing them as sediments on the lowlands. Jungles that subsequently clothed these deposits, together with swamp vegetation, were buried by new layers of sediment to become lignite, a type of soft coal. During their final development clouds of ash from the mountain-forming volcanoes of the West drifted eastwards and settled on this layered residue. In the course of time, the ash decomposed and, today, what remains is exposed in layers of blue bentonite clay. A myriad streams have cut down through the soft strata to sculpture this formation into a lunar landscape and an infinite variety of flat-topped buttes, tablelands, valleys and gorges. Wild, remorseless, dangerous country — the Indians had good reason for giving it its title — the Badlands had us in their grip the moment we clattered out of Medora's wild west façade of saloon bars.

De Mores' stagecoach had daily left town from the Rough Riders Hotel in the main street so we followed suit, trooping down the dusty road feeling like a posse in the celluloid epic 'High Noon'. Others must have thought so too for we drew quite a few sardonic 'Howdy Pardners' and 'Which of you guys is sheriff?' Most of this was aimed at Steve who, taking things more seriously than Mike and me, insisted upon wearing an outsize stetson and fancy boots. I rather let the side down with my brief shorts, sandals and little else for the late spring sun was warm.

There is a conflict of opinion as to the exact route of the stage over the first section of its course, much of this due to the renaming of certain localities. But a dust road, seeming to know where it was going, led us in the right direction and, eventually, to Gully Creek but, thereafter, an oil company track of recent origin pulled us southward into untracked, untamed country of rocky crags and outcrops of bracken. An antelope bounded gracefully across our path to turn and stare from what it judged to be a safe distance. I was relieved to discover that I had not quite lost all the horsemanship drilled into me as a youth though my narrow saddle was already giving pain. My optimism took a knock, however, when Trixie stopped with such abruptness that I found myself hanging from the underside of her neck.

By turning my head I gazed, eyeball to eyeball, at the first rattlesnake I had seen outside of a cage. The shock over, I slid to the ground to take some fine close-up photographs unaware of the fact that when a rattler fails to flee it is because a mate is working its way round to attack from the rear. We were to meet more such 'critters', for the Badlands are renowned for rattlesnakes but, this initial encounter over, our main concern was that of keeping direction across a series of gullies laced with boulder-

35

strewn streams. It made particularly difficult walking for Bill, encumbered with his load, and he objected most strongly to negotiating the half-hidden streams.

Our pace was dead slow since we could only move at walking speed, and that dictated by the willing Bill. In such manner we pressed on, aware that the original trail lay parallel to our left, to find ourselves in a wide valley which, for several miles, was the route of the famous Custer Trail. Clumps of primroses and gumbo lillies made splashes of colour against the coarse burnt grass as a late afternoon sun dipped below low hills. Another dirt road appeared to show us a large rock upon which had been preserved the graffiti of two of Custer's troopers together with the date in 1876. (A year later I was to stand upon the colonel's last battleground, that of Little Bighorn in neighbouring Montana.)

Since we had left Medora late in the day the estimated twelve miles we covered to Davis Creek by the end of the afternoon was, by universal consent, deemed satisfactory. Here, in a hollow in which a half dozen dead trees sprouted, mute and grotesque, we made our first camp, setting out our bedrolls directly under the sky for there seemed little chance of rain. Our marked maps showed the first stage station to be little more than a mile ahead but, with an abundance of dry timber on tap, we were not tempted further. Water was, however, not so easy to come by but by dusk we had a fire crackling merrily and a meal of beans in the making. Breakfast that morning had been substantial but lunch had never materialised so our appetites were healthy.

As darkness fell we retrieved the horses from a patch of grazing on which we had tethered them and it was while I was changing lead reins that I remembered a lesson of my Pony Club days. The trouble was my re-education came an instant too late. Perceiving a chance of freedom, Trixie bounded away like the wind and disappeared into the gathering darkness, the drumbeats of her galloping hooves a tattoo of despair in my ears. My companions stared at me aghast. Steve was no encouragement whatsoever with his gruff 'She'll never come back y'know', but Mike was more philosophical and simply shrugged his shoulders. To lose one's horse the first day out was shame indeed and I lay down on my sleeping bag to bask in self-pity. Twenty minutes later came a sound of trotting hooves and Trixie was back, seemingly unable to sever contact with her four-legged friends. Mike cautiously approached the nervous animal, comforted her with soothing noises and firmly gripped the flowing mane. The crisis over I fell asleep a happy man but awoke soaked by dew, thus learning another lesson the hard way. Even Mike and Steve broke the Boy Scout camping code by laying themselves directly beneath the overhang of a dead bough. I had already aired my suspicions of the beaver-gnawed tree trunks and naked branches so when a wind arose to bend the brittle timbers ominously they saw my point and moved out of range.

Steve had elected himself to the position of cook for which there was no contest. His breakfast offerings were ash-covered omelettes and burnt bacon on which we aired no comments in case he resigned. Our ablution and washing-up water was one and the same. We had slept intermittently, listening to the fidgetting of the horses and the creaking of the skeleton trees as the wind played amongst their bones.

My attire had shocked Steve to the core so he insisted I wear his spare cowboy boots 'for the look of the thing' as he put it. These had soon rubbed sores into my feet where their pointed toes failed remotely to fit my own and, to my mind, looked the more ridiculous still when worn with shorts. He'd have had me in chaps if he'd thought to bring some along. My saddle showed no sign of moulding itself to the angled shape of my hindquarters but, these inadequacies notwithstanding, my spirits were high as I limped about repacking provisions and loading our respective steeds. These antics were watched in some amazement by a pair of antelopes artistically situated against a blood-red sunrise.

The new day's ride began by following a dirt road that paralleled the original route and about a mile out of Davis Creek we changed course into the swell of hills to determine the possibility of there being anything remaining of the stage station. But nothing showed so we returned to the road. The countryside flattened out as if the exertion of raising even the suspicion of a hill was too much for it and permitted unseen ranchers to zealously pen their herds of cattle on its abundant grass. But if these grasslands offered no sign of human activity this was not quite the case with the rough and ready road. Occasional vehicles passed in balloons of dust, their drivers invariably stopping to ask the reason for our journey. One kind fellow produced nectar in the form of three cans of cold beer, from others we received offerings of water and even a bag of oats. Half-empty creeks grudgingly gave up water for the horses and with temperatures mounting into the high eighties they needed it. Bull snakes squirmed purposefully across the roads as did big jack-rabbits who leaped up from beneath our hooves to lope across the pastures like bloated hares. For miles we, ourselves, walked in a sheen of sweat to give relief to the horses, a mode of progress that also gave relief to my buttocks if not my feet.

A deserted and out-of-season camp site that rejoiced in the name of Burning Coal Vein made our pad for the night. Trees — young shady evergreens — clothed the gently undulating landscape but the nearest water was a murky liquid in a muddy creek over a mile away. Supper was bacon and mashed potato and it was all we could do to find the energy necessary to attend to the welfare of the horses before crawling into our sleeping bags.

Again we chose to sleep under the stars. 'It won't rain; just look at that sunset', concluded Steve, who liked to think of himself as a backwoodsman. It was he who always found the water; looking for it in the right places while Mike and I thrashed about searching where any real backwoodsman knew it couldn't be. But weather-forecasting was obviously not one of Steve's talents. About two in the morning the heavens opened.

The only permanent fixture on the site except for the 'no out-of-season camping' signs was a dilapidated cabin, securely locked, with overhanging eaves and beneath these we took refuge, our damp sleeping bags draped around our shoulders. We attempted to lie down again, hugging the lee of the wall but the slope of the ground sent water seeping surreptitiously towards our prostrate forms while the eaves periodically unleashed a deluge from above. The pre-dawn hours found us huddled miserably round an extinguished camp fire, vainly trying to coax its damp embers into flame. These efforts finally succeeded (Steve again, of course) and a strong cup of tea raised flagging morale.

We were now but eighteen miles from Amidon a village on Highway 85, and, breakfastless, we set out confident of attaining it by virtue of our enforced early rise. I was the only regular early-riser of the trio; the other two being confirmed lie-abeds of a morning. Another dirt road stayed with us all the way to the township but our progress was baulked by the frequent lack of a rancher's gate at points where cattle grids and fencing barred the way. Over much of the Dakotan ranchlands a grid of barbed-wire divides the land and where a road or public right of way crosses such a 'border' a cattle grid is positioned. Usually a gate or moveable section of fencing is positioned close by since a traveller on horseback too has the full right of transit. However, in spite of a law that insists upon such an arrangement, not always does such a 'gate' exist. This was the case beyond Second Creek and because the horses were unable to negotiate the grid we had no alternative but to follow the fence up into the hills in the hope of finding one — and the hills here had abruptly become as marked as the Sussex Downs. Further fences then deflected us from our course and when finally a 'gate' was discovered it led only into another wired compound. Exasperated beyond measure with playing a kind of mounted snakes and ladders and hopelessly lost we finally had to re-pack Bill's load which chose just such a time to part company with its bearer. Had it been Beauty acting as packhorse I dread to think of what might have happened but Bill, bless him, stood docile while we painstakingly sorted things out. Upon regaining the road at last the whole business of zig-zagging about the hills had to begin again to add at least half a dozen miles to our day's total.

The last two to Amidon were by way of Highway 85, a traffic-laden artery but blessed with wide grass verges along which we were able to break into a trot for short spells. Another rattler caused Trixie to shy and me a near-heart attack prior to our entry to the village.

'Capital' of Slope County the place gave little indication of so high an office but among its few dwellings were three vital components: a rodeo stadium, horse pens and a bar. From the office of administration — a room at the back of a bungalow — we obtained permission to bed ourselves and horses in the stadium and pens and, the horses attended to, made tracks for the bar.

Virtually the entire male population of Amidon hung out in that little saloon. The arrival of three strangers — one of them a Brit — caused an unnerving silence broken by intense competition to supply us with booze. As if my nationality was not enough our project and method of accomplishing it produced incredulity and the issue of further liquid refreshment so that, within minutes, each of us had amassed a line-up of Budweisers. As supply outstripped consumption characters wearing outsize stetsons on the back of their heads staggered unevenly up to us to commiserate, congratulate or offer zany advice. Few had even *heard* of the trail and those that had put it the wrong side of town. Running out of thirst we dined on hamburgers.

It rained again in the night but the morning dawned dry if a little chilly. A tap made a convenient water source for the horses but by the time we had smeared our faces with soap it ran dry. Breakfast was thick glutenous porridge and strong milkless tea and before leaving for the open country we called at Amidon's only shop for supplies. The proprietor was surprisingly know-ledgeable about the trail and excitedly pointed out the way we already intended taking. 'You're the only folk I know who've thought to do this', he exclaimed with not a little envy.

Our maps and sketches put the stage station of Rocky Ridge right on the site of a homestead at which we arrived twenty min-utes after setting out from the village. The farmer, a red-faced in-dividual with beady eyes, came rushing out of his front door in great excitement. 'I knew you'd be coming, Boys', he pro-claimed, 'my wife works behind the bar in Amidon', he added as if in explanation. News travels fast in such tight little commu-nities as Amidon.

The track we were following lost us amongst a series of narrow valleys veined by rivers and streams objected to strongly by the horses mainly on account of the marshy ground around them. Trees with low-slung branches did their best to unseat us but by dint of much urging, thrashing and cursing we got through the morass with nothing worse than wet feet. The weather continued cool and breezy with dark clouds scudding across the sky.

We lunched on corned beef and an apple in a waterside grove. Steve, munching away, began reminiscing about his railroad days, treating Mike and me to a mental picture of our serious-minded companion in his cowboy outfit heading a repair gang on the down-line to Jamestown.

Our whereabouts had become a mystery and with thickly-timbered hills and more fencing hemming us in we were forced to retrace our steps back over some of the waterlogged territory we had taken such pains to traverse in the first place.

A woman at a tiny Mark Twain farmhouse could offer no

assistance but our eyes caught sight of a big open-backed Cadillac bouncing along a track so we made haste to intercept it.

The driver could have been Steve's twin. Beneath the regulation stetson was a cigar clamped between bared teeth and, further down, a cartridge belt straining around the beginnings of a pot belly. He actually said 'Howdy Pardners', adding, 'I'm Chris Roan, ranch boss around here. What can I do for you?'

Steve was in his element. 'Mighty glad to see you Chris', he replied in the exaggerated drawl he was happy to effect on such occasions. 'We're on the trail of the de Mores stage outfit', he went on, 'and got ourselves a mite off limits. Any ideas how it runs?'

Chris was full of ideas. He expounded them for the best part of half an hour interspersed with anecdotes of life on the plains. 'Gee Boys I'm danged if I wouldn't hitch up a moke and come along with you but time is dough and I've not got enough of either.'

Steve positively glowed. We'd heard variations on this theme before and we were to hear more in the days to come. I like to think our little hack might have started a sort of nostalgic cavalry charge across the steppes. But I doubt it.

With Steve as spokesman we hardly got a word in and it didn't matter a lot. He introduced us a shade hesitantly, trying not to look at my bare legs encased in his boots. Chris had no such inhibitions and pumped my hand for all it was worth. But the delay paid dividends. The very track we stood on was part of the trail and another stage station lay close. 'Some call it "Roberts Springs", others "Springdale", I guess you can take your pick but there's nothing to see', volunteered Chris who added that, if we kept going we'd eventually hit Bowman.

Under clearing skies we made exhausting but rapid progress along a dead straight grassy route that sped us towards limitless horizons. Jack rabbits, prairie dogs and the occasional antelope bounded across the pastures. In the far distance almost out of vision we could see strange hillocks protruding, like boils, from the flat landscape.

Now that we had gauged the walking and trotting paces of our respective mounts we had evolved a formula for our order of march. Trixie, I found, liked to lead but, once in front, needed constant urging. Mike on the nervous Beauty, was inclined to

41

lag. Thus Steve or I usually led though sometimes Trixie moved better as Tailend Charlie. Everyone took turns to lead Bill.

We made camp late in the evening beside a brackish pond that formed part of Buffalo Creek and close to the only two trees on view within a five-mile radius. Supper was a hurried affair of ham and eggs made in competition with darkness which won hands down. Mike and I, with painful memories of the previous night, pitched our lightweight tent. The sunset was one of those that have to be seen to be believed but we weren't putting our cards on its promise.

Dawn was equally sensational but, temperature-wise, freezing. Through chattering teeth we forced down a spoonful or two or milkless, lukewarm porridge and called it breakfast before continuing on our way aware that our camp site was at Cold Turkey Creek where, once, another stage station had served its quota of travellers.

Bowman, a small town that heads Bowman county, was off the trail but our stores needed replenishing. Much of the six miles we had to cover to reach it was via Highway 85 again, a necessary detour. Upon tethering the horses beneath the big grain elevators near the town centre we were ambushed by a bevy of local reporters who had learnt of our mission and wanted to take pictures. Re-stocked from a supermarket we clattered out of town bringing play at the golf course on the outskirts to a halt as the players crowded round to express their varied views. Such an enterprise as ours in Britain would not have raised an eyebrow but here in the United States it is a very different story.

There followed a grim evasion exercise, the point being to escape from the traffic-snarled clutches of Highway 85 obstinately claiming the way we wanted to go. In desperation we took a side road, this one more pleasantly peopled with meadowlarks, redwings and yellow-wing blackbirds, the verges ablaze with prairie roses, that, alas, led us only to a gravel pit. Beyond the pit another cats-cradle of fences pushed us, eventually, back to the 85.

This accursed highway was to be our cross to bear for much of the way to Deadwood as it turned out, with only brief respites. Its verges became known to us as 'Beer Can Alley' by reason of the litter discarded by uncaring motorists. This included glass bottles, broken and unbroken, which, more than once, cut open one of the horse's hooves. Every milepost a taunt, we were goaded into an average rate of four miles an hour which, with a packhorse in tow and under an ever-hotter sun, is hard going. Bridges forced us onto the hard sticky tarmac and vehicle drivers, shouting their words of encouragement or derision, occasionally drove deliberately close with the object of stampeding the horses. The sores developing on my backside and the strain on my calves when attempting to alleviate the pain of the former became agonising. To dismount and proceed on foot for a mile or two was like taking a holiday.

But on this fifth day the North Dakota—South Dakota state line was to mark a turn-off into territory known as the Flint Hills. A series of false trails and the usual deflections caused by fences led us astray but at least we were away from the 85. A herd of playful bullocks mock-charged the horses causing even Bill concern and Trixie too I had to keep under a tight rein. A river, winding and deep, had us meandering along its course in all sorts of directions before a fordable crossing-point could be located.

I was leading Bill when we finally attempted the crossing and while Trixie bounded eagerly across, Bill took two steps into the water and refused to budge. Steadfastly I refused to let go of the lead rein — remembering the near-loss of Trixie the first day out — and so was dragged from the saddle into the frog-laden river, much to everyone's great amusement. In such manner we reached Crooked Creek where the halfway station was recorded as having once been and here we thankfully hove to for the night.

It was a warmer dawn and the porridge of a more edible consistency but, during the night, the foolish Beauty had succeeded in cutting a fetlock. Mike bathed and bandaged the wound but this all caused delay and, when we finally moved off, our speed was much reduced. Trotting was out of the question for plainly the leg was painful. With sinking hearts we reverted to the 85 as the most direct route to Buffalo, a fact that had been taken into account by those who had forged the stage line.

By the time we had plodded into a hamlet called Ludlow we knew the worst. Beauty was limping badly and was not going to stay the course. Furthermore it would have been cruel if we had tried to make her do so. We therefore decided to leave her in care in the town of Buffalo, a destination at which we had planned to spend a rest day.

43

Ludlow was no more than a church, a bar, a garage, a confectionery shop and a post office. We made use of all these facilities except the church. With every mile the sun became hotter with the hump-backed Butte country shimmering with heat but the long drag to Buffalo was, nevertheless, punctuated by a few light moments. A driver stopped to offer us copious swigs of rye whisky which I'm sure did us no good, a police patrol slowed down, hesitated and halted to enquire of our actions, plainly puzzled as to what state law we could be breaking; a gazelle stood and watched with a quizzical expression.

The last six miles of the day we were able to divert to another dirt road into Buffalo. A squall caught us before we reached the town, serving to cool our shoulders with a sprinkle of water, and was gone.

Buffalo is an agreeable little town, widely spread and aware of its situation as the geographical centre of the United States. It was a Saturday evening which meant that all offices were closed but our enquiries nevertheless produced a mayor, a town clerk and more newspaper men who took photographs of us in the company of His Worship. From him we obtained permission for ourselves and the horses to doss down in the Hardy county sales barn, the equivalent in Britain being a cattle market centre. With hay and oats for the horses, a gas cooker, abundant water and trestle tables on which to sleep we couldn't have asked for more. At dusk we celebrated in style by taking ourselves to a quality restaurant and putting down some enormous steaks. We even found time to wash some of the grime from our bodies in honour of the occasion.

Nowhere else have I encountered such a 'laid back' township as Buffalo on a Sunday. Nobody but nobody made a move until nearly midday. We, at least, went to work in the afternoon arranging for the well-being of Beauty, overhauling our equipment and deciding upon which items of gear we could leave behind and how to festoon what remained about our persons and respective horses. We had slept well bar the occasions we had rolled off the tables and were much refreshed. The local museum was a mine of information on the subject of the trail; the lady curator being intensely interested in the details of the ride. And as well, perhaps, for it was she who we persuaded to be Beauty's keeper for the period of our absence.

Monday morning the heat really came on and by nine the day was sweltering. Somehow we attached bed rolls, spare garments and vital stores and provisions to our saddles and about selves to proceed into the shimmering horizon along the ubiquitous 85. Without a packhorse we made better progress though speed, in the new circumstances, meant broken eggs which dripped depressingly down saddle bags and horsey flanks. The loss of the eggs brought our rations to the bare minimum; a few tins of beans, some wads of pre-cooked buffalo meat and a supply of tea-bags.

Snakes, including rattlers, were much in evidence, slithering through the grass verges to upset the horses. Trixie suffered a severe attack of nose-fly for a while and became very difficult to handle. A golden eagle spiralled in the sky and coyotes, racoons and deer made fleeting appearances to add a faint aura of menace to a burning land of strange unreal hillocks devoid of succour.

Redwig was marked as a hamlet on our maps but, in fact, was no more than a 'gas' station. We reached it following a journey of 23 miles from Buffalo and the kind-hearted proprietor allowed us to utilise his sheep-pens as a roof for the night since we no longer possessed tents. Furthermore his wife and daughter insisted upon us joining them for supper. The evening was a social one; conversing contentedly amongst ourselves, the family and the occasional clients calling in for petrol. Only with darkness did the temperature, which had risen to the high nineties, begin to fall.

The night, however, was anything but tranquil. I suppose the thunderstorm was inevitable but what came with it had me in a cold sweat. We in Britain are fortunate not to suffer the threat of tornadoes and the one that was forming amongst the huge grey-black bruise of angry clouds in the sky had us worried. Both Mike and Steve recognized the symptoms and we spent the night heaped together in a dry ditch in preference to the more exposed timber-roofed pens. Having securely tethered the horses and battened down everything that could be lifted by a rising wind we lay uneasily awaiting events. No rain fell in our vicinity but the night sky was vivid with perpetual lightning while thunder rolled across the huge ethereal battleground in the manner of a gigantic artillery barrage. We watched, in awe, as first one, then two, 'twisters' — the cylindrical-shaped phenomenon of dust and

45

wind — formed and expanded, screeching with mad banshee howls out of the tormented heavens. But neither of them developed long or low enough to strike the ground and, gradually, the wind decreased, the scream died to a whimper and only silence — uncanny in its intensity — remained. We slept.

We were on the road again by 06.30. The day was warm and sunny; just like it had been 24 hours before and the storm might never have been. The sky was smiling, peaceful and serene with not the slightest hint of the terrible wrath it had exhibited earlier.

Two hours later we were passing Crow Butte, a larger edition of the other inexplicable flat-topped knolls that pushed up from the plain. It was, allegedly, a hive of rattlesnakes but its fame stems from less prosaic reasons. The region was the scene of a celebrated battle between Crow and Sioux Indians which ended with the former being besieged and starved to death.

Another stage station was marked as being at the bottom of a two-mile driveway to a lonely farm but the likelihood of there being anything to show for the detour was so remote as to preclude the need to take it. Instead, we turned off onto a country road that not only followed the trail but took us, gratefully, off Highway 85 for a dozen or two miles. The new road's tarmac had worn away in places and was used solely by the few ranchers who lived along the way. The thin ribbon stretched away, straight as an arrow, for as far as the eye could see.

Again the heat was murderous — relentlessly it toasted my bare shoulders as I rode or walked. The agony of my hindquarters had reached well-nigh unbearable proportions and to walk was the only relief. And then I had a brainwave. Together with my sleeping bag I possessed a small inflatable pillow; not much good for the purpose for which it was designed but maybe it held a hidden use? I brought out the square of yellow canvas for re-appraisal and, inflating it lightly, lay it between the high pummels of the saddle and my rear end. The result was startling. Gone was the pain from the rash of white-tipped blister-like sores and gone too was the ache in my calves from constant attempts to stand in the saddle.

Macey's was the name of the subsequent station and its remains were, amazingly, in existence. Close to the Moreau river the broken-down structure looked no older than other more recent dilapidations around it. We eagerly went in search of the

46

Moreau at the bottom of a creek, our minds full of visions of cool clear water but we found only a dry river bed. A nearby pond holding a puddle or two of alkaline moisture at least seemed to satisfy the horses.

We were now reduced to a lethargic plodding, both the horses and ourselves wilting in temperatures well over a hundred degrees. The water in our waterbottles had become warm and unpalatable but, ten miles on, we were in for a treat. The gates of a ranch tempted us to detour in search of cooler liquids and we thus made the acquaintance of one, Fritz Fonk, manager of the Moreau River Grazing Association, who resided in a large caravan in place of a ranchhouse. He expressed considerable interest in our undertaking having heard of it through the grapevine. At his invitation we sat with him under the shade of a tree telling him about ourselves and sipping cold fresh lemonade. Fritz lived alone with his dog and his horses and a herd of cattle, seemingly well content with his hermit existence. He gave us the name of his nearest neighbour another ten miles on where he judged we could camp for the night.

The fever of the day's heat broken we moved off once more, escorted to his gate by Fritz on a fine black stallion. A lonely figure, he stood there waving forlornly until we were no more than specks in the vastness of his beloved Dakotan prairie. General Custer supposedly made the sometimes quoted comment that the Badlands look like 'hell with the fires put out' and I was inclined to agree with him. But writer Frank Lloyd Wright's counter comment that 'communion with what Man calls 'God' is inevitable in this place' had, possibly for us, a rather different meaning than intended. Yet there was no denying the delicate beauty of the strange buttes and a barren labyrinth of pinnacles and bizarre shapes washed into existence first from the high levels of the ancient Black Hills, and then carved by the elements. Now a country almost devoid of water, this region once must have had ample moisture for it was initially a haunt of the three-toed horse, the camel, the rhinoceros and the sabre-toothed tiger.

We found the home of Fritz's friends to be a prosperous-looking ranchhouse approached by an imposing drive. But there was no response to our knocking so we took it upon ourselves to lay out our sleeping bags close to their garden lake, a seemingly idyllic setting for a camp. Supper of beans warmed up on Mike's kerosene stove made poor restitution for stomachs denied both breakfast and lunch but it was all we had. We were even reduced to eating the beans with the blades of our penknives, our cutlery having been discarded at Buffalo. The pond might have made an attractive backdrop for the night but its vicious breed of mosquitoes made painfully aggressive bedfellows.

Attempting to sleep suffocating beneath the folds of our bedding we heard the return of our unknowing hosts but, being out of sight of the house, remained where we were, setting out early in the morning to avoid being run for trespass. We were now in missile country, passing by any number of well-guarded Minuteman silos which only served to accentuate the remoteness of the territory. All too soon the sun was belting out its heat which, together with a hot wind, made conditions insufferable. Slumped on the horses like drunken men we made slow progress back to the hated Highway 85.

But hope lay on the horizon. A faint swell of land all but lost in the haze proclaimed the Black Hills. Between them and us lay the town of Belle Fourche, a sizeable place by all accounts and allegedly well-stocked with bars. We determined to reach it by nightfall.

The town slowly materialised as we pressed on down 85, counting milestones and telegraph poles. At midday we halted in a glade of long-dead trees to sit out the worst of the heat and consume some cold beans and buffalo meat but clouds of biting insects drove us out of their domain. In all it took eight hours to attain Belle Fourche when a car could have covered the same distance in minutes and the shadows were perceptibly lengthening as we clattered noisily into its urban heart.

'Bell Foosh', as the natives call it, was once the scene of a range war between cattlemen and sheepherders and its annual rodeo is looked upon as one of the finest in the West. Otherwise I would call it a place of no great distinction but plenty good enough for us. We lay out our beds in a deserted meadow close to the arena, obtained water and oats for the horses, then made a beeline for those bars to replenish some of the liquid our parched throats craved.

The night was well nigh as hot as the day — we were told the day temperature had risen to an unprecedented 111 degrees —

but the cool fresh smell of the Black Hills was in our nostrils. Breakfast was no more than a swig of water — heat nullifies hunger as nothing else — and we trundled out of town before many of its citizens were out of bed.

The new road was a delight when compared with the ruthless 85, a country lane that switchbacked playfully into a scenery that reminded me of Lowland Switzerland. Furthermore, it was also the stage route. As soon as we began climbing gently the surroundings became imbued with clumps of trees that, mile by mile, blended into ever-thickening forests of Ponderosa Pine clothing granite slopes. Behind us the flat eternity of the prairie faded into the same haze that had initially hid these friendly intimate hills from our longing gaze.

Midday brought a mirage but one that stuck to its guns. Not always do I look upon a Holiday Inn with euphoria but differing circumstances turn pumpkins into golden coaches. The hotel was situated two miles out of Spearfish, just short of Interstate 90, and we could afford no reason for passing by on the other side. Lunchtime business diners were thus treated to the spectacle of three horses being 'parked' amongst the Cadillacs and Chevrolets and their dishevelled riders — including a near-naked cowboy — entering the hallowed portals. In the hotel swimming pool and jaccuzis we soaked away dirt and fatigue of days before partaking of wads of pancakes, fried eggs and syrup — an all-American mixture for which we all unaccountably craved.

Crossing the multiple highway we crept back to the hills as if to conjure forgiveness from nature for our excesses and excursion into man-made luxury, our dirt road pushing us towards pine-soft peaks, idyllic lakes and sparkling streams. Our last night's camp was amongst trees adjoining a miniature cascade, its waters clear and fresh and tinkling. But nothing is perfect in this world — and the mosquitoes ensured an element of discomfort.

Until the morning's sun could fumble its way into our glen, emerging from our warm bags was purgatory, such was the unaccustomed cold but it had us on the road to Deadwood bright and early. Macaroni cheese was Steve's final breakfast masterpiece and no disrespect was intended when we repeated the performance later at a café in Central City, a Deadwood suburb. Our way led through the alpine village of Maitland brandishing its historic beginnings in the form of a crop of old lumber camps and gold mine workings. Somewhere close by was the last of the stage stations but its location was lost in trees and the mists of time. But who cared? Certainly not the stolid denizens of Maitland, nor Central City, astride a lethal highway — our arch-enemy, the 85 — and certainly not Deadwood, famed for such characters as Calamity Jane, Preacher Smith and Wild Bill Hickok, aglow with the commercial benefits of preserving its riotous past.

Around midday we clattered into town and no one took the slightest notice of us since we blended into a place that continues to mirror the lawless community it used to be.

Our ride was over. We had broken no records, notched up no great achievement, won no prizes. But, nevertheless, the soft glow of pride and triumph that suffused our minds for reaching the end of an old trail nobody had thought to follow offered reward in plenty.

There is a brief sequel to the tale. Fresh — if that's the right term — from our Medora—Deadwood hack I was pitched into another horsey perambulation into yesteryear, the mode of transportation this time being a covered wagon. Returning with my companions to Enderlin I continued to Jamestown there to join the annual Fort Seward Wagon Train for its week-long, 100-plus mile excursion into the North Dakota countryside and American folklore.

The previous year the first replica wagon train had rolled out of Jamestown as a one-time experience by a committee of history-conscious citizens but, because of multiplying enthusiasm and support, it blossomed into an annual event.

On this year's train were 130 'wagoners' and our route was a circular one, much of it following and crossing the course of the James river. Participants had the option of riding a horse, riding a wagon or walking or a combination of all three. My anatomy's more tender portions being where they were I chose to walk. No twentieth century facilities like radios are permitted and everyone is encouraged to dress in the garb of the old wagon train days. Being, again, exclusively British, I was excused the fancy dress, my shorts and a dab of woad offering a glimpse of *my* very earliest forefathers.

50

The chore of organising a wagon train in the 1980s is not all that different from what it was a hundred years ago. Much of the equipment and supplies procured for the original pioneer wagon trains are still needed today. One of the major tasks, both then and now, was and is to organise the crew. The pioneer wagon trainers knew that the success and safety of their train depended upon good marshalling and discipline. More often than not the wagon train leaders were elected from the participants. Today the leaders have to be volunteers willing to put in a lot of time and work to the venture. But similarly the modern train has to have its wagonmaster, ramrod, trail boss, quartermaster, head cooks, programme directors, medical staff, etc. In running a wagon train in the 1880s and 1980s, efficiency and safety was possible only by having experienced people in positions of leadership.

Wagons used are similar to those of the wagon trains crossing the Dakota prairie a century before; some, in fact, *did* carry pioneers into North Dakota and are still operational. Many of the pioneers used oxen instead of horses and mules to pull their wagons. Oxen were able to subsist better on the short and rough grasses of the plains and had no need of grain to supplement their diet as do mules and horses. Furthermore they were cheaper to buy and, later, could be slaughtered for food. Today only horses and mules are used and arrangements have been made to supply hay and feed for them. As in the old days a great deal of food has to be gathered and prepared for the trek. Wagon train food was not as harsh as is often thought. Pioneer families stored away supplies of flour, dry beans and peas, cornmeal, oatmeal, rice, rye, biscuits, sugar, tea, coffee, salt pork, cheese, onions, potatoes, root vegetables, dried fruit, pumpkins, sweetcorn and jars of preserve. A good number of these items ring familiar with the present-day wagon trainers.

Tents were as common in the days of the pioneers as they are now. Every evening our wagons were circled together in the form of a corral and the animals staked near the tents pitched around the wagon circle. In this respect today's wagon trains remain authentic — even to a few grisly teamsters sleeping in and under their wagons as their fathers and grandfathers did before them.

Travelling is a little easier and faster nowadays. The old wagon

51

trains usually put in five to fifteen miles per day depending upon the terrain, weather and Indian interference. Today — with no Indians — twelve to twenty miles is the daily norm still allowing an early camp with time to wander off and explore, swim in the river and prepare an evening's entertainment around the camp fire. With a hefty meal stowed away the evening gathering drew the spontaneity and creativity out of many a weary but contented wagoner.

While walking, most of the times behind my allotted wagon, I occasionally partook of a lift on the padded seat or the step when the pace became too fast or the way too muddy. I found a great sense of 'togetherness' on the trek. Families kept together and everyone participated in building fires, cooking, chopping wood, serving meals and, upon early morning departure, clearing camp. Our 'wagon people' came from all over the United States; from as far away as California and New York. Ages ranged from six to over seventy. The route varied in scenery and condition with several stiff hill climbs and exciting river crossings on most days. To see the long lines of wagons, preceded by upwards of a hundred mounted horses stretched out against the horizon was a stirring sight. As the lone Britisher within this dedicated but heartwarmingly friendly band of Americans I felt that I too was part of the heritage of their great country though they thrashed my forebears in battle. America may not possess a history as old as that of Britain and Europe but what she's got is worthy of remembering with humility and pride.

Among the assortment of wagoners was a poet, Betty La Fontaine, who wrote thus about the trek:

'We creaked and rumbled from horizon to horizon,
Reflecting on those who had gone before.
What power drove them to the farthest sky?

Perhaps we envy hopes so high,
And following their path, expect to win
New lands for the soul, to build new homes within.'

3

Round and about the Sahara

DESERT TRAVEL IN NORTH AFRICA

The deserts of this world are cause for a special mode of travel. I have an affection for deserts that surpasses that for every other form of landscape though my knowledge and experience of them is, I would say, the slightest. Come to think of it, my knowledge of most of the world's landscapes through which my wanderings have led me has been hardly of the fullest but this never dissuaded me from travelling to them.

I am not alone in my affection for deserts but, quite certainly, their environment is an acquired taste. The lure of the sea and the mountains is far more universal and conventional. As Quentin Crewe remarks in his *In Search of The Sahara*, 'Any old fish, as it were, can live in the sea, but it takes a very special fox or gazelle or even scorpion to survive in the desert.'

So many people on this earth dismiss its deserts as a wasteland to be avoided or, at most flown over. How wrong they are. Harsh and terrible a desert can be but beautiful and fascinating too. I have touched on or been to a number of deserts and semi-deserts about the globe such as the Gobi in China and Mongolia, the Arabian in North Yemen, the Nubian in the Sudan, the Indian in Rajasthan, the Mojave in California, the Syrian and others but it is the Sahara to which my footsteps return again and again; not only because it is the nearest and most accessible. That it is makes for a bonus but, additionally, it is the most intriguing, as well as the largest though, surprisingly perhaps, not the most dangerous. But let no one in his right mind approach a desert carelessly for there is too much empty space and lack of life-sustaining essentials for even the smallest navigational error or casual mistake. Three million square miles in size — twice that of Europe — it covers almost the entire northern end of the African continent, from the Atlas Mountains in the north to the beginning of the dry savannah fringe of tropical Africa in the south. In the west it reaches to the shores of the Atlantic and in the east to the coast of the Red Sea. A gigantic desert indeed is the Sahara, one that occupies a sixteenth of the entire land area of the earth and is a sure-fire magnet for the traveller with the slightest penchant for adventure.

My introduction to the Sahara was effected in the same manner and via the same road as that for the many tourists who are interested enough to want to take a peek at the desert while holidaying in nearby but more temperate climes. For most visitors the introduction is as far as the relationship goes. But not all.

For those who come to relax in North Africa the proximity of the great Sahara is nowhere so compelling a draw than in Tunisia. It can be reached by car or bus (and, once upon a time, by narrow-gauge train) with no trouble at all from towns and resorts like Sfax, Gabes and Sbeitla. I first took the road to the Sahara in 1969 and having looked upon it I was conquered.

A sunset equalled only by the sunrise, a distant sound of barking dogs, the drums and voices of a faraway festivity, and the incoherent rumblings of a town relaxing upon the dying day. These are the sights and sounds that greet the first-time visitor to the desert.

It is at Nefta, a township of mosques, close to the Algerian border, that the Sahara and its strange compelling remoteness can be sampled even by the most comfort-conscious of us. Overlooking the town on a neighbouring hillock stands the Hotel Sahara Palace. It is a luxury hotel by any standards and two of its qualities are a modesty of size and a serene unpretentiousness. A beautiful building of Tozeur brick, it has a grace that blends with the majesty of the surroundings. But it is the startling significance of the desert unrolling from the front door that gives an impact few other hotels in the world can achieve. From the private eyries that are bedroom balconies, the strange sounds of Gafsa and the pulsating silence of the desert will blend to haunt you at eventide.

Another pre-Sahara experience is to be found with the Tunisian *bled*, a land of nowhere, a desert with no sand, a flat treeless plain that turns briefly green in spring, is parched in summer and is bleak and windswept in winter. The earth is scarred by *wedds*, dry eroded gullies that suddenly become raging torrents in the rare but violent rainfall. A lunar landscape, its frightening emptiness occasionally broken by sagebrush and wormwood, can be home to few. Yet lost settlements do exist in this land of mere subsistence where a traveller seldom proceeds alone.

Here is also the country of the mirage where the sun and air play games as you look out across the half-world in which you find yourself. A Bedouin tent becomes a clump of cactus. A herd of camels is no more than the ruins of a Berber village. Driving along you shake your head and watch the road run straight into the blurred horizon as if into eternity. And when you get there nothing has changed; the road still runs into the blurred horizon.

Occasionally a dirt track wanders off the main road to disappear into the *bled* towards some nameless community of mud-walled houses and unsmiling people huddled in earth-coloured *jebbahs* and blankets. But the folk most at home in the *bled* — as they are in the desert — are the nomads.

The Bedouin are not a race but represent a way of life. The men are tall and lean with deep-set eyes, high cheeks and hawk-like noses. The women are often strikingly beautiful with fine features and a poise that would be the envy of a ballet dancer. But like the brief flowers of early spring their beauty all too soon withers under the yoke of work and rheumatism. Their chins, cheeks and foreheads bear tattooed markings and they are loaded with silver jewellery which is the family fortune.

To the Arab as well as the European the Bedouin is a remote and mysterious figure. The townspeople speak of him in wonder, a little fear and probably a lot of ignorance. Visitors are always being offered a visit to a Bedouin encampment which underlines the air of mysticism that surrounds them. But no self-respecting member of the Bedouin community would tolerate this intrusion by a gaggle of gawking tourists and I suspect that those who do are not typical of their race. The Bedouin women never veil and all, including the children, keep themselves to themselves living in ragged tents and, when travelling, never acknowledge you as you drive by. Tales of wedding night beatings, of vicious customs and pagan rites tell of a life that is scarcely human and unchanged since the Dark Ages.

Bedouin, Berber, Tuareg. Desert names for a desert people.

Their lives — to the outsider — are something of an enigma that, for some, sharpens still further a thirst for knowledge of the vast, terrible and inspiring land behind the *bled*.

It was in 1972 that I made a land circuit of the Mediterranean and touched upon the Sahara to feel, again, the lure of its infinity and taste its sandy wastes in my nostrils. The journey carried me along the whole of the Maghreb, between Casablanca in Morocco, across Algeria, to Gabes in southern Tunisia. From Gabes I continued into Libya and onwards to Egypt and Jordan, there to gaze towards the horizons of another great void.

The railway lines of the Maghreb — where there were any — do no more than skirt the northern perimeter of the Sahara, their ill-laid tracks hugging the coast and burrowing into the thin strip of vegetation bordering Mediterranean shores. Only in Algeria do adventurous branch lines sneak inland to the Sahara proper. From Mohammadia one snakes out to Bechar, of Foreign Legion fame. Another, to Touggourt from Constantine, lunges into low hills to offer a panorama of the burnt cubic cliffs and deep *wadis* of the Grand Erg Oriental where sand creeps up to nip at the track bed.

In the oasis towns new hotels offer a surprisingly high standard of comfort for those who can't do without it. There is the Okba in Biskra, the Oasis in Touggourt, the Trans Atlantic and el Mehri in Ouargla. It is a half-day drive from one town to the next and in between is the stony, hostile desert criss-crossed by camel trains, flocks of goats and nomads in their black tents. Thus again the expected ingredients of the desert are conveniently to hand, this time just a few hours' train ride down the line.

But back on my circuit Gabes was emphatically the end of the line. The Sahara invades Tunisia from the west. Like a tide, via the great salt lakes or *chotts*, it advances to well nigh cut the country in two. It clogs the valleys near Gafsa, brushes the foothills of the high steppes, and rivulets of sand dribble to the sea. Huge herds of camels dot the landscape. Medennine and Ben Gardane are outposts of a lost world. Sabratha, in Libya, is another. Once it was a fine Roman city but today its bones bleach in the desert sun.

I resumed my journey by road and the road offered more adventure than the railway. Tripoli, Libya's capital, I attained balanced high above the swaying cargo of a wildly-driven lorry and thereafter followed a heavy dose of taxis, the communal sort shared by the world and his dog.

Tripoli to Benghazi is all of 650 miles and it made a quite remarkable night drive. The vehicle's clientele were a mixed group of five and we stopped at Homs, close to the remains of Leptis Magna, to eat a hearty meal in a simple stone restaurant that looked more of a ruin that did the famous Roman structure. The driver was a friend of the management so we ate in style in the kitchen-living room seated around an ancient stove while, outside, rain beat upon the tin roof.

The rain gave way to wind, a hot searing torrent of air called the *ghibli*, which stirred up sand and dust into disconcerting whirlwinds not all conducive to safe driving. In more compassionate mood the moon rolled out from behind departing clouds to illuminate the desert in a silvery pallor. We bowled through palm-fringed Misurata to enter the Syrtic Desert, an arid crescent of the Sahara lacking in fresh water but immeasurably rich in crude oil. Beyond Sirte our progress was made painful by the presence on the tarmac of hard-pressed wedges of sand blown across it by the howling wind. Each wedge had to be circumvented or driven over in bottom gear (for they were capable of breaking an axle), while all the time a fog of grit crept into the car to sting eyes and clog mouths. For one who had hardly seen a desert before, it was an alarming introduction.

From Benghazi onward I was packed into an old Packard, with five new companions for the 350 or more miles to the Egyptian border. Most of my fellow travellers left at Tobruk leaving me to continue with the grizzled driver. I entered Egypt alone across what I would term a 'sticky' frontier.

To wander about the battlefields of El Alamein forty years after the events is to marvel afresh at the folly of men. But, as had been the case in Tobruk, Salloum and elsewhere along this fabled shore, I felt an intruder, a trespasser into other people's memories. The desert here is dreary scrubland, the untidy village of Alamein containing little more than a couple of petrol stations, a snack bar and a museum. Memorials, erected by every nation represented in the vital World War Two battle, are scattered like shards over a dozen miles of desert.

The Siwa Oasis was an inland destination I had hoped to reach. It is linked by a 200-odd mile south-bound track from Mersah

Matruh but since both this port and the oasis lie close to the hostile Libyan border they are classed as restricted zones. Every authority to whom I applied for permission to go shook their heads in stern admonishment. The very idea. Though I did manage to get into Mersah Matruh I was soon directed out of it. Siwa Oasis, lying in a depression nearly 60 feet below sea level, the seat of the Siwans of classical times, would have to wait for another time.

The Nile Valley is a green and lush strip of land that lies within the aura of the Sahara though it cannot, in itself, be classed as desert. But, pressing in from east and west, the tides of sand seas penetrate close to the great river in an ever-present threat. Strictly-speaking a journey along this river hardly constitutes a desert pilgrimage but it provided another vehicle from which to observe these incursions and cover a further perimeter of the Sahara.

Virtually all the Egyptian archaeological sites of the Cradle of Civilisation are located alongside or close to the Nile. Some are to be found around Cairo but the bulk of the wonders of ancient Egypt lie between Luxor and Aswan. With three other like-minded travellers — a New Zealander, an American and a Briton — I set off to add to my observations the treasures of antiquity preserved for us in sand.

By Egyptian standards Aswan is an exceptionally well laid-out town fronting the wide river. Its *raison d'être* is the First Cataract, the name given to the rapids obstructing navigation to anything but small boats. Ten miles south is the Nasser Dam that harnesses the waters of the Nile and created Lake Nasser which spreads into neighbouring Sudan. Half an hour's flight away is Abu Simbel where the temples, threatened with submergence by the man-made flood resulting from the dam, have been painstakingly re-assembled. I visited both edifices as most tourists do, the country surrounding Abu Simbel being near desert.

For the 200 miles back to Luxor and beyond towards Cairo we pinned our faith in the crew of the Nile's traditional felucca. It promised to be an original and restful voyage; a change from overcrowded trains and *servis* taxis.

Our craft awaited us at the quayside among a concentrated fleet of similar vessels of varying size and state of seaworthiness. It was one of the smaller of the species; barely twenty feet from stern to prow and equipped with a single sail that could be swivelled to catch the wind from any direction it came, and a keel that could be raised or lowered for shallow or deep water. There were no living quarters as such. Close to the prow was a tiny galley — no more than a space for the cook and his apparatus and provisions housed in a dank cupboard — otherwise passengers and crew lived and slept, sardine-fashion on deck over which an awning could be stretched if required. En masse, riding at anchor at the quayside the felucca looks quaint; romantic even; a breath of ancient Egypt still in operation and not squeezed out of the country's heart by brash modernity. But, closely observed, the vessel displays its nautical limitations and lack of creature comforts all too readily. Our craft had the name *Yournni* painted crudely on her side and, plainly, she had seen better days to judge from the faded and scoured paintwork and the patched and ragged sail.

The same description could almost be levelled at her crew. The skipper was a dark-skinned, moustachioed figure, handsome in a superficial way in his jellaba and head-dress, who spoke the rudiments of English. His name was Sayed Mahmoud Ali. And there was Abdul, the cook and general factotum, a youngster afflicted with a hearing defect that disorientated him to the point where his conversation (mostly to himself) emerged as a series of rhythmic babblings. Whatever accomplishments he might have possessed, cooking was not to be one of them. A total complement of six meant that living conditions were going to be decidedly cramped. Foam rubber mattresses and rugs littered the deck.

We set off from Aswan in bright sunshine against a light head-wind which necessitated tacking from one side of the half-mile wide river to the other. The wind was to remain head-on for much of the voyage but, fortunately, the current was with us. Though the sun remained brilliant the wind was icy enough to have us cocooned in rugs all the afternoon. At dusk the wind dropped for a while to offer a change in the method of propulsion. It was a case of all hands to the oars for the considerable distance to Kom Ombo and with just one set of oars, our rate of progress dropped, with the wind, to almost zero.

Hoving to on an island opposite the famed temple we dined on generous helpings of vegetable stew which even Abdul was

unable to spoil. The night was bitterly cold but by lying feet to head, smothered in rugs, sleep came easily. Janette, the American and the only woman, made the mistake of sleeping alongside the skipper and so fell victim to his amorous gropings.

Next morning, unwashed but well breakfasted, we crossed to Kom Ombo to spend a cultural hour visiting the Ptolemaic temple in company with a battalion of freshly-laundered tourists from a luxury cruiser. The edifice is situated on a lofty knoll half encircled by a bend of the Nile to give the effect of a sort of acropolis against the desert skyline. Dedicated to two gods, Sobek and Haroeris, the former a crocodile god, it contains a small chapel stuffed full of mummified crocodiles.

We left Kom Ombo beneath the bows of the cruiser from which many a tourist enthusiastically photographed us under the

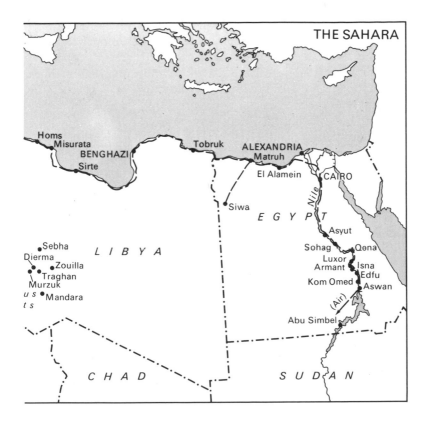

THE SAHARA

mistaken impression that we were colourful locals. Again the wind died and Sayed reluctantly decided to accept the indignity of being towed by a barge. It was the first of many such encounters.

These great monsters, clumsy but fast, form the main traffic of the Nile though before a suitable tow could be spotted by the lynx-eyed Sayed we could only drift in mid-stream being hooted at by the ruthless vehicles of the waterway. A 'tow' selected, much shouting and gesticulating ensued between the two skippers as the distance and fee were negotiated. Bargains struck, Sayed had to bring the becalmed felucca close up against the high steel sides of the motorised barge which made not the smallest effort to reduce speed or detour for our benefit. This skilful manoeuvre accomplished, a line was thrown and secured and our

61

tiny craft positioned behind the huge stern close — too close I thought — to the murderous screw. We took our lives in our hands crossing the gap to the larger vessel there to support our skipper in his final negotiations with his opposite number. These negotiations were cut-throat affairs, the skippers — grizzled, unshaven veterans of financial encounters upon which the quality of their lives depended — haggling to the last sou, their voices rising and falling together with their gesticulating arms for services requested and rendered. Supported by idling members of the barge crew — ruffians all — Sayed was in danger of being overcharged; hence our attempts to offer him moral backing even though we understood not a word being spoken.

We were abandoned at the town of Edfu after nightfall and went ashore with the intention of downing a beer or two. But Edfu by night is even less fruitful than Edfu by day so, parched, we returned disconsolately to bed. However the place does hold an architectural gem in the Ptolemaic temple, a far grander affair than that of Kom Ombo. Described as the most perfect of Egyptian temples it is, astonishingly, almost intact and towers over the mean adobe dwellings of the twentieth century around it. We toured its dramatic columns soon after dawn next day so that we could enjoy the edifice by ourselves.

Under a freshening wind we sailed beneath Edfu's Nile bridge and soon were keeling over at an alarming angle with the four of us, under orders from a worried skipper, moving from side to side of the deck to counter-balance the boat's tilt as we tacked choppily towards Esna. Only once were we in danger of being swamped, but it was enough for Sayed. Thereafter we played safe and took shelter close to a sandy beach to await calmer conditions.

We waited in vain so eventually returned cautiously midstream to take up position for another tow. A gravel-loaded barge signalled its willingness to oblige but this time Sayed muffed the approach and the barge — not wishing to lose a source of easy extra income — slowed and turned thus resulting in both vessels circling each other, caught up in a ponderous ring-o-ring-o-roses with their respective skippers screaming their terms to each other across the waters. Finally we got a rope across and were pulled into a towing position to receive a dousing from the thrashing screw. The 'small print' of the financial hagglings concluded, we made a good rate of knots through the choppy waters to reach Esna just as a golden sunset melted the horizon to turn the Nile into a sea of blood.

Hardly had the first buildings of Esna appeared on the shore when we were abruptly discarded like an old glove and so had to make our own way to the huge Esna barrage that is the main feature of the town. We tied up to another barge which, like us, awaited the morning's passage through the lock.

Following a supper that consisted chiefly of under-cooked potatoes we accepted an invitation to the barge captain's cabin for a round of hot sweet tea and a turn at the communal bubble pipe. Blue hashish smoke lay heavy on the air as the first mate deftly loaded the hot charcoal and kept the 'fire' stoked. With nothing more exotic than a sore throat for my pains I crawled, with the others, into our blankets long after midnight though an early rise loomed to meet the schedule of lock-opening.

Emerging on time we nevertheless had to wait hours before we could finally enter the lock in company with our huge neighbour and a tourist cruiser. A dangerous manoeuvre this, for we could so easily have been crushed and it was a relief when the opposite gates opened to allow us to escape into the wide river.

Esna town, however, promised a change of environment for a couple of hours and so drew us ashore again. The place contains another temple that is the creation of Ptolemaic and Roman times but there was little else to hold us it being an aggressive, smelly, noisy town with its suburbs petering out into the sands of the desert. The highspot, for us, was the invitation to 'take tea' with a local schoolmaster in his simple one-room home where, squatting on the carpet, we passed the time of day.

Our host was the most unlikely of schoolmasters; young yet knowledgeable, aware of his country's shortcomings but not critical of them nor in any way fanatical or revolutionary in his opinions. His single room abode was devoid of furnishings except for a rickety bed, a pile of well-thumbed books and, in place of pictures on the grimy wall, were cuttings from a variety of newspapers of very differing political hues. In his soft voice he told of his life and plied us with questions about our own, all the while pressing us to innumerable glasses of sweet tea as if desperate to hold his guests for as long as possible. His thirst for knowledge was prodigious and I hope we satisfied at least part of it.

Here was a man who was a credit to his country even though it rewarded him so abysmally.

Eventually the tea ran out and we returned to the *Yournni* in time to witness an altercation between Sayed and Abdul that well might have had serious consequences had we delayed longer in Esna. In the fracas the cook had bitten the skipper and the skipper was now twisting the cook's nose. The cook then threw the raw stew he was preparing at the skipper and things reached a climax when Sayed drew a knife. We intervened quickly to drag the contestants apart, allowing the row to subside in a welter of oaths and bubbling insults. So angry was Abdul that, upon emerging on deck, he missed his footing and fell overboard and had to be dragged out of a particularly oily and polluted patch of the Nile.

Except around towns and villages we found the condition of the river to be reasonable enough for the occasional swim which was the only means of washing. All water for cooking and tea-making came from the Nile anyway — and Abdul was never too fussy as to where he drew it even if the liquid took on the colour and texture of brown Windsor soup.

'Aubergines for lunch and wind drops', reads my notebook; hardly an original entry. With the aubergine and potato hash disposed of we caught another tow but barely had we got into position behind the coal barge when the tow rope snapped and we were adrift once more in becalmed waters.

There followed hour upon hour of sustained rowing and this went on well into the night since Sayed was determined to reach some mystical island alleged to be the home of a fisherman friend of his. Our exertions were enlivened when Abdul, attempting to climb the flimsy mast, brought down the sail and, with it, fell into the river again. Fast-flowing here, we had quite a job to get him back on board for he floated downstream as fast as we did. At being accident-prone our cook showed at least one ability.

It must have been about the middle of the night when we tied up at Sayed's island, suffering from overworked muscles and calloused hands. The fisherfolk had long gone to bed but were roused by Sayed to be put to the inconvenience of cooking us a quite delightful catfish supper made the more appetising by being washed down with local brandy.

The late supper precluded the necessity for breakfast by

Abdul's reckoning and a gentle breeze offered opportunity for idyllic progress with *Yournni* gently corkscrewing down the river catching and revelling in every puff of wind. The sun was more than warm by midday so that we were able to bask on deck and at last enjoy the sort of conditions I had always imagined accompanied felucca-sailing. On the opposite shore the industrial town of Armant discoloured the river in a great arc around it and here Abdul broke the idyll by performing his 'man overboard' act yet again but this time dragging me with him. The cause, on this occasion, was a simple joke I made against the skipper who lunged at us in mock fury. Abdul, overcome by paroxysms of bubbling laughter, retreated to the side of the boat, grabbed me to maintain his balance and into the Nile we went.

Banana Island, quite close to Luxor, made a perfect night's anchorage and its abundance of the fruit, after which the island is named, made the sole ingredient for supper that evening. Babbling with pleasure Abdul produced a three-course meal; fried banana hash, banana fritters and bananas, neat, for desert. He never knew how close he was to being *thrown* overboard.

The climax to any archaeological-minded visitor to Egypt has to be Luxor. The enormous temple of Luxor itself and that of nearby Karnak provide the highspot of this vibrant town. Both temples offer the ultimate in sightseeing, the drama of Karnak, the world's largest religious building, being overpowering even in its ruined state. On the west bank lies the Valley of the Kings to which we galloped on frisky donkeys. Once the region called The City of the Dead, the barren satanic hills contain a wealth of tombs including that of Tutankhamen, the only sarcophagus to escape the attentions of tomb-robbers. At the head of an adjoining valley, burrowing into sandy cliffs, is the vast temple complex of Hatshepsut, the funeral temple of Rameses II, the Tombs of the Queens and, alone in a field of corn, the astounding granite Colossi of Memnon.

> I met a traveller from an antique land
> Who said: Two vast and trunkless legs of stone
> Stand in the desert. Near them in the sand
> Half shrunk, a shattered visage lies whose frown,
> And wrinkled lip, and sneer of cold command...

With Luxor behind us we had reached a no-nonsense section of river neither infested with tourist cruisers nor bordered by antiquities of crowd-drawing grandeur. Sometimes in tow behind barges, occasionally moving only through the sweat and 'skill' of our oarsmanship, but mostly by eternal tacking to catch a fickle wind we progressed towards Cairo. On the banks stood unimpressive towns some of which became replenishment centres for our daily bread. Qena, Dishna, Girga, Sohag and, finally, Asyut; none were of great sightseeing potential but they were the real Egypt. Many hold relics representing all ages of Egyptian history but they are scattered; the domain of the local inhabitants and the destination of but the most determined of archaeologist. We managed to keep Abdul more or less dry over the six further days it took us to reach Asyut and restrain both members of our gallant crew from going for each other's throats, an achievement of some magnitude.

I remember Asyut in particular. It is the largest town of Upper Egypt and we approached it through the lock of the Asyut Dam, a legacy of the British though my recollections of it will forevermore be tinted by the colourful outburst of fury forthcoming from both Sayed and Abdul — for once in harmony — directed at a lock-keeper who let other vessels through the gates before *Yournni*. The town itself is by no means unattractive whilst its rock-tombs of Twelfth Dynasty vintage are the chief reason why non-Egyptians occasionally visit the place. But the four of us got no further than the town for here Sayed had relatives and of course we were invited along to be shown off as his friends. And what a pleasure it was. So often visitors see only the superficial, commercial and ugly side of Egypt. Yet here in Asyut, eating and drinking with a people who had little enough for themselves let alone for foreign strangers, we were treated as honoured guests and not permitted to make even the smallest contribution to the offerings. Tea and refreshments while sitting crosslegged on a rug was becoming a regular occurrence and I was glad that I had more or less mastered the technique of squatting for considerable periods in such a position without succumbing to the agony of cramp. We were a fruit salad of nationalities: American, New Zealand, British, Egyptian, Armenian, Sudanese and Turkish, unable to comprehend each other's tongues yet bound together by something that transcended mere language.

Returning to *Yournni* after one such social gathering a small boy had detached himself from the huddle of people outside a bar to stab his finger in the direction of a fat girl in a green shift nearby who must have weighed at least sixteen stone. When I shook my head politely, the girl smiled and said, 'Never mind', with no hint of rancour for business lost, and waddled away. Somehow this small incident too personified Asyut to me as nothing else can. A place of no great beauty but a heart of pure gold.

And with Asyut came the parting of the ways, Sayed and Abdul to their respective homes, my companions south by bus back to Luxor, and I, by train, for a return to Cairo. Before we crossed *Yournni*'s gangplank for the last time Sayed hugged me and Abdul, bubbling incoherently his farewells, burst into tears. I was going to miss that pair.

But it was time to leave a river that is not a component of the Sahara. I'd had enough of teetering about on a desert's edge; it was time to try a penetration.

★ ★ ★

There is a physical barrier to the desert in Morocco. The High, Middle and Anti-Atlas Mountains, commencing in the north-east on the Algerian border to run in a huge rim ending at Agadir on the Atlantic coast, allow penetration only by way of tortuous mountain passes.

Easier approaches to the Sahara there may be but the drama of the mountains make a spectacular prelude to the ensuing drama of the desert. The land beyond differs completely from that of the southern flank of the Atlas. There is the land of the *ksar* — the fortified villages, the oases and a narrow band of faltering green along the capricious *oueds* (dry river courses) which have somehow managed to gain a foothold in a territory of sand and rock.

Three roads pierce the mountain barrier to reach Zagora in the centre, Goulimime in the west, and Rissan in the east. From Zagora a track heads out to Mhamid, a true desert community close to Algeria's north-western border. A traveller may go there by a rickety bus if so desired but I chose a more traditional means of transport when in February 1974, came my initiation to the art of camel travel.

My mount, nameless in the beginning, became known, for no accountable reason, as 'Plastic Charlie'. He was a king of camels; the strongest, fastest and, a rare attribute, almost white in colour.

He was also bad-tempered, fierce and afflicted with the habit of leaping to his feet just as I was attempting to get into the saddle. This had the effect of projecting me skywards like a renegade missile; an additional hazard to others that are part and parcel of mounting a camel.

But I soon got the hang of it. Rising to all four feet involves a 3-part zig-zag, the first propelling you forward over the head, the second making you tumble backwards over the rump and the third throwing you forward again — if you're still there that is. And should the gurgling, foaming beast fail to catch you unprepared on the ascent it'll get you for sure when you dismount.

My companions for my two-week circuit in the Moroccan Sahara were Brahim, the resourceful young Arab son of the owner of a camel herd who spoke fluent French when he wasn't singing bawdy Arabic songs. And Lute, a bearded, moustachioed, desert Tuareg usually high on *kif*, a popular stimulant in these parts. With them I was to make a journey taking in Mhamid and the Algerian border, returning via Jbel Bani to Zagora.

Some people insist that riding a camel is positively soporific but I'm not one of them. Being pitched backwards and forwards like a fly on a piston rod is not my idea of an inducement to slumber. Breaking into a trot has you bouncing around until your teeth almost drop out. 'Grip with your knees', came a voice from afar which sounded remarkably like my long-suffering Pony Club instructor of aeons past. But how the hell can you grip with your knees when they're stuck out in front of you? And the steering gear's all wrong. A length of cord attached to the beast's left nostril is supposed to cater for both a left- and right-hand turn, the direction depending upon the angle of pull. Going left was no problem but pulling right simply seemed to activate the beast's head which swivelled round on its long neck so that a hate-crazed face glared malevolently at you. The words of command are 'Ha!' (move, blast you), 'Shshsh' (stop) plus a tap on the small of the neck which is supposed to indicate that you require him to sit down (if he hasn't done so already). A series of variously-pitched clucks supposedly effects an increase or decrease in speed.

For those enamoured with the notion of camel-riding for any appreciable distance let me offer a morsel of advice. Very early in the proceedings pad your saddle. It won't be of a design anything like any other saddle you know but it'll inflict indignities upon human hindquarters such as you have never previously experienced. And you'll soon learn why Arabs envelop themselves in so much linen when the wind gets up and blows stinging clouds of sand at you.

We left Zagora around mid-morning with the sun high, its brilliance severing the demarcation line between the horizon and the sky. And as if to prove that variety is the spice of life the night that followed was freezing. Brahim and Lute, between them, determined the length of the day's plod, the odd waterholes and the time taken to travel between them, being the regulating qualification. Between the fry and the freeze the pace of progress rarely altered and, that first day out, my sense of values underwent a sharp revision. Life in the desert demands an existence of complete simplicity that releases an instinct for survival. In a Western world suffering from over-indulgence the transformation becomes a remarkable lesson in humility. Stopping only to draw water that is little more than liquid mud and to give the camels a snack off the occasional clump of prickly desert shrub, we went right through to evening before Brahim designated a camp site in the middle of nowhere. The evening meal was carrot stew, multiple glasses of sickly-sweet tea, and the odd date from a sticky brown paper bag. New bread baked expertly between hot sand and ashes was full of grit but delicious. The camels were hobbled and left to their own devices.

Our route followed the dry course of the Drâa river marked by a few empty *ksars* and the skeletons of deserted villages of mud that petered out by the end of the first afternoon. The sombre heights of Jbel Tadrart and a hidden pass led us eventually to a land of dunes eerie with silence. We slept in the open, each of us scooped into an indent of the soft, initially-warm, sand, our clothes on and rugs piled upon us.

Four days out from Zagora had us in Mhamid where I became the guest of the village head man. For two further days we remained here and for all of it I was bidden to share his home, his food and his life as if it was the most natural thing in the world (which it was). In the humble dwelling I was content to sleep upon the floor, eat upon the floor and meet members of his considerable family upon the floor for that is how it is. Together with them I ate *cous-cous* with fingers that attempted to emulate those of the others by forming the damp warm millet into a firm ball for

69

transfer to the mouth, consuming vast amounts of green tea and, with the nightfall, joining in the Berber dances that had me prancing about like a member of the chorus of the London Palladium.

The third morning we loaded the camels, bade our hosts farewell and lumbered into the wilderness, pitching back and forth in the gait that is peculiar to camels. Flat sand and rolling dunes gave way to desolate rock gullies with the approach to the inhospitable Jbel Bani, a 3,000-foot mountain rising if only to prove that desert is neither flat nor solely sand. Brahim intoned one of his interminable Arab ditties and Lute, his eyes glazed from a surfeit of *kif,* led without enthusiasm or complaint towards the stony uplands. When the going got really rough we dismounted to lead our reluctant beasts over a hard uneven track that had them stumbling and nervous; not at all their former haughty selves when sand was underfoot.

A nomad family, relatives of Lute, sheltered us for the night. We spread ourselves over a none-too-clean carpet in company with an assortment of children, goats and sheep exuding equally powerful smells. Meat — rare on a desert menu — formed the main ingredient of the evening meal and this, as is the custom, was removed from the blackened cooking pot, portion by portion, and handed out according to age and seniority; each fragment, in the handling, congealing and collecting liberal coatings of sand and grit. The taste was in fact not at all that bad — rather like elderly mutton. A watery vegetable stew followed by endless servings of green tea preluded a series of mammoth belches and we all lay down to sleep where we sat, a young goat just behind me making quite a passable pillow.

In the morning we came down from the mountain to be claimed by the great plain of Zagora which held us in its sweaty maw for two days until journey's end. Zagora town took on the aura of a metropolis.

My farewell to Plastic Charlie was a private affair between beast and rider. His gurgle was no less musical than the plumbing of a Kensington hotel I know but the bite he gave me held, I'm positive, an inner meaning. Brahim hugged me and Lute became maudlin but I think their verdict was approval.

To a new-found felucca-sailing proficiency I could now add the qualification of camel operator.

* * *

70

Three years later I was to return to the Sahara to make a deeper penetration. The popular 'overlander's' route into the desert's interior is that which leads from Ghardaia southwards through Algeria's Hoggar Mountains to Tamanrasset but, for me, a lesser-known route through Libya's Fezzan promised both exclusivity and an added challenge, the main challenge being the country itself.

Libya, these days, hardly lays down the 'welcome' mat for British visitors bent upon such frivolous projects and things began to fall apart the moment of my second arrival in Tripoli. The simple requirement of a hotel room for the night had me tramping the streets in vain and in spite of the advance booking confirmation I was able to brandish to all and sundry, 'government delegations' it seemed, held a monopoly on Tripoli's bedrooms. My solution was to lay out a sleeping bag in the lush gardens of the city's central square and prepare for a perfectly satisfactory night under a jasmine bush. As half-expected, along came a jeep-load of machine-carbine-toting militia just as I was settling down for sleep. 'It's forbidden to sleep here', they barked. 'You must register into a hotel'. 'Find me one and I will', I countered. And they did — by the simple expedient of ordering one to take me in.

Sebha — no more than a small oasis when I was last in Libya but now the country's third city — is an ugly place of unfinished roads, broken pavements and mind-boggling rubbish dumps. It was from here that I was to begin my long journey to the Wadi el Ajal which contains the records of ten thousand years of man's history.

There is probably no other stretch of country in the Sahara so rich in historical monuments. And to go with the concentration of history is a concentration of geography whereby all the differing constituents of a true desert are present within one comparatively small area. Rocky uplands called *hammada* give way to the gravel-covered plains or *reg* and vast sand seas of fragile beauty — the *erg* — wash against lofty mountain ranges. All the world's deserts — their drama and their poignancy — are in the Fezzan.

To reach the treasures of antiquity in the Wadi el Ajal we had to drive our Landrover more than seven hundred miles across a flat and desolate landscape that can only be described as semi-desert. Once off the Italian-built coastal highway the route

71

became difficult and muddled with the road in existence only in patches and, even then, so pitted and pot-holed as to be almost impassable. Thus we frequently steered a course across the open plain following myriad tracks of drivers with the same idea. An exhausting drive indeed but it is a price we had to pay to reach the core of the Sahara.

My companion was John, an Irishman with a yen for desert travel and considerable knowledge to match. At Sebha we picked up Gamal, a Tuareg guide who had once lived at Siwa Oasis on the Egyptian side of the Libyan-Egyptian border. John had long wanted to run Landrover tours for desert-interested tourists and, on learning of my own interest, had invited me along to share in the reconnaissance of routes and methods.

The smooth tarmac that led out of Sebha was a mirage come true; it was almost ethereal after the excruciating earlier desert 'highway', but, like so many projects in the Arab world, the black ribbon was to turn to grey dust before many miles had passed. Bounding and bouncing along, sometimes choosing our own 'road' in the hard flat terrain, we drove a great figure Z to cover all that is of historic interest in this ancient valley. At the end of the day we searched out a site for an overnight camp that could offer, if possible, a tree or a boulder for shelter.

In spite of a savagery of desolation the long wide valley aspires to surprising beauty with strips of green fertility prized from the waterless sand by the patient hand of man over the centuries.

The Fezzan has nurtured five capitals; quite a number for a desert. Such an abundance of cities is an indication of the importance once enjoyed by this region of the Sahara. The first was Garama, now Djerma, capital of the Garamantes with links emerging from pre-history. To this day the people of this pre-Roman civilisation remain a mystery nation of the ancient world, a tribe who 'pursued the Ethiopian troglodytes in four-horse chariots' and left behind a legacy of irrigation systems far in advance of anything even the Romans could devise. Very little else is known of the Garamantes except, maybe of the land in which they lived, depicted in the ten-thousand-year-old rock carvings in the Wadi Mathendous and elsewhere.

Mathendous, a gash in the harsh grey clinker of the *Hammada*, contains the most exciting and prolific rock art galleries anywhere. Here displayed for posterity, lies a record of what this barren land was like ten millenia before. Few people take the trouble to view these granite canvases and the oasis-dwellers in the valley can raise no curiosity in etchings of elephant, giraffe and cattle. Yet here is proof that, once upon a time, this was a land of forests and rivers inhabited by wild beasts long since moved south to the interior of Africa.

Old Djerma is now a dusty ruin. Thick walls and ramparts, some of Roman construction, remain but new Djerma rises from the decay for, as with all these long-dead Fezzan cities, the new generation of inhabitants are being afforded homes fit for humans to live in.

As Garama, the city was destroyed and raped by hordes of Oriental nomads with burning aspirations to spread the word of Mohammed through the language of the sword. By the eleventh century Garama was a capital and source of influence no more. Of the secrets of the Garamantes the Arabs retained only that of an itinerary towards the south. It was they who henceforth controlled the Sudan trail, a trail that was to create the riches of the new capital, the Islamic capital of Zouilla.

From the eighth to the twelfth century the city functioned primarily as a slave market. From this inhuman commerce Zouilla drew its luxury in a welter of debauchery and ferocity. But the Berbers were architects and gave to their new capital a belt of fortifications and a row of fine tombs that stand to this day. One obtains a strange impression from the solitude of the ruins; high walls brought low by time and the elements. It is the image of a city accursed within the heart of a silent desert. At nightfall scorpions by the score emerge from its remains.

The new enemy came from the south, and the aggressor was Negro. It was the black sovereigns of the Kanem who, from the beginning of the thirteenth century, became the successors of the Garamantes and the Romans in this trans-Saharan corridor. They established themselves in the Fezzan and made their capital Traghen, 40 miles west of Zouilla.

As it stands, Traghen is but another network of ruins close to the new town of government-built bungalows entangled in a skein of lamp standards which modern Libya deems a necessary adjunct for burning off its excess electricity. Amidst the hard-baked mud are vestiges of irrigation canals, guard towers and circular ramparts of long gone epochs.

73

But the struggle for this Saharan cross-road did not end with Traghen. In the fourteenth century it was the turn of the Moroccans who established yet another capital, Murzuk, where the last slave caravan passed through as recently as 1929. To the student of Saharan history, here stands a milestone in his journey. This small oasis presents, in microcosm, another lost African world — the world of the slave trade. The place still reeks of the misery of its inglorious past, symbolised by the Turkish citadel and Arab fort. If film producers are still interested in Foreign Legion epics and are looking for locations the Libyan Fezzan is the place to go. From Sebha, through Murzak and Ubari, guarding the entrance to the Wadi el Ajal on the desert track to Ghat, there are splendid examples of legion-type forts. Few of them are old but all are richly endowed with crenellated walls, redoubts and embrasures.

Another 'art gallery' — of paintings this time as opposed to rock carvings — we found in the Acacus Mountains. These mountains are remote and hard to find since only wind-swept sand tracks lead to them. Even Gamal lost the way on the flanks of the great Murzak Sand Sea and it remains uncertain whether or not we inadvertently entered Niger territory for nothing marks the border. But a night among the great dunes of pristine sand came as a privilege for their ethereal shapes by moonlight make a picture of fragile beauty. In the heat of the day mirages paint a scene of lakes out of which the sand mountains rise and so real do they appear you want to run down to the water's edge. On the way to the Acacus were hazards of soft sand to be negotiated and we inevitably became bogged down, an oft-repeated event that had us all straining to push the vehicle out of deep ruts with, on the worst occasions, sand mats utilised to extract deeply embedded wheels. Close to the border we were apprehended by a motorised detachment of Libyan frontier troops bristling with suspicion and weaponry. But their hostility quickly turned to a concern for our welfare and we were presented with tins of food and a recently-shot gazelle that made a most sumptuous supper that evening.

The Acacus Mountains were well worth the effort of reaching them. Black eroded ridges rose in jagged folds for as far as the eye could see to make a lunar landscape of weird intensity. And within their cracks and crevices and wondrous caverns were cave paintings from 10,000 BC, depicting life as it was then as clearly as if created yesterday. Two days we spent exploring this evocative sierra and delving into fissures gouged by time.

Living beyond the enormous dunes stretching along the north side of the Wadi el Ajal is a tribe called the Dawada, or literally, the 'worm-eaters'. For countless centuries the Dawada have been isolated from the outside world, safe from their enemies but captives of their own security. They live around a miracle of water, a shy timid people retaining their charm even when their privacy was rudely invaded by the likes of ourselves. Their chief food is derived from a kind of shrimp obtained from a lake that only women may enter. They own nothing but their thatched huts, a cooking pot or two, a few vegetable plots, a share of the date palms that surround the stagnant lake and the rags in which they clothe themselves.

The journey to the Dawada was an experience in itself. It was made in an open Landrover owned and driven by a local Arab with lifelong knowledge of driving in the treacherous conditions of a sand sea. In his vehicle we hurled ourselves at ridge after ridge deep into the stationary ocean of sand. The skill centres around an ability to generate enough power to attain the ridges by momentum and then halting on the knife-edged crest, there to tip forward to roll down the opposite slope. Our objective was the Dawada village of Mandara and we made it surprisingly in one piece even though some of us were suffering from sand sea sickness!

And this, quite assuredly, is the only method by which a motor vehicle can reach the Dawada. Atop the last dune that marks the southern limit of their domain the scene is at once the most beautiful and awesome. There before you is a landscape indescribably desolate, composed of sand hills rising ever higher until they appear to reach the height of distant mountains. Not a blade of grass or any living thing is to be seen in the enormous desolation, and unless one knew otherwise, one would be forced to conclude that there was no possibility of human life beyond or amongst these towering dead hills. That there is, is nothing short of a miracle.

The first view of the lake confirms it. And this is no mirage though at first you won't believe it. An oval sheet of water, lilac and sapphire blue in colour and encircled by dark-green palm trees, it is an impossibly unreal jewel in the middle of a waste-land.

As we approached we saw the habitations of the Dawada scattered about the sand hills; little huts called *zeriba* made of the fronds of palms set down in the sand. We saw, too, the tiny gardens watered by wickerwork baskets lowered on the trunks of trees weighed at one end by chunks of natron or hydrated carbonate of soda.

Once the people would have fled from such a visitation but now they stand and watch; nervous, apprehensive but wanting to be friendly. Several women stood in the dank waters netting for *dood*, as the 'worm' is called. It is actually a sort of brine shrimp, blood-red in colour that lives in a water heavily charged with natron, and is comparable in density with the Dead Sea. How any creature can exist in such a strong brew is a mystery as is how it got there in the first place. We watched the women, up to their waists in slime, undertaking their exclusive and soul-destroying task. And the taboo is such that not only must it be a member of the female sex that enters the lake but this only on alternate days. In addition, no woman can enter until 41 days after childbirth and following purification with incense. The lake is very deep in the centre; the Dawada insist it is bottomless.

For cultivation and cooking the Dawada make do with the same implements that their forefathers used 2,000 years before. It is like stepping out of the twentieth century back into the Middle Ages, the purity of their way of life guarded by the sand sea lapping at their doorstep. Questions flew to our lips. Where does the water come from? Why doesn't it drain away in the great heat? Why is the water so cold? But nobody knows and the mysteries give an added dimension to a desert's wonder.

The village headman bade us welcome and, sitting on rush mats in a compound, we drank tea with the elders and played hide-and-seek with children whose initial fright soon gave way to raucous laughter. A school had just been formed and the school-master knew a few words of English so that a faint dialogue could be maintained. We asked our questions but obtained no answers; only smiles and more tea.

Back the way and by the method we had come to forsake one Landrover for another and that one in turn for the services of three camels with the object of heading for Ghat. From a journey back in time to the Middle Ages it was only appropriate to proceed onwards by the traditional transportation of the desert.

My camel was a moulting, tick-infested beast with none of the attributes of Plastic Charlie beyond the ability to bite. We rode steadily, that first day out, and the going was faster than I liked. Throughout the morning I had trouble keeping my mount at the trot and trailed badly behind the other two. But then I discovered that if I gave the animal a belt with my riding stick he would, after a protesting snarl, break into a gallop and recover the lost ground. What was more, I found that by crossing my feet over the neck, gripping the pommel of the saddle between my thighs, I could ride at the gallop without feeling so precariously perched.

We had hundreds of miles to go before we would see the Landrover again and I had private doubts about whether it would ever find us in the weeks to come on the track north from Ghadames. But I'd put my life and trust in the hands of John, Gamal and Allah and their arrangements for our future.

We met many nomads in the days that followed for the desert is a surprisingly populated place. Not a day passed without our seeing at least a dozen humans tending their herds of flop-eared brown sheep and we spent as many nights in the company of others as we did alone in our solitude. Either a small tent was raised for our benefit, or we slept in the lee of a nomadic tent. It was the unwritten rule of the desert that we should be fed and housed by these nomads to a degree that made me feel extremely uncomfortable but there was simply nothing to be done about it. Offering money is taken as an insult and money was the only commodity that John and I had to offer.

Everything in these nomadic lives was bent towards a preoccupation with food for man and beast alike. Food of every kind was their obsession. They were particularly avid for meat which represented to them the most nourishing as well as the most satisfying form of food. This desperate desire for meat, I soon realised, explained their habit of merely singeing it in the flames of a fire as soon as they had hacked a lump off a butchered animal: they simply could not wait to get their teeth into it.

Upon arrival at an encampment the process of greetings commenced and it seldom varied. Throughout the Arabic-speaking world this begins with 'Selehmoo alaikum' — 'His peace be with you', which is exchanged for the responding 'Alaikum wa seleh-moo' — 'Peace to you too'. But a shorter recitation is used in differing circumstances, such as when two strangers pass and here 'Le-bas' — 'No evil', is the operative phrase.

Again our itinerary and rate of march was dictated by the availability of wells, and seemingly Gamal had a built-in map inside his head for we always came upon the vital source of water even when the track was obliterated by sand storms. The second day we moved from the plain into low dunes, scattered thinly above the bedding of hard rock. For five hours we slogged wearily up and down mounds of sand which was always soft and which, in the hollows, was never deep enough to prevent our feet bruising upon stone and clinker. A wind arose, blowing grit into our faces, to add to the discomfort. But we had to maintain the pace to reach the well before darkness, a hole in the sand, perhaps four feet wide and twenty deep, which, the thought kept occurring to me, we might so easily, with the best navigation in the world, pass by. The only clues were a criss-cross of tracks leading to it but, again, this could be blown away by the next sand storm.

We sloshed water into the cooking pots so our beasts could drink, and a great deal of it dribbled back into the well each time, taking sand and muck with it. After sucking noisily at the proffered liquid, the animals appeared to be satisfied, so we turned to filling our guerbas, I was drinking five or six pints of unclean water a day quite apart from the liquid intake from tea and that used in the cooking.

We pressed on into a series of days that became blurred by the thickening haze of our weariness. The most eagerly awaited moments were those at midday and evening when we drank the first glass of syrupy tea, knowing that there was plenty more to come, each loaded with properties that would restore energy to our wilting bodies. But then the dragging agony of movement would begin again, the grinding ache where the left leg joined the pelvis, a sore on my buttock and the pain of cracked and dried lips whipped by blown sand.

For myself, I was happiest when we spent our nights alone, for my nerves became frayed by the uncongenial atmosphere of the camps. That we were in debt to our hosts who had so little for themselves, I was aware, but I found the perpetual staring and cadging for items we had to keep for ourselves hard to handle.

We reached Ghat close to the Algerian border and on the edge of the Tassili n Ajjer Mountains on the twelfth day. The mud-walled houses, the new but empty hospital, a modern school occupied by boys but no girls, and a garish necklace of slender concrete street lamp-standards welcomed us back to present-day Libya. The minarets of half a dozen mosques made the only distinguishing feature of a town that fights for existence against the sand.

One of the most substantial dwellings was that of the town hall. One of its elders received us on the premises and allowed us to sleep and feed in the corridor of the courtyard. We cooked our evening meal of left-overs from our provisions; hardly a distinguished menu but, this notwithstanding, the headman eagerly joined us and seemingly enjoyed the ill-cooked fare.

Ghat, served only by desert tracks, to Ghadames (through which a paved road runs), is all of 250 miles distant to the north and we were uncertain how many of these miles we would have to ride before we were met by our vehicle. Should the condition of the tracks preclude the Landrover using it then we were in for a long ride. But Gamal was confident that the track was passable to vehicles of four-wheel drive at the very least for fifty miles south of the little town. As we set out to close the gap we were aware that a good road lay not many miles to the west, between Djanet and Ghadames, along which we could have driven in comfort. But a border lay between and in countries like Libya a border is inviolate.

The first afternoon out of Ghat we had ridden across glaring sand, then over a range of dunes which the wind had carved into a series of fantastic shapes, full of enormous overhangs that put me in mind of a stilled ocean, its waves frozen solid as they broke over a groyne. The dunes were very steep and we were moving across their grain, which taxed both us and the camels to the limit. The beasts grunted with the effort of uphill struggle, which they made in jerky bursts with each of us leaning far forward to put maximum weight over the shoulders of our respective mounts. Riding downhill was even harder, for the camels, moaning softly, ran stiffly in long strides to avoid losing their control while we, leaning backwards now, our arms braced against the sides of the saddles, had our spines and shoulders jolted unmercifully.

A night on our own made for a restful sojourn but our proposed early morning start was confounded by the temporary loss of the camels. Though their forelegs were always tightly hobbled together, they could move extraordinary distances with unexpected speed in their search for food, proceeding with the determined shuffle of a sand dancer or a series of comical bunny hops. When we were guests of the nomads the children of the family took it upon themselves to rise early, track them down and return them to the camp but, on our own, the chore was ours. On this occasion the beasts had broken all records for wandering and half the morning was gone before we could continue on our way.

We traversed more dunes and their negotiation induced in me an alarming sensation of foreboding. In the hollows between the dunes it was as though I was very close to the edge of the earth. There was no vista beyond that undulating ridge just ahead, nothing but flawlessly blue sky; gain it and I would drop off into eternal space. But at the crest of the ridge a vista did appear, and it was even more intimidating than the illusion of space. A repeated sequence of this and the mind became dazed by the sameness of these elliptical shapes; a sort of fascination that became hypnotic.

We came out of the dunes at last and moved across a flat pancake of gravel for all the world as if a village had once been here but had been wiped clean from the face of the desert. I shivered but not from cold. Tired though I was I'm glad we did not have to camp there though I can give no reason. Instead we rode for two hours and then, seeing a dark tent, decided to camp near it hoping for the company of fellow men but not their attentions. After a while a woman and a small boy appeared, bringing some milk. While we prepared a fire a man joined us for our evening meal and we were pleased to have an opportunity to return some hospitality even if it did expend our limited provisions the faster.

The next day was unpleasant. We were riding directly into a strong wind which continued right through to nightfall, the flying sand flaying our faces. The particles found their way into my nostrils and into my system so that I was eternally spitting out the stuff. We camped again with nomads, this time in their tent, the only advantage being that we had no need to set up our own refuge for the night (though we only did so in a sand storm). The effort of doing anything was getting beyond me; it was more than mere weariness for several parts of my body had begun not to function properly. I found myself blinking rapidly to bring things into focus, and my limbs were trembling with excessive fatigue.

Once again, our days became a long drawn-out agony of perpetual movement under a blistering sun that never, for a single second, hid itself behind a cloud. For me, measurement of time became a simple matter of countless obscure hours of movement punctuated by the relief that resulted from a meal or snack stop and, the climax of the day, the events brought about by dusk. Looking back, I count the days of the journey by the differing end-of-day occurrences. There was the evening when we rode up to an encampment where three men lounged and a woman sat apart, nursing a baby. We paused to exchange greetings before riding on, but the men seemed anxious that we should stay and talk. This we did, eventually accepting their invitation to share their meal though, on closer acquaintance, we took an inexplicable dislike to them. They seemed shifty and their perpetual talking about money seemed strange for a nomad. None of us slept that night but no harm befell us. And there was another evening when we rested with a band of friendlier folk who erected a small tent of hides for our benefit and then entertained us to a musical evening; their bevy of children were still dancing when my eyes finally closed. And came the evening when we learnt that our vehicle was waiting at the next encampment. Such occurrences as the coming of a car are cause for much speculation and news of its arrival spreads far and wide.

We estimated that we were now within a hundred miles of Ghadames and it had not gone unnoticed that the track had begun to improve and was the more pronounced. But the news of the proximity of the Landrover had us in high spirits that last night in the wilderness. It was spent with our informants, a ragged bunch of Tuaregs and we treated them to much of the remains of our provisions cooked over their fire. Together with them we laid ourselves down under the patched and frayed roof in a fog of acrid smoke from both the fire and a battery of cigarettes.

The last camp, the last well. There was a small crowd of Tuareg drawing water, stripped to the waist in the shimmering heat. It was the first time I had seen such men out of their robes, which normally left only the eyes and the bridge of the nose visible. They were a friendly lot who helped to refill our guerbas and speed us towards a village they said was not many hours hence.

A clear morning gave way to a sandstorm in the afternoon and visibility dropped to no more than a few yards. Although the wind was hot I felt fingers of cold playing about my body as if I had a fever and was glad to keep moving through the lacerating void for fear that if I stopped I'd never get going again. By mid-afternoon a line of rocks showed through the driving sand, no more than a low shelf with a few stunted trees standing by it. Jubilantly we settled under a prickly bush and contrived a fire using the saddles as wind breaks. On this we made unsweetened tea with the last of our water.

Hardly had we resaddled the camels than we found ourselves in the village; a white village, its street deserted as a result of the storm. Because of this too we nearly missed the Landrover parked prudently in the lee of a wall away from the near-vertical sweep of sand. The driver must have heard our approach for he emerged from a doorway hurriedly wrapping swathes of muslin around his head. His momentary look of guilt turned to relief as he perceived our pleasure at the meeting.

I never did learn the name of the white village. It was old, constructed of uncemented stone flags to form box-shaped houses and its mosque had a solid square tower that made a bastion out of a church. We spent the night in the guesthouse, a stark building of empty rooms.

The wind dropped during the night and, with no camels to locate and load, we were on the road with the dawn. Gamal stayed behind to spend his rest days in the village with some of his numerous relatives and these now appeared in a great phalanx of varied humankind to wave farewell.

The track, washed clean of prints, was marked at intervals by stone cairns and poles and made effortless driving. By midday we had Ghadames on the horizon.

With its white stone buildings within a thin forest of palm trees, the town likes to be known as the Pearl of the Desert though I wouldn't put it as eloquently as that. However any oasis has a certain charm after days in the pitiless outback, particularly when attaining it across an endless plain with green trees and white houses in sight of one's mirage-tricked eyes for miles beforehand.

An hour north out of Ghadames, very close to the Algerian border, we were again marvelling at the beauty of the dunes now that we did not have to urge camels over them. Just across that border was the fort of Michaguig, one of many French Saharan forts long fallen into disuse we had seen elsewhere. At Michaguig, however, the fort stands proudly on a hilltop very much alive, with soldiers on its battlements watching the border, a bare four hundred yards away. Below the fort is to be discerned the remnants of a village and nearby a mound topped by a classical obelisk: the memorial to the Marquis de Mores who died courageously furthering the Saharan interests of the French a long way from his one-time enterprises in the American West. His death at the hands of a large force of hostile cameleers is the stuff of glory, with the marquis, outnumbered and outgunned, taking many of them with him to his death. Said King Edward VII, 'If he had been English, I would have made him a viceroy'.

We were in Tripoli two days later, my Saharan travels at an end. But a few discomforts and shortcomings cannot dissuade me from a desert's call. 'The desert is the most beautiful of all things', wrote Collette, an opinion that cannot be denied by anyone. Assuredly I'll be back.

4

Mountains are for Madmen

MOUNTAIN TRAVEL IN MOROCCO, INDIA AND NEPAL

In the realm of popular conception the opposite of the hot, dry, flat desert is the cool heights of the mountains. In point of fact this is not strictly true as I was to discover in the Sahara and although desert mountains do not have the height and grandeur, nor summits of virgin snow, they are emphatically mountains all the same. Conversely, deserts and semi-deserts can be found in surprisingly close proximity to some of the world's great mountain ranges.

About the one talent I can claim is the modest one of being able to walk. But whether trekking, hiking or back-packing I do prefer my progress to be made on ground that is not too far in excess of 45 degrees from level. In other words I am no climber though, in the course of my mountain travels, I have found myself getting uncomfortably close to it.

For this mountain travel chapter I shall chronicle three of my mountain journeys that took me across two mountain ranges. The three and more months I spent stumbling along Inca roads in the South American Andes have been narrated in my previous book *Journey Along the spine of The Andes* so I shall concentrate solely upon the Atlas and the Himalayas. For the former my peregrinations are helped along (or hindered) by the idiosynchrasies of a mule and a Bedford truck, this last a mode of conveyance ludicrously unsuitable for Atlas negotiation. And as I am frequently asked by would-be participants about the conditions likely to be met on a Himalayan trek so the narrative of my two more recent journeys — one a gentle introduction; the other a little more rugged — amongst the highest peaks in the world might serve a useful purpose.

First then, to take us neatly from the preceding chapter, to the Atlas which forms the northern bulwark of the Sahara.

The track, ill-defined, disappeared into a great tongue of steeply-angled scree. My mule hesitated but a fraction of a second, then lunged onto the treacherous stair-carpeting of stones. Instinctively I shut my eyes expecting to be swept, mule and all, downwards amidst a cascade of loose rock but the steady clip-clop of hooves continued unabated and I perceived my mount picking its way daintily across the muddled path.

This was but one memory that has stayed in my mind of a mule trek I made in the sullen landscape of the High Atlas. Perched atop a mule brings a new dimension to the experience of four-legged travel. And a mule train winding its way through a defile has something timeless about it; only the plodding camel trains of the desert can offer the same awareness of the surroundings and insight into a life where speed is an unknown word.

A mule is not a difficult animal to ride, nor is its back so far from the ground as is a camel's hump. But there are surprises. There is no saddle in the accepted sense but a hard pack-like device made for the attachment of pannier bags or baskets and any cargo you care to name. It is this cargo that counts and if this is — and it is — an impediment to a comfortable ride then it's just too bad. A mule, as we all know, is a stubborn animal, and some are more stubborn than others. To counteract this factor, the muleteer's bark of command, together with the application of a stick or boot, produces spurts of acceleration usually at precipitous spots on the mountainous flanks where you least desire it.

The year was 1974 and I had come once more to Morocco to help out with another reconnaissance, a friend of mine being anxious to run mule treks in the mountains of the Great Atlas chain. We were a group of ten; five men and five women, and we were spending our nights at Berber villages half-hidden among valleys, in mountain refuge huts, or simply beneath the open sky. The nights were cool, the days hot and, all the while, our cheerful muleteers, from the moment of starting out on a cold dewy morning to the moment they jumped up behind one on the mule to ride the last miles to their home village or the day's destination, sang lusty songs and attempted complicated conversation.

Our general route lay along the westerly axis of the mountains, avoiding the great massif of Toubkal, and taking us alongside rushing torrents and bone-dry *wadis,* through stunted undergrowth alive with lizards and the chirp of crickets, and by strange villages of mud brick and wattle — each house a stepping stone supporting another in the manner of a child's pyramid of bricks. And, all the while, those chasms and precipices were ever around the next switchback corner to keep the heart firmly in the mouth.

Food was the simplest, much of it being bartered for at villages. These provisions were shared with our Berber companions and eaten in the Berber manner squatting round the *cous-cous* bowl or camp fire. We were fortunate to be present at one village at the end of Ramadan and to be able to participate in the all-night eruption of festivities celebrating the end of the feast. In the darkness the fervency of the mass-praying and fanatical ritual of devotions had been almost frightening in their intensity. Ranks of men prostrated themselves, intoning the words of the Koran to themselves, their eyes unseeing but aglow with emotion while, all the time, the preparation of the *mischouvi* — the communal consumption of a whole roast sheep — proceeded against the rising crescendo of the rhythm of drums and wailing women's voices terminating in unearthly screams.

Our transfer from mule to truck came about only because of an administrative necessity of getting the vehicle, in which we had driven to Morocco from Britain, from one point to another. It was never intended to be part of the reconnaissance. Someone had facetiously suggested we drive it to Imlil at the base of the Toubkal massif by way of the backbone of the Atlas and, all of a sudden, the suggestion became a proposal and a challenge. Our leader — one Rene Dee of my own hometown, Brighton — initiated the idiotic project with a harmless question, 'I wonder if it'd be possible to reach the base of Toubkal from here?' 'Here' was a village called Agouim and behind us was the Tizi-n-Tichla Pass through which the road had coiled.

At the junction at Agouim a signpost indicated a place called Sour to be 26 kilometres distant; the map assured us that a road of sorts led to it. Thereafter the road expired and even the enlarged inset became very vague at positioning the various tracks that led in the direction of Toubkal.

'Perhaps we would learn something at Sour', I observed doubtfully. 'We can always come back'. As I said it I foresaw we were in for a rough ride. As if Rene would ever turn back. Ex-overland driver, soldier, traveller and budding explorer, defeat was a word foreign to his vocabulary. He turned the Bedford into the dirt

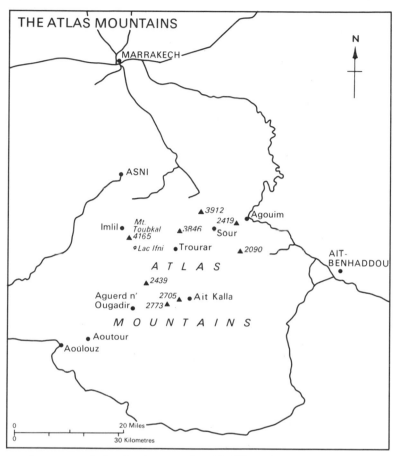

THE ATLAS MOUNTAINS

MARRAKECH

N

ASNI

▲3912
Imlil•   Mt.   2419▲   •Agouim
Toubkal   ▲3846   •Sour
▲4165
○Lac Ifni   •Trourar   ▲2090   AIT-
BENHADDOU
•
A T L A S

▲2439

Aguerd n'   2705▲   •Ait Kalla
Ougadir•   2773▲

M O U N T A I N S

•Aoutour
•Aoulouz

0   20 Miles
0   30 Kilometres

road, surveyed the horizon and said, 'Yes, I suppose we could'.

The road to Sour wasn't exactly the M1. Clouds of dust billowed up and enveloped us all in a grey film. The canvas sides of the truck were furled to allow for extra ventilation under the hot sun and because, at the reduced speed, the exhaust fumes had a sickening habit of seeping back into the buck instead of dissipating at the rear.

We never actually discovered Sour. Two baked mud dwellings marked a junction of the dust road and a local bright boy sent us rattling along the left fork towards a further couple of houses on the skyline. Halfway there a passer-by confirmed our suspicions that we were on the road to Ait-Kalla and that we had passed

Sour. So we returned to the junction and took the other fork, which is how we came, eventually, to Tiourar. And we *knew* this was Tiourar because all nine inhabitants were bunched together with nothing to do except enthusiastically affirm to bewildered travellers that this was indeed Tiourar.

The condition of the track deteriorated further. Veins of rock stood out on its surface and crevices lay in wait for a moment of careless driving. Corners never planned with 3-ton trucks in mind had brought our speed down to a crawl. 'Can we get through to the Azrou?' Rene enquired of the nine wise men. Solemnly they gazed at our vehicle, went into a huddle and emerged with their verdict. 'No', said four of them. 'Yes', said five. Encouraged by a majority of one on the side of what he would do anyway, Rene continued.

Or at least we continued to the river. Small stream if you like but it ran deep in a fissure and required a bridging party to effect its negotiation. Twice the wheels stuck; the third time we took it at a run for it was a downhill gradient.

The cold of early evening forced the battening-down of the canvas. Diesel fumes swirled in the buck. Sweat and dust-stained handkerchiefs became plugs for foul-tasting mouths. Smarting eyes cascaded crocodile tears. Choosing to freeze rather than asphyxiate, I balanced myself precariously on the rear of the chassis and, standing on the tailboard breathing God's fresh albeit frozen air, rode out most of the frightful lurches. Then we plunged into a hole and everyone was on top of one another. I was lucky to escape with a badly scraped thumb and a bruised rib. Thereafter, I chose asphyxiation as the old Bedford ploughed on with darkness adding a new hazard.

Each hairpin bend subsequently took three and even four shunting movements to negotiate. Too far to the right and we scraped the rocky wall; too far to the left and our wheels were in thin air over a forty-foot drop. Only one headlamp worked, the other having been extinguished by a well-aimed stone from a small boy in Agouim.

Somewhat the worse for wear we arrived at what purported to be Azrov and negotiated the overnight hire of a bare room in a stone and mud building. The arrival of a truck-load of visitors from another planet would not have drawn larger crowds and, under their intense scrutiny, we cooked our stew and prepared for bed. With no water available and it being too cold to undress, such preparations were minimal but certain calls of nature had to be answered. 'Mind the dogs', warned the villagers and we found out what they meant when two members of the party, ashen-faced and clutching various items of apparel, threw themselves into the room ahead — but only just — of half a dozen snarling beasts. During daytime, stupefied by heat, Atlas village dogs are subdued, cringing creatures but at night their more ferocious instincts return. In a state of siege — two of us in the truck — we spent an uneasy, freezing night.

Early next morning we continued to what we termed the Imlil junction though 'continued' makes it sound like a spin down the road. The track narrowed to little more than the width of the Bedford, which was satisfactory on the straight, the complications only arising on the bends. Most of the time I was — thankfully — out of the truck walking backwards ahead of it watching the inches between the off-side wheels and precipitous edge of the track and trying to judge if the edge would hold as the vehicle inched forward.

One of the hand signals arranged between Rene and I consisted of a quick flip of the fingers which meant 'accelerate like hell' because the edge of the track was collapsing into the chasm below. Fortunately the innocents in the back remained ignorant of the reason for the many sudden bursts of speed!

Thus we crawled thankfully into the village of Imlil, lying inert at the foot of Mount Toubkal. The mission was accomplished. But now we had a new decision to make — to go on and try to link up with the main Ouarzazat-Agadir road. 'We *could* go back,' Rene suggested gently 'or we *could* carry on; it's about the same distance.' Nobody was enthusiastic about going back and on the basis that at least the horrors ahead would be novel, we decided to carry on.

All around, the great bulk of the High Atlas loomed threatening and indignant that a motor vehicle had had the nerve to invade its wild domain. Little boys emerged from mud dwellings to stand amazed rooted to the spot or excitedly draping themselves along the truck's sides, depending upon their degree of boldness. The village elders were coerced into admitting it *might* be possible to get to Aoulouz, which was astride the Agadir road. It was enough for Rene.

With Toubkal on our doorstep at least we knew where we were. The map showed Aoulouz to be some 50 kilometre distant. As the crow flies. A dotted line on our map linked a number of village names which grew more numerous some ten miles before Aoulouz. In the usual bottom gear we ground out of Imlil and took the left fork. Ten minutes later we came to the trees.

The first — a fine walnut — flung a heavy bough across our path. There was no getting by, though we tried for nearly an hour, and no detour was possible. Or so we were gleefully informed by our retinue of young Berbers. A child emissary was sent to Imlil and a delegation arrived to ponder our fate — and to bargain the price of tree surgery. Five pounds it cost us and two hours of time before the offending limb was axed to the ground.

Thereafter we were frustrated by a succession of large overhanging trees, many of them requiring three males of the party to lie athwart the canvas roof and bodily lift each branch away from the framework as the vehicle inched forward beneath. Twice a companion and I were swept painfully back across the sagging canvas through a breakdown of communication between roof party and driver.

A river successfully forded, the villages of Assarad and Tanmitert negotiated, we made our way past more obstructing trees, until we hit the rock.

To cross a damp patch of sand we had accelerated, got stuck and reversed straight onto a huge, partly-submerged boulder. It promptly showed its wrath at being so rudely disturbed by upending and wrapping itself around the rear axle and other vulnerable mechanisms in the belly of the vehicle. Checkmate. Everyone disembarked and lay flat beneath the Bedford to push at the stone — but nothing happened. Reinforcements arrived. Even in the remotest districts of the world people will suddenly emerge from nowhere at times of crisis. One of them had an entrenching tool with him and soon he and his colleagues had scraped a hole into which the boulder could be laid again to rest, thus freeing the vehicle. An issue of cigarettes all round, accompanied by expressions of thanks to our Berber working party and we were again on our way.

Beyond Tizourine the excruciating track could be seen wandering down the side of the right-hand shoulder of the valley to disappear into infinity. The countryside was magnificent; but most of it was a hundred feet sheer below us and, more alarmingly, but four inches from the offside wheels. Feeling like the man who used to hold the red flag in front of Victorian trains, I continued my truck-conducting task (which at least kept me out of the vehicle) guiding its wheels away from that nightmare edge. Eagerly we peered ahead as we rounded each spur only to see the track stretching endlessly ahead to the next one.

The Bedford was taking ferocious punishment. Lurching, bumping, skidding, its engine sometimes screaming with pain as it took some horrific incline, we ploughed on. Surely, if nothing else, the vehicle would run out of diesel fuel, a prospect that frightened the life out of us. It was not one that escaped Rene either but he forbade anyone to take a dipstick reading. Bliss can sometimes be ignorance.

And so we came to the township of Aguerd n'Ougadir which boasted a mosque and some whitewashed buildings. More significant there was a *car* standing in the main square. And indeed the road out of Aguerd n'Ougadir *was* an improvement for a mile or two though it deteriorated again at Tamaout.

It was darkness that finally defeated us; not any malfunction on the part of that courageous old Bedford. We spent the night uncomfortably on the stony bed of a river hoping it wouldn't rain.

In the morning, damp and bleary-eyed, we gained Tasdrent but the thicker line on the map was a fallacy dreamed up by the optimistic cartographer. 'Aoulouz four kilometres down the road', affirmed a squatting Tasdrentian, and ten kilometres later we reached it.

We had broken no records, nor had we negotiated the full length of the Atlas by a long way but, assuredly, we had accomplished a drive quite certainly no Bedford truck has ever attempted before. The hard tarmac that swished beneath the tyres was music in our ears.

Perhaps it comes as no surprise when I tell you that Rene's tours by mule (or truck) in the Atlas never blossomed into the greatest holiday venture ever. Next time I'm about the Atlas I'll stick to my feet.

★ ★ ★

When I told my wife that we had *both* been invited to join a trek in the Himalayas she visibly paled. Not, I hasten to add, because she dislikes walking — far from it; her daily shopping incursions in Brighton town clock up a mileage of some twenty a week, half of it uphill, while the renowned Undercliff Walk between Brighton Marina and Saltdean is her happy tramping ground whenever the sun shines out of a clear blue sky. No, her initial reaction was that of any comfort-loving being when presented with the prospect of a first visit to India. Marble temples but mostly mud huts, maharajas but mostly beggars, lepers roaming the streets and handcarts making dawn rounds gathering up the bodies of those who'd died on the pavements during the night; sweating jungles, baking deserts and icy mountains. These were the images that flashed through her mind. Additionally she didn't like camping and, most daunting question of *la femme* anywhere: what *was* she going to wear?

The list of participants was not at all revealing. Every name was prefixed by a sober Mr. Mrs. or Miss, with one captain. Only Mr. Stratte-McClure and Miss Chabot-Le-Conte offered a partnership that aroused some interest. For an expedition into a fastness of the Imperial Raj and one of its cherished hill stations we appeared to be a modestly down-to-earth little group.

And so it came about that, under the initial jurisdication of Richard Waller, botanist and ornithologist, Anna (now suitably booted and spurred) and I became fused into the party of twelve. For the first part of our journey we took the toy-like 1903-built Viceroy's Railcar from Kalka up into the hills to Simla — just as the Viceroy himself would have done to escape from the summer heat of the plains.

With its green meads of asphodel, of hyacinth and celandine, of carmine rhododendron trees surrounded by solemn forests of deodar and spires of pine, Simla still retains the ghost of its past splendours. To me it was a smiling caricature of a small Sussex town, its church a faithful copy of those I've seen at Burgess Hill or Uckfield. Yet when did Burgess Hill sprout a bazaar? Inhabiting it were very un-Sussexlike characters; stately Punjabis, southern Indians with dark faces and rapid gestures, hill people with their Mongoloid features, and the occasional *Lhama*, complete with his prayer wheel, tinder and flint.

Based for a couple of days at the elegant Woodville Guesthouse, a Rajah's former private residence, we took stock of both Simla and ourselves. We strolled the Mall, looked over Scandal Point, gawked at Vice Regal Lodge (now the Indian Institute of Advanced Studies), learnt that the church was in fact a cathedral and walked, daringly, to Jakko Hill on the outskirts of town. As for ourselves, no interesting eccentricities initially blossomed. The Stratte-McClure/Chabot-Le-Conte partnership turned out to be two young Americans, but the army captain showed distinct promise of odd behaviour and a 'Mr' Champion gave out that he was once Governor for the Outer Hebrides. An addition to the group was Kranti Singh who was to lead us on the trek. A tall sophisticated Indian, his attentions were all too soon focussed upon the female Chabot-Le-Conte half of that partnership. At a round dozen we were all set for a hike labelled 'Venturing to Kulu'.

It would have been no arduous undertaking to have walked to Dalash in Outer Saraj from whence the trek commenced but with a road that runs through Narkandah it was thought beneficial to drive us to see a view that is reputed to be ultra-spectacular. If so it was diluted by a heat-haze but the delicious coffee in the guest-house made amends. The drive into Narkandah was typically hairpin with frequent notices on display in both English and Hindi exclaiming 'Safety Saves' and 'Make Safety a Habit'; advice steadfastly ignored by Indian drivers. The village is a tiny hill-top place with a little wooden Tibetan shrine, a school, post-office and a few primitive shops. The view, if we could have seen it, looks across the deep Sutlej valley towards the eternal snows of Spiti and Rampur Busahr.

From Narkandah the road continued along the bottom of the Sutlej valley alongside, and occasionally crossing, the river. We are, we were told, on the Hindustan-Tibet road and, in keeping with its impressive but unkempt image, had to push our bus over portions liberally doused with encroaching sand. Maybe the omitted walk to Dalash would have been less energetic.

Dalash village has been accessible by road for not many years so visitors there are still looked upon as a pleasant novelty. At one time a traveller could follow mule tracks south to the old-established mission station at Kotgarh or north over the Jalori Pass where we were going. The village contains an ancient temple which we dutifully inspected en route, up a steep footpath, to the resthouse all the time in the boistrous company of some quite delightful schoolchildren.

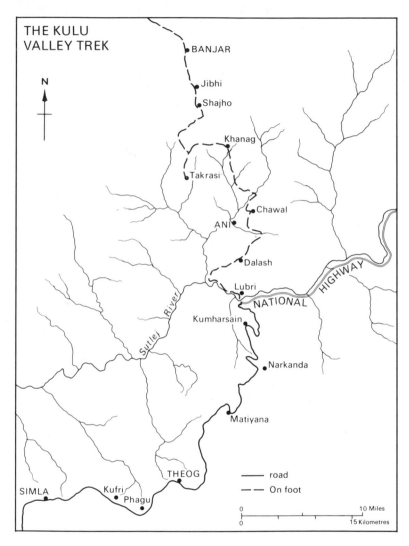

THE KULU
VALLEY TREK

N

BANJAR

Jibhi

Shajho

Khanag

Takrasi

Chawal

ANI

Dalash

Lubri

NATIONAL   HIGHWAY

Kumharsain

Narkanda

Sutlej River

Matiyana

THEOG

——— road

– – – On foot

SIMLA   Kufri
           Phagu

0   10 Miles

0   15 Kilometres

The big attraction of this particular trek to many arises from the fact that there are resthouses, constructed by the then British-run forest administration, sited in commanding positions at extremely convenient intervals along the whole route. That of

Dalash was a typical example. Built in what might be described as Victorian railway-station style, with regular blocks of stone and thick mortar layers, each has two or three sizeable rooms, plainly furnished. At the rear were small storerooms and bathrooms — with or without running water — and at the front was a wooden verandah. A discreet distance away were the kitchen and staff quarters. Most resthouses are now deserted, although the provincial government retains a caretaker at each one.

Until the end of the British Raj they were in continuous use, and equipped with all the minor luxuries of a now vanished society. Some of the items of furniture survive; armchairs with extension foot-rests and *chaise-longue* type sofas upon which the sahibs could recline in varying forms of horizontal pose while sipping their *chota-pegs*. The resthouse here had none of these refinements but we were to come across and appreciate others of old-fashioned, strangely out-of-place comfort at a later stage in the trek.

As was to be the case on all such sojourns there were always too many of us for the resthouse to accommodate in civilised style so the overflow had to make do with a tent. And with these erected in advance by our cheerful team of cooks and porters we were relieved of the task of raising or striking camp at the end of a day's walking. A team of packhorses carried our heavy baggage so all that was required of us to give an impression of backpacking was to carry a miniscule knapsack containing no more than a waterproof, pullover and one's picnic lunch.

Puritans may deplore the idleness of such an expedition but then puritans don't have to do as we did. I found the undeniable sensation of luxury on trek extremely pleasant and though I normally abhor the thought of other people having to do my dirty work the route was so easy and our porters so obviously content with arrangements that I could raise no guilty conscience.

We met our staff at Dalash and were introduced to the chief cook as well as a Tibetan-featured individual called Lama who might well have been a wandering holyman when not humouring the likes of us. With no electric light, bedtime universally came with darkness and we drew lots for a room or a tent.

We rose at five, helped by a cup of tea, to a prepared breakfast of cereal and scrambled egg with *chapatis* and we were on our

95

way well before the cool of early morning had dissipated. Although Dalash itself was high on the north wall of the Sutlej valley there was still a steady climb ahead for the first hour or more to gain the contour-following forest tracks connecting the ridge-top villages. Thereafter the walking became more or less level at around 7,000 feet and, though only the first day out, the pattern of the trek began to materialise. Straightaway the American couple proceeded to forge ahead at great speed perhaps to dissociate themselves from the remainder of the group all of whom were well into middle age. I have to admit that the pace was too slow for me but, being middle-aged myself, and noting that Anna thoroughly approved of the relaxed atmosphere, I was more than happy to go along with it. Richard Waller soon came into his own, gathering about him those interested in flowers and birds, to dawdle and detour into the undergrowth after particular specimens. This made our progress even slower but since the day's trek was of only five hours duration anyway, time was on our side, and we could enjoy the detours.

The forests through which we walked were mostly of large pines, including the vast deodars; but also ilex, chestnuts with flaky barks, and some bamboo. Through them flitted yellow-billed blue magpies with their distinctive long tails, tiny nut-crackers and white-capped redstarts while overhead, soaring against an eternally blue sky, were griffin vultures, lammer-geyers, peregrine falcons and kestrels. Botanists amongst us released cries of joy — to the dismay of the bird-watchers — as they sighted iris, ground orchids, geranium and primula.

Thus we advanced in a spasmodic manner, usually in three separate groups with the Americans always in the lead and only letting us catch them up at junctions of the path where they had to wait to discover which direction to take. Only at lunchtime would we all congregate to spread ourselves on a ridge or in a clearing to consume our tinned fish or meat paste *chapati* sandwiches.

The second resthouse, called Shila, was situated among trees and so was in permanent semi-darkness but it afforded a fine view across the valley to the snowy peaks of the Spiti and Kinnaur mountain range far beyond. Darkness turned it into a magic landscape of grey undulations, like a stilled ocean, with the phosphorescent ribbon of the Sutlej river winding, serpent-fashion, at its base. Anna and I picked a tent for the night; not a success so far as my good wife was concerned since the issued sleeping-bag was one of those resembling a straightjacket. But dinner of soup, curry with vegetables and salad in unrestricted quantity made an appropriate end to the day.

A series of villages provided the high spots — literally — of the next day's six-hour perambulation. The houses were of stone with timber bondings and roofs of slate. A lower roof afforded cover for animals and an upper floor provided living quarters for the family — more often than not a pretty populated one. Around the upper floor were primitive wooden balconies, protected from winter rain by the overhanging eaves of the roof. Many houses had fine stone courtyards adjoining and forty or fifty such dwellings huddled together at different levels formed a picturesque urban complex of which the central feature was a tall tower of stone and beautifully-carved wood used as a central store. Many such villages possessed a local temple reverently set apart on its own piece of ground; sometimes in a sacred grove.

There was always time for a pause amongst these communities thus providing opportunity to meet the inhabitants and, occasionally of being invited into a school or home. All were immensely friendly and our appearance among them seemed to offer as much pleasure to them as they gave to us. Children were released from school to greet us while the head man invariably arrived to lead us on a grand tour of his domain. The older men of the village were dressed in undyed woollen trousers and coats, the women in brightly-coloured cottons, long dresses and shawls; their shoes made of hemp. Generally-speaking their life, although extremely poor, seemed to be above the misery level; certainly better than that of the teeming millions down on the plains.

Each village community cultivated a series of tiny, painstakingly-made terraces on a bi-annual crop system: a summer crop of maize harvested in October, and a winter crop of wheat, harvested in April. They also possessed cows, sheep and goats; but no poultry or pigs which are considered unclean. Drying corn cobs, laid out on every available flat roof, made a vivid splash of orange against a predominantly brown background.

Margi resthouse lay at 7,500 feet, amongst apple trees and a belt of cosmos daisies. Flowers that would have cost a small fortune if purchased in a British florist sprinkled the ground like confetti among rhododendron trees, dardamon and a profuse selection of mushrooms, one gigantic specimen of which Anna, who has considerable knowledge of mushrooms, cooked for supper. Nobody else trusted the thing and even our Indian cooks were horrified at our intentions to eat a growth they plainly thought would cause instant insanity, even demise. The trek was taking us into semi-tropical forest, damp and cool under the canopy of foliage but abruptly hot in clearings upon which a warm sun concentrated its power as if in revenge at being denied entry elsewhere.

A steep climb to the ridge at over 9,000 feet was a feature of the third day but this was accomplished mostly beneath the shade of the trees. Moreover much of the way was laid out as if by a landscape gardener with roses, clematis, orchids and gentians excited into exuberant growth. The American couple had been brought to heel by an exasperated Kranti forced to make an energetic detour in search of them when they had anticipated — wrongly — the route at a junction of the path. They now remained with the main party which was a mixed blessing since they seemed rather resentful. The captain too began to behave most strangely though it was not until later that we discovered he was suffering from some serious malfunction.

The ridge we now straddled was one of hundreds that interlock with one another in the Western Himalayan foothills. From them, particularly in the evening and early morning, the other tree-covered ridges look merely two-dimensional, like the teeth of an undulating saw, flowing from their higher ends in the north, to where they expire in the south into the chasm of the Sutlej. During the day a heat-haze softened the outlines though the effect was still discernible.

An abrupt and stony descent led to the Taralla resthouse from whence the sound of a rushing stream was tantalising though the source was invisible. Mountain torrents had been a feature of the walk over the last couple of days but they had always appeared in the cool of morning when we least desired a dip in their cold clear water. But near Taralla a torrent coincided with a midday sun-ravaged patch of path and most of us took the opportunity for a refreshing swim.

The evening meal consisted of an assortment of curries a regular contender being a lentil curry known as *dahl* which varied in popularity among the group. Anna adored it but repeated appearance on the dinner table earned the dish the title of DDD or 'damned dull dhal', inspired, I think, by Lady Betjeman, a regular guide on this route. But against any accusation of slight monotony of fare must be recorded an improvement in living conditions with resthouses increasing in stature at each consecutive overnight sojourn.

A case in point was that of Karnag where we were to spend two nights, with a rest day between. Here was not only the luxury of running water and bedrooms with toilets but a superb view from the verandah to go with it. But such luxury has to be earned and the catch was the longest haul of the trip, an unshaded tramp over a 9,500-foot pass and some uncomfortably-rocky walking. But, again, there were compensations en route such as a village temple sporting original and particularly handsome door-knockers, a perfectly-situated pool tailor-made for bathing and the ruins of an old fort each offering every reason for a prolonged rest.

I have met rest days before on group treks. More often than not they become the most energetic days of all as enthusiasm overcomes fatigue. Anna firmly resisted the temptations of the environment and remained behind to wash her hair while others climbed to a holy lake high above a forest of brown oak, its cold but not entirely unswimmable water guarded by a tiny temple. The village of Kot was only two miles distant too and its *bhandar* (temple) of striking design made another objective.

The altitude was enough to ensure nights that were decidedly nippy and, with plenty of logs available, we indulged in the further luxury of a dining room warmed by a crackling fire around which we sat long after our usual bedtime. I managed a chat with Lama and some of the cooks to learn that they enjoyed these repeated excursions into the foothills though they plainly found it hard to understand what a European sees in a countryside that, to them, is of no consequence. 'But the pay is good, the food is good, and the work not so hard', explained Lama, adding, what I had expected, that conditions on trek were far superior to life in his village.

From Karnag the route swung southwest to contour through some of the grandest fir and deodar forest in the Western Himalayas. Many villages lay astride the path, their occupants busy with sheep-shearing and tending huge flocks of goats. Some of us made a side-excursion to the extensive ruins of Jalora Fort built about 1840 in the time of Ranjit Sinh, the great ruler of the Punjab. Its broken walls stretched dramatically over a number of hills, the dead carcass of a century gone by made the more eerie by black thunder clouds and lammergeyers spiralling for thermals above the heat-bleached bones.

With Takrasi resthouse — another offering astounding views plus some surprisingly civilised facilities for so wild a spot — and a further night behind us the ridge along the Jalora range led, with only one steep climb, to the pass at 10,280 feet. Actually there are two Jalora Passes, the old one crossing the mountains about a mile and a half to the east. The new one was forged just before the First World War as a continuation of the road up the Ani Valley. A small hamlet now marks the head of the pass and at a rough and ready 'chai house' we sat down to a glass of thick sweet tea while gazing upon spectacular manifestations of the Western Himalayas; range after range receding into the horizon. And beyond the head of the Kulu Valley, now well in sight, were the snowy peaks of Hanuman Tibba, Shukerbeh and Mukerbeh. Few traverse this pass, even by the road that runs over it, thus a view that would become a commercial proposition in Europe is hardly known to anyone here, even today.

The top of the pass marks the boundary between Outer and Inner Saraj and the three-mile walk down the other side is by a zig-zag road pleasantly shaded by silver fir, spruce and occasional wild cherry. Clumps of iris growing on the bank above and below the road mingled with bracken and tall evil-looking cobra plants. We passed several groups of men felling spruce firs destined for a bumpy journey down mountain torrents into the Beas river and along it to the Punjab plains. The captain was now weaving twice as violently as the road and had to be helped along. To everyone's surprise the Chabot-Le-Conte motherly instincts suddenly came to the fore and she helped him for the rest of the journey.

On arrival at the Shoja bungalow, a guesthouse beautifully situated in a grassy glade thick with iris, we found tea ready on the lawn and the caretaker eager to show us our rooms. And no wonder for they were quite the best so far while the wicker armchairs and sofas in the drawing room were positively luxurious.

Thereafter the route was nearly all downhill but made doubly sweet by the glades of iris through which the Jalori river tumbled.

As we descended into lower climes so the temperature rose but the deodars, continued to provide shade while the brown oaks were replaced by green holly oaks, white oaks and huge walnut trees. Patches of cultivation appeared, many plots containing cannabis which we had seen as hemp being made into rope. These embryo ropes trailed along the road from a buffalo cart and my attempted close-up photography of the water buffalo's head startled the beast into lunging at me angrily.

Jibbi resthouse lay at 6,000 feet only two and a half hours downhill from Shoja which made the day's walk a very easy one. Next morning we turned off the road onto a path that led along the right-hand side of the Jalora valley, winding through woods and fields to bring us to Chaini. And Chaini is a very odd-looking village indeed.

It contains a number of 200-foot white stone storage towers — 'sky-scraper treasuries' as they are known — one actually a temple. We were permitted to climb the unbanistered stair-ladders to reach their high entrances, explore their strange interiors and, from the viewpoint of the roof, look upon the colourful but haphazardly-lain tiles of the village housetops, many again the repository of drying corncobs. Another temple to observe, this one recognizable as such but locked and barred, and we slowly wound down to 5,000 feet to enter the township of Banjar, the principle centre for Inner Saraj. The place was hot and oppressive as we toiled down the long village street abruptly aware of snarling traffic and its attendant smells, and of disinterested people whose open-fronted shops and government offices brought us back to the world of commercialism. Outside the urban boundary the air was alive with multi-coloured butterflies — Indian Red Admirals, Painted ladies and Newabs, many of enormous size — but our eyes were on the resthouse, this one flaunting its superior grade, aglow with electric light, hot water at the command of a tap and a lounge of deep-set armchairs in which to wallow.

At the gates of the Kulu Valley we had reached the end of the trek as such though our further northward travels were to bring us a little more walking. Kulu, it should be explained, is an ancient kingdom giving its name to the valley of the Beas river which rises in the Rohtang Pass. The original name of the Kulu Valley was Kulanthapitha meaning 'The End of the Habitable

World' — as anyone who has stood at the top of the Rohtang Pass, bounding Kulu and Lahoul, will understand.

Once more I repeat that true trekkers may deplore the idleness of such an expedition and sneer at the comparative comfort of its nightly stopovers. But the Kulu walk does not pretend to be a test of strength and stamina or a lesson in masochism. However nature and the countryside such as offered by the foothills of the Himalayas need to be appreciated from ground level; not by occasional glimpses through the window of a speeding vehicle. By observing it of an evening favoured by a rising moon and the promise of a myriad stars, pleasantly weary but well fed, is as near perfect a condition for so doing as could be devised. And for those who have their sights set upon the mighty giants of the Nepalese Himalayas it makes a useful run-in to a more gruelling type of progress.

★ ★ ★

When I looked upon the Himalayas for the first time in my life I was in a Russian aeroplane flying from Novosibirsk to Alma Ata in Soviet Kazakhstan. I was looking at the enormous jumble of mountains that went by the names of Hindu Kush and Pamir which, in fact, all form part of the great Himalayan chain that stretches across the thick neck of the Indian sub-continent for 1,700 miles, from Afghanistan in the west to Assam in the southeast. Roughly 100 to 150 miles wide it straddles six countries, dividing India from Tibet and making up three major ranges: the Himalayan, the Karakoram and the Hindu Kush.

First sight of the Nepali Himalaya — while I was on a lowland expedition to that country — was a traumatic moment in my life. Too sharp to be clouds, the huge peaks nevertheless floated above the brown haze of the plains. In both directions the line of great massifs marched away into the distance, growing smaller and smaller until my straining eyes could no longer discern earth from sky. Their scale, their extent and their seemingly complete dissociation from the real world beneath us had me awed and determined to see them from ground level.

I returned at the end of October 1979. On this second flight into Kathmandu I could make out Everest but my eyes were for other summits. One of the world's most wonderful prospects is that of the morning mists dissolving about the glittering ice-hung southern ramparts of the Annapurna Himal rising above the lush green fields of Pokhara, Nepal's second town. Annapurna is more than a mountain. It is a complex of mountains and no less than eleven 23,000-foot summits plus a score of other great peaks adorn this incredible massif. I had been given the chance of making the trek to the Everest base camp, now something of a shanty town so I'm told, but the prospect of trekking only to the *bottom* of a mountain didn't appeal. Not that I had any intentions of attaining any other Himalayan extremity. But somewhere between lay my aspirations and the trek round Annapurna along a trail that passes close to Tibet and through a region only then recently opened to foreigners would serve them.

Trekking in the Himalayas is possible at any time except during the monsoon, the winter months being probably the best walking season. And it is precisely because of the monsoon that Nepal is, basically, so green and fertile both in its sub-tropical lowland and the more arid mountain regions up to 12,000 feet. Cultivation extends even as high as 9,000 feet with rice paddies and terraces of millet, buckwheat, maize and barley thriving in the wildest places. Deep in the hidden valleys are communities of people living their lives in a fastness I had thought to be penetrated only by the occasional climbing expedition.

Our route circuiting the Annapurna massif was to be by way of the Marsyangdi Valley, Manang, the Thorong La Pass and Muktinath then to Jomosom and the well-trodden path through the upper valley of the Kali Gandaki and the Ghorapani Pass; some 200 miles and three weeks of tough walking along ancient footpaths that are vital trade routes still heavily utilised, goods being carried by yak in the northern marches, or on men's backs.

It was this facet of the route that particularly fascinated me. In this instance the trails were commercial links with Tibet though no more than narrow footpaths broken by boulders and with space for only one person to walk comfortably. Until 1959, salt collected from the salt-lakes in the country was exchanged for Nepali rice and barley. Additionally wool, livestock and butter were exchanged for sugar, tea, spices, tobacco and manufactured goods from India as it is, to a lesser degree, today.

Our party was thirteen-strong, including the leader, Everest-climber and world-renowned mountain photographer, John Cleare. Our Sherpas and porters were, initially, three times this

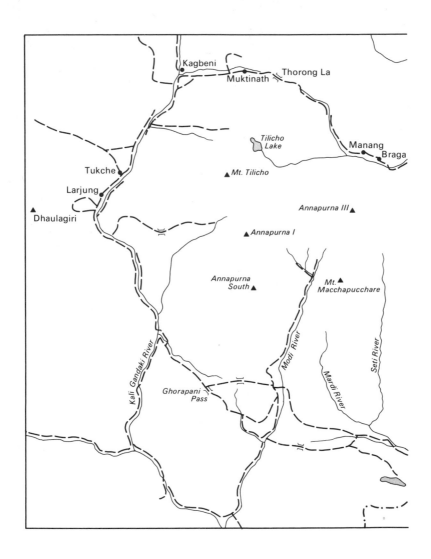

number reducing as the trek proceeded and the amount of provisions lessened. The average age of the group was around 35 with the oldest a spritely if tetchy old gentleman of 74.

We started out on the trek from Dumre, a village on the Kathmandu-Pokhara road, carrying no more than a small rucksack containing rainwear and pullover, the rest of our needs being carried by the Sherpas. My conscience took days to abate on first

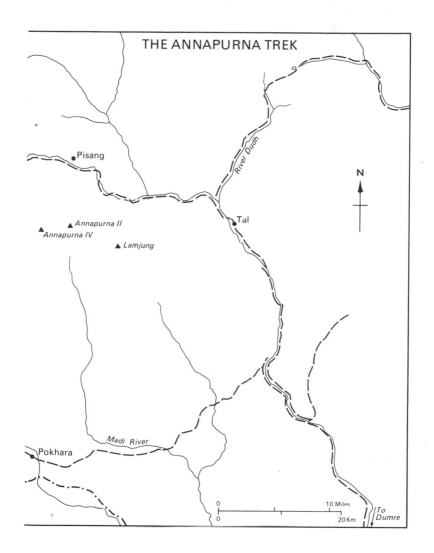

THE ANNAPURNA TREK

Pisang

River Dudh

Tal

▲ Annapurna II
▲
Annapurna IV

▲ Lamjung

N

Madi River

Pokhara

0   10 Miles
0   20 Km

To
Dumre

scing smiling little Nepali men, often barefoot, bearing tents, cooking equipment and provisions on a scale that would not have shamed a royal safari. Among our participants was a doctor who was paid to not only look after the welfare of the trekkers but also the Sherpas, porters and any villager en route requiring medical attention.

At first villages were numerous and large; all were extremely poor. This is a primitive land indeed where only the fit survive but those that do, have sufficient to eat and a capacity for enjoyment.

The trail from Dumre followed the east bank of the Marsyandi river, climbing gently except where it was necessary to cross the steep ridges. Here, in the foothills, the people were Gurungs, an ethnic group known for their loyal service as soldiers in the Gurkha regiments of both the British and Indian armies as well as the Royal Nepali Army and police. Ahead the handsome face of Himachuli smiled in the sunshine providing us with our first close encounter with a great mountain.

The early days were hot and sticky, the hills and valleys corrugated with cultivated ledges while valley beds were chequered with paddy fields and banana plantations. The first camp was a prototype of them all, our porters erecting two-person tents with the speed of long practice and the cooks producing steaming mugs of tea hardly had we removed the equally steaming boots from our feet. The evening meal was usually taken in a mess tent on tablecloth-covered tables and was, invariably, of many courses (lunch was, likewise, a hot meal, the porters racing ahead after breakfast to prepare it at some picturesque spot out in the 'field'). Every morning we were gently awoken by a cheerful Sherpa with a mug of tea thrust into the tent followed by a hurried breakfast of porridge, muesli or *tsampa,* a ground millet-based substance that soaks up prodigious quantities of goat's milk. Such luxury and service amazed me. All *we* had to do was to walk.

With the village of Tal reached after a long and tortuous climb, we entered the district of Manang. Its peoples here are of Gyasumbo stock who hunt musk-deer. They are Buddhists and their features and dress were plainly Tibetan. For days we had been accompanied by the music of running water and now we were to look upon the thundering cataracts of the Marsyandi as it hurled itself through narrow gorges in crashing crescendos. A series of swaying suspension bridges, some of very flimsy construction, carried the path across the river whenever a vertical cliff deflected it from its course. It was these bridges that did more than anything else to separate the sheep from the goats among our group. Although they had spent large sums of money to participate in a Himalayan trek many were to go into a blue funk at the first bridge or ledge overhanging a chasm or precipice.

Vertigo is an unfortunate condition with which to be afflicted — I'm not wholly happy in such situations myself — but, in mountains of the calibre of the Himalayas, heights and sheer drops are to be expected. One of our number had to be escorted and helped over every bridge, her bleats of fear, vaguely appealing at first, becoming a source of irritation to everyone as the days wore on. One man even disclosed to me after the first week that he hated walking! To his credit he never complained during the course of the trek but, on the flight home to Britain, he broke down declaring that it was the worst time he had ever experienced in his life. Yet everyone must have had a reason for choosing the trip.

It was the evening rest periods, before and during dinner and round the flickering camp fire afterwards, that offered the most fruitful atmosphere for getting to know one's fellow participants. Invariably holding forth on any subject raised was the second doctor in our ranks, a lady practitioner attired in a Sherlock Holmes-style walking outfit, who, to her shame, for some reason refused to become involved in the medical ministrations to unfortunate villagers and even our own Sherpas. Worse, she had brought along a library of books which she expected the porters to carry. But on a lighter note I shall long remember our two titled ladies — a Lady Cynthia and an Hon. Mrs 'Double-Hyphen', both of advancing years — reminiscing in loud manly voices on the Second World War Eritrean campaign like a couple of troopers while swigging their respective bottles of duty-free gin which, so far as I could make out, was the sole content of each of their day rucksacks. The older tetchy gentleman usually retired to his tent at every possible moment refusing even to emerge when playfully tempted out by the skittish overtures of the vertigo-prone nurse. They were an unlikely lot to be found clambering around a mountain but it is such characters that add to the colour and interest of a group trek.

Bagarchap had been the first village of typical Tibetan architecture — stone houses with flat roofs packed tightly together. Here too we came across the *gompa* — a Tibetan temple — that is a stock edifice in every village. The Manang Valley, through which we were travelling, starts as a wide plateau, narrowing slowly, its initial stages well wooded with pine and fir that are, alas, being slowly destroyed by villagers in their constant and understandable quest for firewood and the materials for house-construction. At Chame was one of a number of police checkpoints where trekking permits are scrutinised. On the patches of stunted grass, sheep, goats, small wiry ponies and shaggy fierce-eyed yaks grazed with a certain desperation.

Beyond Pisang the land became perceptibly drier. The great bulk of the Annapurna massif now formed the western wall of the valley with Annapurna 2, Lamjung and, later, Chulu, in full view. The crack and thunder of avalanches echoed dolefully in the clear cold air. The heat had evaporated as we steadily climbed to be replaced by the keen air which blew directly off the snow.

The large village of Briga, very much more prosperous than its lowland fellows, was the last before the Thorong La Pass. A remarkable place of square houses packed one on top of the other, each with an open verandah formed from a neighbour's rooftop, the village *gompa* holds an astonishing display of statues, *thankas* (ornate Tibetan paintings) and manuscripts reputed to be up to five hundred years old.

As we trudged through its single street I heard a cry followed by a shocked howl. A woman wearing an opulent necklace of turquoise and coral, symbol of status and wealth combined, had had it broken by the clutching hands of her small son. The mother was almost beside herself with fury. She screamed with rage and attacked her offspring unmercifully, hitting him on the head, back and legs in the intervals of scrabbling amongst the filth in the gutter in an effort to retrieve her priceless treasures. The child screamed at the top of his voice as his mother pursued him, until the child, infuriated and revengeful, hit her back. It was a disturbing scene but one in which we could not interfere.

From the village we could see the enormous peaks of Gangapurna (24,457 feet), Glacier Dome (23,190 feet) and Tilicho Peak (23,405 feet), their snowbound crests rearing skywards. In the evening the sunset threw a veil of deepening apricot over their bulk while the full moon of night made the scene more wondrous still.

The onward route climbs out of the Marsyandi Valley and turns north west to follow the tributary of the smaller Jarsang Khola. Before the region was opened to foreigners in 1977 it saw few outsiders; those that did find their way here being met with hostility. Since then the population has adapted fast to the invasion of Europeans into their territory and now sell trinkets with the greatest of commercial tenacity.

With the exception of a few juniper shrubs and a threadbare carpet of Edelweiss nothing grows in this wild spot where, directly the sun drops behind the mountains, the temperature plummets to zero. Ahead, the scree wall that was the pass indicated the only way out of the narrowing valley. Local traders ride horseback over the Thorong La to Muktinath in a single day but the elevation rising to 17,200 feet obliges most trekkers to take two days for the trip.

The ascent was a long and painful slog, the thin air making breathing difficult. The path zig-zags violently up the steep face and our camp at the top of the pass was made in sub-zero temperatures on a crystal-clear night, the moon offering stupendous fresh horizons of mountains. The way down the other side is equally long and winding but with the warmth increasing instead of falling.

Muktinath, 8,000 feet down, is more interesting than its dreary mud-walled houses hiding a *gompa* or two leads one to believe. The township is located in a poplar grove and is a sacred shrine for Hindu and Buddhists alike. It is an ancient Hindu pilgrimage site mentioned in the *Mahabharata* (a book of Hindu mythology written about 3000 BC) because of the presence of ammonite fossils which are the object of worship. Water is important in ritual purification for Hindus too and the springs piped into the 108 waterspouts near the temple dedicated to the Hindu deity Vishnu are the focal point for the pilgrims. The place is also a Buddhist pilgrimage site; members of this religion revering the fire from the natural gas jets that sprout from earth, rock and water and these 'miraculous fires' can be seen in the Nyingmapa *gompa*.

Tibetan women wearing elaborate head-dresses were much in evidence when we were there and the ceiling paintings in the *gompa* made striking sightseeing. A rest day was held quite close by, the most active of us ascending a hill liberally strewn with fossil ammonites there to behold a panorama that, in all my life, I have seen nothing to equal in splendour. Shining magically in the distance was a mountain of crystal — Dhaulagiri — so beautiful as to leave one breathless. Together with its retinue of crags the great massif overshadowed the Kali Gandaki Valley, its winding river a fluorescent serpent writhing in its dark bottom. Rising from the other side of the valley were the proud Nilgiris — the 'Blue Mountains' — and, far above, the soaring might of Annapurna, resplendent, proud; dominating everything as a goddess should. The wind tore through us as we gazed upon such wonder, spellbound.

The trail continued along the flanks of the Jhong Khola, a narrow stream running through a wide desert-like valley decorated by sand-blasted rocky outcrops. The village of Kagbeni with a red-ochre fort of a *gompa* held us for an hour before we began the unpleasant negotiation of miles of rounded stones of which the valley floor is composed. This was made the more difficult for me since, resulting from an altercation with a yak on one of those swaying suspension bridges, I had sprained an ankle and was now dependent upon a Sherpa-donated stick to take the weight off the injured foot.

The valley of the Kali Gandaki is said to be the deepest gorge in the world. It separates two of the world's largest mountain massifs — Dhaulagiri and Annapurna. The distance between them is 22 miles, and the bed of the river at its central point lies 18,500 feet below.

However the word gorge needs some qualification; it suggests a narrow slit cut by a river between vertical rock walls. The Kali Gandaki is certainly not that for much of its upper course, carved by glaciers in the remote past, is a mile wide, and its banks, though sometimes extremely steep, are more often gently inclined. No road runs along it, but there is a path that can be followed from village to village by men and pack animals, and it has been known for centuries to pilgrims, traders and migrant families as one of the easiest breaches of the Himalayan wall.

The Kali Gandaki claims another distinction. Its upper level is a dry valley. The monsoon exhausts itself against the southern slopes, and although rain can creep along the mountain walls, it does not penetrate the valley floor. A dessicating wind blowing from the south dries it still further, and the increasing altitude completes the process. The valley becomes a semi-desert only 20 miles beyond the point where its vegetation is riotously tropical. In the space of a day's march we were to descend from the sharp dry sunshine and wind-blown Tibetan flora around the village of Jomoson to the steamy humidity and sub-tropical monsoon flora of the gorges below the village of Ghasa. The abruptness of the change was astonishing.

The valley floor swelled into humps like dunes, but there were patches of vegetation that stained the sterile sweeps of sand; scattered pincushions of caragana and bushy junipers that lower down the valley were growing to 50 feet. We were lashed by wind-born particles of sand that had carved the valley walls into fluted cliffs down which sheep and yaks picked their way to the maze of water channels in the riverbed. The Tibetan plateau is said to be the only region on the earth's surface where desert and arctic conditions coexist; the subsequent forest to the north being 2,000 miles away in the wasteland of Siberia.

High overhead, cranes, storks and eagles glided over Jomosom, in their search for thermals as we struggled on leaping from rock to rock, stumbling over sharp broken fragments of stone and endeavouring to keep our feet dry when crossing the myriad streams. At one point we waded the main river, a tumbling torrent grey with cold, to make our way up the east slopes and away from that accursed valley floor. Tiny balls of cloud hung in the sky, as if they had been fired there by anti-aircraft guns. Every sound was audible from a mile away, the clinking of shod boots against stone and the bells of a distant donkey caravan. Growing out of the bank of a small tributary of the Gandaki was a birch with tawny leaves — the first splash of colour we had seen for days.

This day was one of the longest of the trek and as night closed in on us the porters erected our tents and fed us a warming meal of mutton, carrots and cauliflower, and tea laced with rum. We were tired and the night passed quickly. When we awoke the sun was breaking over the eastern crests to herald a fresh new day and by 7 am we were on our way again.

I was scarcely aware of losing height until I glanced down at the tumbling river; progress that new day was very easy along the flats of the widening valley or on a narrow path cut from the cliff walls. In places the path had slipped into the abyss below, which caused considerable consternation for those suffering from vertigo and provided some rock-climbing practice for all of us.

Black juniper came right down to the valley floor at the village of Tukche and buckthorn, vivid with orange berries, grew in sheltered corners. Here the country began to change perceptibly.

111

Along the ridges from the south strode the advance guard of an army of conifers and pine. The path climbed again along the cliff-face towards Larjung, a village that, like its neighbour, Khobang, had streets that were no more than alleyways or tunnels between houses and courtyards designed as a protection from the wind and snow. Wherever we went we were heralded by the indignant barking of dogs.

Came the time when we were to cross into the splendours of tropical Kali Gandaki, and we set off in perfect walking weather, the sun shining down upon us. Although the gorge was still wide and the river comparatively small within it, there was now an urgency about its passage and it seemed to share our enthusiasm to reach green pastures ahead. Even the vegetation pressed in upon us so that the path appeared to run more directly towards its goal. Thick forests of pine clung to the valley slopes and also to the riverbed itself. The drop in altitude — we had now come down to less than 5,000 feet — and the growing influence of the monsoon and melting snows were collectively responsible for the lusher vegetation that was now surrounding us. Oleander, marigolds, dahlias, tobacco plants and poinsettia were everywhere.

The people of the mountains and their villages changed too. Tukuche, Larjang and Khobang had exhibited houses that were miniature fortresses against heavy snow as well as being caravanserai where passing travellers could find lodging and a refuge from the cruel nights. Their inhabitants were Buddhists, whose piety could be judged from the walls of prayer wheels fifty feet long. Our porters — as well as ourselves — never omitted, when passing, to give a joyful turn to the metallic cylinders upon which sacred texts are engraved — a far more practical idea to that of reciting lengthy prayers. Larjang had also displayed its piousness with the addition of sacred streamers flying from its housetops, their prayer texts agitated by the incessant wind. Each village had its *gompa* and numerous prayer wells around which we had learnt to walk on the left so as not to offend local beliefs.

The trail began to climb again taking us through huge rhododendron forests towards the Ghorapani Pass of 9,300 feet. 'Ghorapani' means 'horse-water' from the time when horse and mule caravans used to pass through in larger numbers than they do today, though I was still surprised at the numbers of convoys

112

— each beast heavily-laden and adorned with feathered plumes and tinkling bells — we met on the path through the gloomy arbour of trees. At the summit of the pass the reward is a superb view of Dhaulagiri and the Annapurna giants.

Dawn was intensely clear here, so much so that the sky over Dhaulagiri was black as in outer space. We descended through the woods suffused with the grey-green glow of bearded lichens and misty against the morning sun were the enormous snow peaks. Our path lunged down to a stream where in the gloom of the forest is a bridge, its approach guarded from evil spirits by a roughly hewn wood carving of a nude woman. Above was a village with the villagers standing on the roofs watching our approach. One of the women was combing her hair, then tying it in a bun at the side of her head in the manner typical of her tribe; she wore a golden disc in each ear together with a necklace of silver coins and musk deer tusks. Another woman rhythmically sifted maize flour, while a third emptied a basket of beans to dry on the flat roof of her house. A shrivelled older woman absorbed the morning sun, sitting beneath a bouquet of scarlet peppers drying under the eaves. Each family uses its roof for storing its harvest: walnuts, maize, pumpkins, buckwheat fodder, and piles of cannabis, which, when dried and ground, is smoked in small wooden tubes. The ground floors house livestock, the men now driving their goats and sheep out into the hills for the day's foraging.

I was suddenly noticing things in much closer detail than before; a sure sign of the impending end to a trek. All at once I felt a desperation to store the sights and sounds, that had become too much initially to digest in my memory so that I could bring them back to life when I had time to appreciate them.

Because we were travelling across the grain of the country we were switchbacking from one mountain shoulder to another and, after Ulleri, there came a steep stepping-stone descent to the valley of Bhurungdi affording magnificent views, this time, of Machapuchare — the 'Fish Tail' — of 23,000 feet with its twin peaks; one of the world's most beautiful mountains. This, from some angles is an exquisite single peak and from others a twin-peaked eminence of unsurpassed loveliness.

The Sherpas and porters were in high spirits as, carrying their loads, they neared their homes from which, in a very short time, they would consider themselves lucky to be doing it all again.

The last village. It was flanked by clumps of bamboo and an occasional banyan in whose shade the porters halted to rest their loads by setting them down onto high stone benches. Banana trees surrounded each home, the primitive elegance of their arching leaves offset by yellow-blossomed pumpkin vines growing in careless intimacy over the thatch. Calmly purposeful, village life is not affected by passing intrusion. Children splashed in a sluggish stream around several submerged buffalo to pause for a moment as we drew near. Their almond-shaped eyes sparkled as they called 'Hello' in English, 'How are you?', 'What is your name?' and 'Where are you going?'. At the end of the village was a tea shop similar to the many others along the route. Only an open-fronted shed, a bench, fire-place, two kettles, and half a dozen glasses are needed to establish such a business. It was near lunchtime so I stopped gratefully for a glass or two of milky tea. As I sipped the over-sweet nectar I pondered upon the events of the trek, already planning in my mind a return journey.

Three weeks of tough walking in the company of the same group of Europeans is enough. Another time I hoped to be able to do it the lone way with just one Sherpa, so that I could explore in more depth a country I had grown to love.

5

Roads to Eternity

DRIVING THE HISTORIC HIGHWAYS OF ASIA AND NORTHERN NORTH AMERICA

I have recorded a journey along a dead highway in a preceding chapter. Now I turn to historic roads that, in their living embodiment, have become legendary highways of both yesteryear and today. With Inca roads well chronicled in *Journey Along the spine of The Andes* and my coverage of famed Roman roads as yet incomplete few will disagree with my choice here of the 1,520-mile Alaska Highway as the road with the most evocative image while, not quite so universally known perhaps, is the Karakoram Highway in Pakistan — described as the most dangerous in the world. This road, as a mountain track, once formed one of the threads of the old Silk Route and I was lucky indeed to be able to cover portions of this historic complex too in China on modern roads that have taken over from the old.

As the last chapter was about mountain arteries let's continue the theme by beginning with the enormous Karakorams as the backdrop for a journey I made by bus along what turned out to be one of the most horrific of all the highways I have travelled.

The Karakorams in Pakistan are the north-west extension of the Himalayas. Wedged between Afghanistan to the west, the USSR to the north and the People's Republic of China to the east, these mountains bridge the gap between the Hindu Kush and the Kun Lun range. In this remote location the two giant land masses of India and Asia meet, throwing up rugged peaks to the sky. Among them are twelve of the world's highest summits and some of the longest glaciers to be found outside the polar regions. The collision between these land masses results in the confusion of geography for which the Karakorams are noted; deep river gorges, impenetrable passes and intense earthquake activity. The extremes of the landscape make a breathtaking sight for, in effect, it is a glaciated desert — a mass of bare tortured rocks and unstable scree slopes into which run massive tongues of debris-strewn ice. The annual rainfall averages only four to five inches though flash floods can result in devastating land and mud slides.

Throughout the centuries men have dreamed of a road between China and the fertile plains of the Indus river. Throughout the centuries, too, the harsh and inhospitable mountains of the Karakorams have thwarted them in their purpose. When the Chinese pilgrims such as Fa-Hsien came to Buddhist Swat and from there to Taxila in the fourth, fifth and sixth centuries AD they wrote of the primitive people with goatskins on their feet crossing swirling torrents over bridges made of ropes of willow. In their Imperial Archives they record the use of wooden ladders and wedges used along these track-less mountain walls. Later, the silk, tea and jade-laden caravans from Central Asia toiled, for centuries, over these routes, many perishing along the way.

It was these 'silk road' tracks that formed the basis of the Karakoram Highway (or KKH as it is locally known), construction of which was to commence the second half of the twentieth century. In spite of the most gigantic obstacles with which any landscape could harass a road the project went ahead, first on a piecemeal basis and modest scale but developing into an engineering feat of unprecedented magnitude. It was in 1959 that a single Pakistan Army engineer battalion constructed a 155-mile dirt road between Swat and Chilas, following the Indus river, and then, extended this to Gilgit, another 90 miles. The 1965 war with India halted operations for a while but, with hostilities at an end, it was decided to not only extend the road to the Chinese border but also raise the specification generally to that of two-lane heavy traffic proportions.

The Chinese then came into the picture by agreeing to construct a similar highway on their side, joining up with the KKH at the Khunjrab Pass and linking it to Tashkurgan, Kashgar and Urumchi, capital of Sinkiang and a railhead. A second war further delayed operations for Pakistan but, when it was over, the Chinese government offered help in the form of a skilled labour force to work side by side with Pakistani workers on Pakistan territory. Thus, during the 1970s, the total number of men and women working on the project was around 25,000. Major

116

General Butt tells, in dry military parlance, of the construction work:

'This was a period of intense activity. The road had to be widened to full width, all the retaining walls and protective works completed, culverts and most of the bridges had to be made and road metalling finished by 1978. Truck loads of explosive were expended every day. The peace and quiet of the valleys gave way to the constant shattering noise of explosions reverberating all along the valleys. Stone masons were busy in hundreds, hammer-dressing granite blocks for the retaining walls. Some twenty quarries were being worked at any one time to keep pace with concreting and road metalling.

'This was also a frustrating period for our logistic men. The road was to be kept open only for one week in a month and all the supplies throughout the length of the road were to be made up during this one week. Sometimes, due to heavy blasting, rains and major slides, the road would stay closed for longer durations, when an air lift had to be resorted to. Casualty evacuation was done by a fleet of helicopters which were suitably located close to major work sites.

'Bridge construction on rivers was tricky. High flood-levels were unknown, the deep gorges and the fast-flowing rivers ruled out intermediate piers and the possibility of shuttering. Each site posed different construction problems and, as a result, each bridge is unique. We have plate girder bridges, pre-stressed bridges, RCC arch bridges and suspension bridges.

'The mammoth project of the road has now been completed after twenty years of hard labour... Some of the quantities involved are indicative of the magnitude of the undertaking: rock blasting and earthwork: 27 million cubic yards; explosive expended: 8000 tons; cement: 80,000 tons. There was a transport fleet of 1000 trucks constantly plying to keep the project going.'

A more human view is supplied by Dervia Murphy in her *Where the Indus Is Young*. 'Deeply as I deplore the building of motorways through the Karakoram, I could not but admire the gangs of young Chinese soldiers, hundreds strong, whom we

117

passed at frequent intervals. Seen toiling against the barren immensity of this landscape they seem true 'Heroes of the Revolution' (In deference to Islamic custom, no Heroines of the Revolution work here). Their task is one that makes the combined Labours of Hercules seem trivial and they are tackling it with the minimum of machinery. Today we saw only one generator on the back of a truck, to drill holes in the cliffs for dynamite, and an occasional wheelbarrow. Most of the work is done with shovels, picks, wicker baskets and naked hands.'

With the KKH finally completed at a frightful cost in lives a road, at last, linked Peking with the Indian Ocean, a distance of about 4,750 miles. The mileage from Islamabad, Pakistan's capital, to whence I flew in 1983 to make my journey, to the Chinese border is 545 though the KKH, as such, does not start until beyond Thakot where the ponderous grey Indus sweeps in from the west. A memorial to the dead — Chinese and Pakistani — marks the official starting point of the highway and to gaze upon the bland stone tablet offers a sombre start to what was to become a hair-raising drive that few Pakistanis living in the Plains will undertake. No figures for the dead have ever been given but it is supposed that the human price of the highway is no less than one man per kilometre.

There were a dozen of us on the brightly-painted bus sporting an interior as lovingly decorated as was the outside. The seats were padded but covered with plastic so that, in the heat and a pair of shorts, my thighs and the back of the knees were in a permanent state of adhesive sweat. I was not the only one to express the hope that the driver, engine and brakes had been as equally well maintained as had been the coachwork. We were a mixed bunch of Britons who had collectively hired the vehicle since few scheduled public services maintain more than a link between one village and the next.

The first village astride the KKH is Besham Qala where Alexander the Great crossed the Indus in 327 BC on his way to conquer India. It is a typical roadside bazaar with tea shops and diseased dogs snuffling through the garbage in the road. From the flat fertile fields of the Punjab, the road wound past tiers of paddy fields and into the mountains, twisting a tortuous route parallel to the swirling, silt-laden Indus river. The first portion of the road north had lain in an alpine environment as it slowly

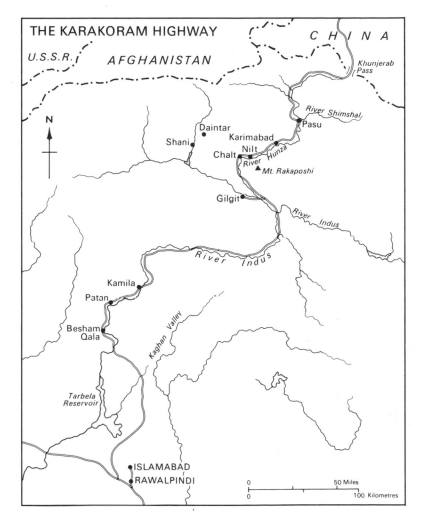

THE KARAKORAM HIGHWAY

U.S.S.R.

AFGHANISTAN

CHINA

Khunjerab Pass

River Shimshal

Pasu

N

Daintar

Shani

Karimabad

Nilt

Chalt

River Hunza

Mt. Rakaposhi

Gilgit

River Indus

River Indus

Kamila

Patan

Kaghan Valley

Besham Qala

Tarbela Reservoir

ISLAMABAD

RAWALPINDI

0   50 Miles

0   100 Kilometres

climbed up and over the foothills. This section was not unlike
any other high mountain roadway in the world and it created the
normal nervousness one would expect from a combination of
Indian driving and bad surfacing. But it had no relevance to the
degree of hazard we were to face beyond Besham Qala. With the
real mountains came the change when the full horror of the road
was revealed. In essence it is a ledge that has been chiselled out of
the cliffs hanging precariously above the Indus and, after Patan

and Kamila — dirty towns with streets awash with filth — runs all the way to Gilgit, the terrain surreptitiously changing from small cultivated squares between widely-spaced pine trees to sheer desert.

Our driver plainly knew his vehicle but, with the beginning of the KKH, even he began to concentrate, staring fixedly ahead through a windscreen half obscured by plastic foliage and psychedelic patterns. He drove fast, the horn constantly blaring even when there appeared to be no reason. I noticed that his eyes were not just for the highway and its obvious perils but also for what lay poised *above* it. My eyes rose likewise to fasten upon the many dangerous overhangs of rock, cracked and rent by fissures. More often than not at these points the pot-holed tarmac had long disappeared beneath successive tons of rubble from previous landslides, mud flashes and cliff collapses leaving a narrow way across the debris which had to be negotiated in bottom gear. On huge scree slopes I saw boulders perched with no visible means of support or reason for not thudding down onto the carriageway. The driver invariably hesitated momentarily at such places prior to a burst of acceleration to take us under and past each threatening slide, an action not lost upon my fellow travellers. Being struck by such a boulder would sweep a vehicle either into the turgid waters hundreds of feet below or, equally likely, onto the morass of dragons-teeth rock that formed the banks. In the 65-mile gorge beyond Kamila, there is no escape from this hideous danger, the gigantic granite walls rising perpendicular from the road; even leaning forward over it. Below, the Indus, flecked white, hurls itself through the narrowing channel as if both river and mountain were combining to crowd out the impertinent highway.

Major General Butt explains — in a gobbledygook of technical phrases — the geology through which the KKH has to pass. 'The rocks are igneous, metamorphic and mafic untrusive comprising granite, gneiss, schist matasedimentary with intusions of granodiorite, granite and diorite. The rock is highly exfoliated' — which is probably what I felt when we emerged from the gorge. These conditions were the major cause, he explains, 'of rock falls and consequential accidents. In simple language this area may well be a paradise for the geologist but is hell for the engineer'.

Apart from the rock there are troublesome stretches of glacial moraine and highly unstable scree and colluvium deposits which collapse without even a hint of disturbance. His words again and he adds that the area is frequently subjected to intense seismic activity. The infamous Patan earthquake of December 1975 released a large number of landslides and blocked the road for weeks, as well as levelling entire villages. Further north are twelve glaciers close to the road which a constant threat. In 1971 the snout of the Batura glacier came down the valley to knock over a large concrete bridge. In 1975 the Momhil glacier activated a massive mudflow which blocked the Hunza river — there accompanying the road — forming a lake ten miles long and the bridge at Shishkot still lies buried under sixty feet of silt. The General observes that 'the terror of glacial movements and mudflows in summer gives way to the threat of avalanches in winter', and, more plaintively, remarks that 'the forces of nature are hard to control'. As we bowled into the next nightmare of rock I pondered upon the likely disaster 1983 might have in store.

The highway crosses the Indus for the second time on a massive bridge and gains high ground again. Far below was the river, deep within the earth's crust, and bordering it the dessicated landscape, its colour burnt to soft tones by the fierce heat of summer. It was a bitter scene, seemingly lifeless except for an occasional tuft of coarse grass, and, overhead, a lingering flock of choughs. My gaze swung in an arc to embrace the mountains behind and upward to a brilliant peak of ice which illuminated the sky. It was not just a mountain but a focal point of the universe. *Nanga parvata*, 'the Naked Mountain', as the ancients called it, rises in one gigantic sweep to a height of 26,660 feet. A Sanskrit proverb states: 'A hundred divine epochs would not suffice to describe all the marvels of the Himalayas'. Nanga Parbat alone transcends description.

It was some ten miles into the gorge that we witnessed our first accident — or at least someone else's accident and a horrific one at that. An open lorry came hurtling down one of the rare straight stretches towards us but failed to take the corner at the bottom of the incline. Riding the buck were a number of people and as the vehicle ploughed through the fence and floated in mid-air, turning slowly over and over, I saw little figures, arms akimbo, flung as from a toy and everything falling, falling like autumn leaves, to smash all of a heap on the cruel rocks bordering the river. My companions, ashen, spoke not a word and I made towards the driver to suggest we do something to help. Helplessly, he gestured that we could do nothing and he pointed to a group of military engineers by the roadside who, plainly, had also witnessed the calamity. We drove on, relentlessly.

The highway has its 'black spots' but these are solely where landslides and avalanches are a recurring theme and we were not to escape their consequences. Army engineer units have heavy duty equipment and many troops standing by at every such known high risk area. Near Chilas the road had been blocked that afternoon by a landslide and lines of vehicles waited on either side of the obstruction. The troops were already at work and we were ordered to take cover in the ditch while a series of charges were detonated to fragment the rubble. The explosions echoed and re-echoed across the chasms and little slithers of dust and pebbles descended upon us from the towering walls above. That the explosions could set off another avalanche was all too possible but Allah was with us that day and to show our gratitude — and to hasten our getaway — we lent the soldiers a hand shovelling the rubble from the carriageway.

Against the tremendous background of one of the world's most gigantic convulsions of nature such happenings take on the ambience of minor incidents. Everywhere were soaring peaks like giant white swords, or colossal squared battlements, filling the sky in every direction. Our whole visible world was a mad jumble of crags, cliffs, rocks, boulders, stones, pebbles and sand. In the river bed detritus of all shapes and sizes had been flung down by avalanches to mix with enormous accumulations of alluvial deposits leaving vivid scars on the awesome slopes beyond the river. All the time, the fractured façades of cliffs promised further disintegration in the future while, below, lay boulders as big as cathedrals, smooth and shiny, and, beside them, gigantic sharp-edged chunks of rock, newly-riven from their parent crags.

For much of the way to Gilgit the road hugs the swift mud-carrying Indus before transferring allegiance to the Hunza. It is only as it nears the one Pakistan town along the way that nature relents to allow the mountains to stand back and green cultivation to take hold in the widening valley. But even here geography and the elements co-operate to battle against the encroachment of man. The winters are bitterly cold and windy, and because of the scarcity of rain and vegetation the valleys below Gilgit are burnt black in the intense summer heat which can rise to temperatures in excess of 120 degrees. As we entered Gilgit a scorching sun which had warmed up the saucer of rock on which the town stands sent the temperature soaring into the 100s turning our bus into a mobile oven. Not even the breeze blowing up the valley could bring relief for it had picked up this heat to playfully blow dust-filled gusts of hot air.

Gilgit spreads itself thinly about two rivers, the Hunza and the Gilgit which meet nearby. Shaded by a double row of trees, the main street is lined with shops and one-storey government buildings with the bazaar the centre of activity and from which the aroma of smoke from unseasoned wood mixes with that of *kava*, a green tea flavoured with cardamon and almonds. It is not a particularly attractive little place though better than some of the unsavoury townships we had seen earlier. A visitor will soon perceive that the town wears an aura of British lineage.

In the heyday of the silk route it was an important staging post but with the decline of the Tibetan Empire it slipped into oblivion surrounded by hostile tribes. But the nineteenth-century British Raj brought a new *raison d'être* and a new prosperity. In 1877 the British established an agency at Gilgit which subsequently became a garrison and the most isolated outpost of the British Empire. Occupied with suppressing the local tribesmen, watching for Russian incursions from their own expanding empire, and involved in devious political manipulations the town's new occupiers brought prosperity back to Gilgit. Now, under Pakistani jurisdiction, trade is once again the order of the day. From the lively bazaars heavily-laden trucks set out for China to deposit apricots, peanuts and almonds in return for rich cargoes of silk from Kashgar. Engaged in this healthy enterprise are a colourful mixture of peoples of many races — Pathans, Kirghiz, Chitralis, Kashgaris, Tshins, Hunzakuts and the pale-skinned Gilgitis themselves, reputed to be descended from the armies of Alexander the Great.

Though their dress was the drab uniform of today the faces of the men spoke of the pages of history. Looking at them the present receded and once again Gilgit was a famous trade centre on the Silk Route. Agents of the Han emperor Wu-Ti first opened the Silk Road in about 120 BC and then patrolled it, protecting it from bandits, as caravans carried silk and other luxuries to the West. It was a difficult route, of 'dark and gloomy mountains', in the words of the Chinese traveller Fa-Hein in the Third Century AD but it persisted. For two thousand years the caravans struggled over the rugged Mintaka Pass on their way to and from Sinkiang. Then in 1949 communist China closed its borders, ending an era.

Beyond Gilgit the KKH battles its way northward through a new storm of mountains, its patchy tarmac surface interrupted for long stretches where landslides have swept away the original bed.

To move off the highway, to explore the byways and smaller valleys leading from the Hunza River became an obsession amongst us. To reach the communities of Guijjar nomads who occupy the summer-only villages deep in the hills it was necessary to travel on foot. Tracks, indicated as 'jeepable roads', branched off the KKH and one of these was to lead a half dozen of us, stuffed into an ancient Jeep moving much too fast around hairpin bends, to the tiny community of Naltar where the Pakistan army has a mountain training camp. We arrived just in time to witness a spirited polo match; the army versus the locals, which offered insight into the expertise of the riders on their tough little horses. The basic difference between 'Karakoram Polo' and the more genteel version played at Cowdray Park is that only six players constitute a team and the side to score nine goals wins. There appeared to be few further rules; it was all a question of nerve and who had the fastest and most controllable mount.

Our trek into the small valley of the Naltar River to the head of the Diantar Pass took all of three days. We bivouacked en route, trying to avoid the treacherous moraines and persisting wads of snow that lay in the path of the glacier-strewn ranges ahead.

The Guijjar nomads remain in the hills looking after their flocks of sheep and goats for the months of June, July and August before returning to their permanent homes in Naltar and other lowland villages. While so engaged they live with their families in makeshift houses made out of any material to hand. In this

124

case it was rock and debris brought down by the glaciers and, though we gazed long and intently at the village from higher up the slopes, it was only when we perceived movement and smoke rising from a fire that our eyes made out the boulder-and-stick walls of individual dwellings.

Though we were forbidden to come close to the huddle of houses and, particularly, the community's womenfolk, most of the male members made their way to see us. Their swarthy faces beneath distinctive flat and floppy hats were wreathed in smiles and straightaway we were invited to a community wedding reception due to be held later in the day.

The makeshift village was called Shani and the proffered reception was like no other that I have attended in a half a lifetime of receptions. And surely no wedding festivity could have boasted of so stupendous a venue as that of the snow-capped peaks and sparkling glaciers of the surrounding Karakorams. In place of the Wedding March there was the incessant rumble of snow avalanches.

Sitting with the semi-circle of men — not a woman, including the bride, was in sight throughout the ceremony — we listened to the intoning of passages from the Koran by an elder, a benign gentleman who reminded me of a bishop I once knew — except for the dagger he wore at his belt. I indicated that I would like to photograph him and he stopped in mid-passage, bowed to me from his sitting position and posed most readily. Everyone smiled and nodded approvingly to me so I went around taking pictures of the whole congregation.

Proceedings were interwoven with dancing and the serving of choice portions of goats-meat, we visitors being offered the special titbits. All the while the silent, overawed bridegroom, colourful in his red and yellow robe, sat impassively next to the elder, occsionally rising to dance in curious jerky movements with his fellows. Never a smile crossed his young and serious features.

The initial proceedings drawing to a close everyone moved off towards the village but for us it was the end of our participation.

The way out of the Naltar valley led over the 15,700-foot Diantar Pass, an exhausting climb that had me on all fours and stumbling about dazedly in snow and ice at the summit. I was suffering from a serious bout of dehydration which additionally made me slightly delirious. On the other side of the pass was the Diantar valley, a replica of the Naltar and a botanist's joy of exotic wild flowers. The gorge of the Diantar too had to be negotiated, the path overlooking a thousand-foot drop as it zig-zagged to the vivid green and yellow oasis surrounded by eternal grey buttresses, a tiny portrait in an oversize frame.

The climb over the pass and the precipitous way to the village of Diantar took another two days, our camp the further side of the pass being made close to a settlement more permanent than Shani. Two of us were invited into a mud-and-wattle house the owner of which lived alone in the most dreadful squalor. From Diantar a 'jeep road' led back to the KKH and along it we were whisked at a murderous pace to resume our broken journey along a highway that now seemed safer than before we left it.

But first a night at Chalt, a large village containing a few shops, just short of the highway. Ahead the ice spire of 25,550-foot Rakaposhi filled the valley and sky making the perfect setting for a night's camping in the garden of a locked and barred guest house occupied only by a hunchbacked caretaker.

Northward now, the Hunza river leads the KKH along its tortuous course, and I found myself in Valhalla. On one side of the river lay the territory of Naga, a small state in its own right, within the Hunza valley dotted with a few trees and the occasional cultivated plot. Included in its boundaries is not only Rakaposhi's incredible bulk but also Dumani peak (23,600 feet) and the 38-mile Hispar Glacier all dwarfing the valley with their magnificence. The bread-basket of Naga is directly across the river where Hunza's fertile land spreads out like a colourful apron from the waist of the glacier-clad gorges and knife-edged summits beyond. This one-time kingdom is celebrated for its happy, healthy people who never suffer from disease, particularly tuberculosis and rheumatism.

Experts differ about the causes of the alleged phenomenon. Some see the Hunzakuts as a superior Aryan strain isolated from contact with the germ-laden outside world. Others point to their food which has influenced 'natural' diets in the west. Whatever the reasons, it must be said that the Hunza people seem to be of an intelligence and integrity far higher than other Karakoram denizens. It shows in their husbandry and thrift. Nothing is left to chance and each minute portion of land is carefully sprayed and seeded every year. The slightest wastage of land or time could be fatal in their eyes. When supplies are running low, the head of the family ordains that it is better to fast than dip into stocks reserved for planting. These facts I learnt from Qudratullah Beg, a former Hunza State minister of education who, with his charming family, has lived all his life in Karimabad, the capital.

Karimabad offers an awe-inspiring view of Rakaposhi at the further end of the valley, a valley overlooked at the opposite end by Ultar Nala, both a ravine and a multiple peak. Directly beneath it stands the fairytale castle of Baltit, for 600 years the home of the Mirs — or rulers — of Hunza. Slowly rotting on massive timber pillars the castle's wooden bay windows, ingeniously carved, add a touch of history to the magic of this secret world.

I walked again and again through the big village among the laden apricot trees. *Was* this really a Valhalla? Downstream the shining mass of Rakaposhi pervaded the valley. Behind me, high above, was the whitewashed fort looking down at the huddle of drab houses and chequerboard of fields. It was a typical Tibetan fort, vaguely ominous with its high walls and narrow windows; wild dark crags towered above it. Rows of poplars along irrigation canals added a touch of gentle elegance to the stark scene. I found it easy to see why Western visitors imbue this valley with a romantic aura, infusing a scenically lovely spot with their dream of a Shangri-la where everyone possesses the secret of health and tranquility and lives to ripe old age. Yet, assuredly, the people of Hunza differ little from those in the other valleys in spite of the fact that the former is more scenically and fruitfully endowed. Hardly is it likely to be happier or sadder, healthier or wealthier. Men and women were toiling in the rocky fields barely able to subsist on a sparse diet of unleavened bread, potatoes, and dried fruit. Foreign visitors, such as we, may be entertained in the wealthier homes like that of Qudratullah Beg which have been set up here partly because of the extraordinary beauty of the surroundings. They are served such rare delicacies as meat and yogurt and jump to optimistic conclusions. Yet the word of Ashraf Aman, a conqueror of K2, the world's second highest mountain, who accompanied us on our trek, could not be ignored as just wishful thinking. A native and resident of Hyderabad and an intelligent and sincere man, he spoke often about the superiority of his race and their undoubted blessings.

On the move again, motivated by the impatient demands of the KKH, we journeyed another 60 miles to the small community of Passu and the great Batura Glacier. To the north of the Passu plain a ridge comprising a score of pinnacles dominates the view. Behind them run the Shimshal river, entering a valley that is the epitome of remote but inhabited areas in the Karakoram where the snow lasts all through the year on its northern slopes and avalanches thunder down its slopes well into spring. 'If you want to find our traditions alive you must travel to more difficult valleys like Chapursan, Naltar and Shimshal' advised the last Mir of Hunza. I was doing just that. But here in Passu village, its own glacier scarring the slopes on which it lies and the sun-burnt walls of the continuing Hunza valley showing the way forward for both river and highway, we came to a halt. In a sheen of sweat I had walked a mile down the road to the military-guarded bridge. One can go no further; not, at least, with my colour of skin. A few dozen miles on and I could be in China's Sinkiang. A point had been reached where politics provided a more effective barrier than had nature in all her fury.

★ ★ ★

Very few months were to pass and I was in Sinkiang but, alas, not by way of the KKH and the Khunjerab Pass where the present highway enters Chinese territory. Instead I had had to fly to Hong Kong, and from there make interminable train rides via Canton, Peking and Sian into Sinkiang and its unlovely capital, Urumchi.

Which explains how I came to be standing at a dusty crossroads in the middle of Urumchi. I was astride another section of the Silk Route, older in conception than history. On this road across the mountains and deserts, the people of the Tigris and the Euphrates, of the Mediterranean countries and the Nile, were in contact with the people living around the Yellow river long before our written history had begun. From the mountains shimmering in the distant heat haze towards Pamir, lapis lazuli was taken in Badakhshan and brought west to Sumer and Egypt five thousand years ago. And jade from Khotan was carried to the Yellow River. When the road was first described in chronicles, it was already an

128

ancient one. Yet only a little over a century ago it became known as 'The Silk Road.'

For those interested in archaeology there is, in Sian, something very special indeed. Once capital of the expanding state of Qin, its leader was Qin Huang Ti and his tomb, a man-made hill, rises from the Wei Valley. Close by is one of the most dramatic discoveries of the century; the army of life-size pottery figures drawn up in battle array still being unearthed from the rough wet earth. The sight of these individually-carved figures of men and horses, emerging from the reddish Yellow river soil, is unforgettable — the replica retinue of unified China's first emperor.

Sian itself is now the chief city of the province of Shensi and one of the few cities in China where city walls still stand though these were much reduced from the extension dimensions of the Tang city, when Sian was one of the largest and most cosmopolitan cities in the world. Today the crenellated walls and high city gates rival the towers of the new telecommunications building and other less edifying examples of twentieth century architecture.

Since my particular interest at this time was roads I would have enjoyed travelling to Sinkiang even on the modern highway that links Sian to the province simply on account of the fact that I would have been following the Silk Route. But in the year I was there — 1980 — travel by foreigners was considerably more restricted than it is now. That the trains were decreed as my vehicle was at least better than having to fly and, because the railway ran close to the historic route, I had little reason for complaint.

My rail journeyings from Hong Kong — including a diversion to Inner Mongolia — had been made in large roomy carriages with compartments exquisite with lace curtains, pink-shaded table lamps and leafy plants. Nobody stole the issued thermos flasks of jasmine tea and my overnight bedding came tastefully wrapped in a dainty lace coverlet. From the window I watched China unfold, the timeless landscape being tilled with instruments unchanged through the centuries. Chinese trains are inclined to dawdle, a pace that, in this instance, suited me well.

While en route to Huehot, capital city of Inner Mongolia, I was able to spend a whole day at the Datong Steam Locomotive Plant which, to anyone who is inspired by the sight of large steam engines, is Mecca indeed. Datong town is not a pretty

129

place; then nor, I suppose, is Britain's equivalent — Crewe. The shop floor of the Datong works is immense with more than twenty workshops and, in company with my retinue of guides, interpreters and office staff, I managed to get round most of them. Outside the main factory is the shed where newly-outshopped engines are prepared for their first steaming and I was permitted to accompany the driver of one shining great black monster on its initial trial, trundling sedately some miles down the line. Afterwards I was asked to take part in a works committee discussion with drivers, workers and staff. This started firmly on railway subjects but curiosity about Britain and the West got the upper hand with, surprisingly, politics well to the fore.

At Huehot it is horses, not locomotives, that are all the rage. Another rather drab town, most of its seventeenth century Buddhist temples have been utilised as much-needed accommodation or back-street factories. But at the city's sports stadium an equestrian event was scheduled and I was invited along to watch. Living near Hickstead I have spent years successfully avoiding horse-shows but I got caught at Huehot. The display started in the traditional mould, then livened up with acrobatic riding and ending with a war-like exhibition of submachine-gun firing while standing in the saddle at a full gallop — which makes Hickstead's offerings very tame indeed.

Inner Mongolia being famous for both horses and riding skills it was not long before I found myself astride one of the fast little ponies legging it, bareback, across the Mongolian plains. Staying in a *yurt* — a traditional octagonal tent — at the People's Commune of Ulan Turger I was able to glimpse something of the life of the region.

But I digress and have got off the Silk Route. To reach Sian I had to return to Peking and, beyond Sian, an overnight journey to Lanzhou brought me with a bump to the end of my luxury rail travel. Thereafter the train accommodation was of a more spartan nature with hard wooden seats and no bedding for the final 36 hours to Urumchi. And, with no steam locomotive plants or horse shows to provide a distraction in the city, my guide press-ganged me into endless tours of schools, hospitals and workers' flats.

The political banners and slogan hoardings of China's cities wear a weathered look and new ones are few. Together with most countries of the Socialist camp the age of attempting to capture people's minds by poster display is dying. But the liberalisation in China has taken a new turn. One carefully framed and eye-catching notice I saw proclaimed an excerpt from one of Mao's more gentle messages: 'Of all things in the world. . . people are the most precious'. But it was in the autonomous region of Sinkiang and its capital that these words struck me as the most incongruous. Here, far from the centre of authority of Peking and very much off the beaten track for foreign visitors, live a people of multiple tongues and nationalities. Bordered by the Mongolian People's Republic, Kashmir, Afghanistan and the central Asian republics of the USSR, Sinkiang has some difficult neighbours. Here Uigurs, a Moslem-Turkic-speaking race, are the largest ethnic group but there are also large numbers of Kazakhs as well as Huis, Kirghiz, Mongols and Tadzhiks. All are very different in looks and temperament to the ordinary Han Chinese while it did not take me long to discover that the fierce and wild-eyed Uigurs were not particularly enamoured with their Chinese brethren into whose territory they were incorporated. A short walk in Urumchi's dusty streets quickly raised a crowd of several hundred companions, friendly, curious, sometimes bearded, all wearing patterned skull caps as a kind of minority flag of defiance and telling me how much they despised the Hans. Dissent or the slightest breath of it is, however, a capital offence in the Sinkiang Uigur Region that roughly covers what was historically known as Chinese Turkistan.

The Uigurs once ruled this arid land until it was conquered by Genghiz Khan and his successors and later by the Kalmucks. Sinkiang eventually came under Chinese control in the seventeenth century during the Manchu Dynasty and, in 1884, it became a Chinese province. During the Nationalist period warlords held intermittent sway with Soviet support and today it is a fact of life that Russia is only too happy to stir the mud that lies quietly at the bottom of the people's minds. There's nothing to stop her walking in either, I was told, but she doesn't want another Afghanistan on her hands.

Resistance to both invaders and occupiers has been a thread right through Sinkiang's long history. For centuries the Han Chinese regarded the people of Sinkiang as barbarians and though, before the 1949 liberation, the Han constituted a tiny

131

percentage of the population they ruled the province either by force or guile.

The simmering animosity is discernible in the big industrial cities like Urumchi but more strikingly in Turfan, a town of 20,000 inhabitants that lies, likewise, astride the old Silk Road between Hami and Kashgar. Turfan, too, is the name of a remarkable depression in which the town is situated and is supposed to be one of the deepest and therefore the hottest places on earth.

To reach it necessitated a 130-mile drive by springless bus from Urumchi over a heavily-rutted but undeniably Silk Road route through the Tien-Shan Mountains which, around the 15,000-foot peak of Bogda and the Tien Chi Lake, look enchanting. The Tien ranges stretch from east to west across the region, dividing into two, with the Dzungari Basin to the north and the Taklamakam Desert and the Tarim Basin to the south. The word *taklamakam* means in Uighur 'once you go in, you never come out' — a sinister name for this massive, impassable area of uninhabited desert, the second largest in the world. It divided the old Silk Road, and travellers would be forced either to pass from oasis to oasis on the south of the desert, along the foothills of the Kunlun Mountains or follow the northern route, crossing the Tian Mountains and the Yili River and continuing westwards to the Black Sea. From the cool of the highlands we descended a coil of a road to cross a dust bowl; a shimmering plain of bone-dry grit and gravel that spreads out to limitless horizons.

Turfan town, when we reached it, I found to be only pleasantly warm. It comprised an old and a new town though, at first glance, both looked equally aged. The bazaar could hardly have changed over centuries gone by and a number of mosques still stood to give a faint shadow of glories shared by Isfahan and Samarkand. One particular mosque, just out of town, was being restored. It was the Mosque of Amin Hodja complete with slender minaret untiled but nevertheless attractively decorated in mud and sun-dried brick. In the hottest months of the year the citizens of the old town retire underground or to vine-shaded courtyards at night since their mud houses become veritable ovens by day. Scorpions, big hairy spiders and Turfan cockroaches two inches long with red eyes are good reason for the hard wooden beds with no bedding — on which the whole family sleeps — that can be seen in every courtyard.

I was taken to see row after row of big pockmarks in the desert and learnt that these were the holes through which the men of Turfan descend to clean their *karez*, or underground canals, dug to bring irrigation water from the Tien-Shan. Something like 950 *karez* converge on Turfan and many date back to the Han Dynasty, when the concept first arrived in Turfan via the Silk Road from Persia. There they are known as *Qanats* and it is these underground canals that make possible the oasis that the Turfan region has become; a green island in a sandy wilderness with a fertility that is a complete contradiction to the barrenness of the surroundings and the extremes of temperature to which it is subjected.

Since the 1950s the Han Chinese have begun to revise their opinions of Sinkiang and have sent colonists en masse into the region. More than four million Han now live in the province. This influx of 'foreigners' aroused resentment as did the Cultural Revolution's eagerness to wipe out old customs and cultures. Today the Chinese government is playing it cooler and making serious efforts to placate and promote the Sinkiang minority. However a purely Chinese face is a rare sight in Turfan as is a European one. All those I saw carried the features of Bokhara, Samarkand, Kabul and Uzbekistan. Yet Turfan appears to be so isolated — especially now with a closed Soviet and Afghan border to the west — though for so many centuries, when caravan commerce thrived, this grape-growing oasis was one of the cultural cross-roads of the world. The ancient Han ruled Turfan as did numerous central Asian peoples who migrated through and got lost in history.

Old cities have been discovered in this fiery basin and one I saw was Kaochang beneath the so-called Flame Hills against the dry furrowed gullies on which the sun's rays strike giving the quivering effect of rising flames. Plainly a large population once inhabited this lonely land. The sense of antiquity was strong and the ruins I was to see were massive and extensive. Kaochang was founded in the first century BC and abandoned in the fourteenth after 1500 years as one of the cultural, political and economic centres of ancient Sinkiang. During the Han Dynasty it was a garrison town and at the time of the Eastern Tsen Dynasty it became capital of the feudal separatist Kaochang Dynasty. The mid-tenth century saw it as a capital city of the Hsi Chou Uigurs and amidst the ruins can be seen a Buddhist temple dating from the fourth century, when the faith of India was spreading feverishly across China. When Islam arrived the temple became a mosque.

Today's faith is communism but the authorities are becoming increasingly meticulous about preserving what remains of a more capitalistic past. A great amount of repair work and excavation is going on amongst the old cities of Turfan including Kaochang which once consisted of an outer city, inner city and the palace city with a total circumference of about three miles. The towering walls of stamped clay remain and are startling in their completeness. The original openings where the city gates once stood are gaping holes and the structure is veined with fissures in and out of which snakes and lizards squirm and scurry. The ruins have a symmetry which indicates a well-planned town and the outline of the main thoroughfares are plainly discernible. In the centre are the remains of the Padshah's palace and around it the handsome stupas decorated with arched niches inside of which decaying figures are crumbling to dust. Before the present government decreed the place to be an archaeological monument a great deal of destruction took place with local people using the material for building their own houses and for this reason it is surprising that so much of Kaochang remains to this day.

Mummified bodies were being unearthed and cave paintings discovered even while I was there, to make the ancient site another archaeologist's dream for those who get there before the casual treatment I saw being afforded these priceless relics destroys them forever.

One thing communism clearly has brought to Turfan is more trees. I noticed extensive forestry which has helped fend off the ferocious hot winds that blast the depression between March and May killing the grape-vines and melons that otherwise grow in profusion in the oasis. I was invited to a picnic at a People's collective — another product of communism — where I drank tea sitting on the ground beneath an arbour of grapes in the company of members of the staff. Little wine is made, they told me, the grapes being turned into raisins. Wine-drinking was considered a frivolous occupation — or at least that was the official opinion.

In spite of my pleas made to various authorities, Kashgar,

further west, was firmly denied me so any notions I may have entertained about attaining the Khunjerab Pass and regaining the KKH were quickly scotched. But even if it had been on a piecemeal basis I had been able to glimpse stretches of the old Silk Route and that would have to satisfy me for the moment.

* * *

If there is an elusive pot of gold at the bottom of the rainbow then there must be reward at the end of the Alaska Highway, or so the notion came to me as I gazed at Milepost 0 in the centre of Dawson Creek.

For years only a dream of far-sighted engineers of the north of North America, the highway is, today, not only another dream come true but a vital artery of travel connecting Alaska and Canada's Yukon territory with the Lower 48 states of the USA and the southern provinces of Canada.

By agreement between the two governments, the highway was built by the US Army Corps of Engineers as an overland lifeline to relieve Alaska from the World War Two hazards of shipping and as a military supply route to counter a threatened Japanese invasion through the Aleutian Islands. The initial road was completed in eight months. This pioneer artery was then turned over to civilian contractors for widening and gravelling, replacing of primitive log bridges with structures of steel, and re-routing.

Since that bitterly cold pre-dawn hour in March 1942 when the vanguard of the US Army Corps of Engineers arrived at the 'end of the steel' — the railway — at the then remote British Columbian frontier village of Dawson Creek, the Alaska Highway has become another legend in the annals of road building.

Crews worked north and south from Whitehorse in Yukon, north from Dawson Creek, and south from Delta Junction in Alaska (where the new road — then called the Alcon Highway — would connect with the existing Richardson Highway). The north and south construction crews connected the road in October 1942 at Milepost 588 where a bridge crossed Contact Creek in British Columbia. Beaver Creek at Milepost 1202 was the second link between the two crews.

On 20 November 1942 in nine degrees of frost, 250 shivering soldiers, civilians and Royal Canadian Mounted Police watched officials from the United States and Canada cut the ribbon stretched across the frozen road at Soldiers Summit. From this wind-swept hill opposite Milepost 1061 on the southern end of Kluane Lake, the highway was pronounced open for business. Fear is a mighty stimulus to achievement and for such a road to be hacked at such speed through a savage wilderness was nothing short of a miracle.

The Alaska Highway is like no other road in the American continent. Others are built through populated areas; they link small towns and great cities; they bear a substantial human traffic and enormous burdens of freight. The Alaska Highway is an artery running inside Canadian territory for over twelve hundred miles and Alaskan territory for more than two hundred more. It has a beginning and an end and almost nothing in between. It is a road without people and very little history. The Japanese threat ebbed and died; the war drew to a close. The Highway remained.

Give or take a mile the recorded length of the road is 1520 miles or 2446 kilometres between Dawson Creek, British Columbia, in the south and Fairbanks, Alaska, in the north.

Most of the miles through Canada are gravel surfaced while the Alaska portion is paved. No longer is this Highway classed as a true wilderness road in Canadian/US motoring circles though, with petrol stations and facilities sometimes hundreds of miles apart, pampered drivers from Europe might not agree. Anyway, before the 'black top' (as our American friends call road paving) spreads the full length of the route I was determined to discover how it felt to drive this astounding artery.

My vehicle was, ironically, a small Japanese Toyota and I left from Edmonton in the spring of 1981 adding 367 miles to my journey.

There is a unique attraction about the Alaska Highway which every traveller must feel as he wheels out of Dawson Creek and prepares to head up the long stretch leading into the wilderness. Nearly all of Canada's roads run east and west, or south across the border. The Alaska Highway is different. It is the only road on the continent that points to the High North. It stirs unfamiliar emotions, excites strange dreams for it leads to far-off places of earth that few of us have ever seen. In the land through which the Highway runs, and beyond, there are great forests and wild animals and strange peoples. We really know very little about them; and the empty regions they inhabit. To those of us who have never seen it close at hand the vast landscape seems alien, inhospitable, progressively more and more barren and empty of life, until at last it falls away into the chill grey waters of the Arctic Sea.

Dawson Creek is a town of some 11,000 souls perched on rolling farmland and though it retains an aura of the frontier it boasts all the comforts of a small city. North of Dawson the scenery of the road changes little. Much of it reminded me of Siberia with which the land has geographical links, with trees, trees, trees — mainly spruce — marching into endless horizons. Fort St John is the subsequent centre of any consequence with, again, a Wild West façade hiding a highly civilised heart. Set in low rolling hills it is a rich hub of grain, cattle and sheep farming but the original Fort St John, established in 1806 on the muddy banks of the Peace River, ten miles south of the present townsite, was no more than a trading post for the Sikanni and Beaver Indians.

Beyond Fort St John the farmlands peter out. The wilderness takes over, heavy forest lines both sides of the road, with here and there, through a break in the trees, glimpses of far-off hills painted a deep, impossible blue that merges into the purple of hills yet more distant.

For the driver conditioned to paved roads, the gravel highway may at first seem something of a trial. However the surface is kept in generally excellent condition by a large fleet of road maintenance equipment so that the driving hazards resulting from those defects common to gravel roads everywhere are reduced to a minimum. Flying stones are the biggest menace and many vehicles regularly using the road have wire mesh screens over windscreen and headlights.

At mile 296 a bridge carries the road across the Muskwa River, at one thousand feet above sea level the lowest point on the Alaska Highway, and into Fort Nelson, another one-time fort, this one to become a railhead in 1971 with the completion of a 253-mile extension of the British Columbia Railway from Fort St John. The township is now a focal point for exploration for natural gas and oil.

With the replacing of miles with kilometres in Canada but the retention of miles on United States territory a certain amount of

137

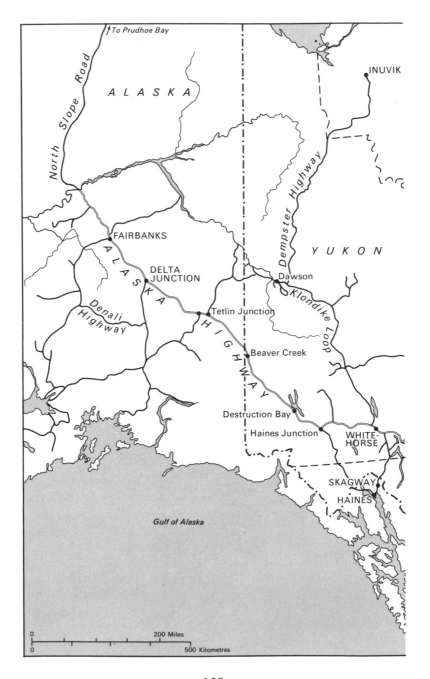

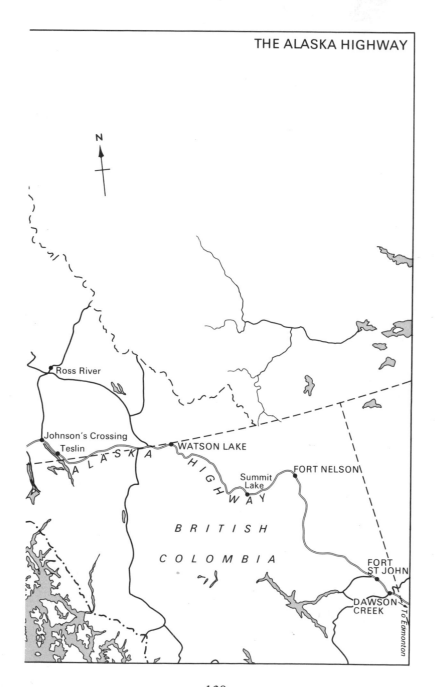

THE ALASKA HIGHWAY

N

Ross River

Johnson's Crossing
Teslin

ALASKA

WATSON LAKE

HIGHWAY

Summit
Lake

FORT NELSON

BRITISH

COLOMBIA

FORT
ST JOHN

DAWSON
CREEK

To Edmonton

confusion is arising along the road. The new Canadian kilometre posts are being installed but some mileposts remain for the simple purpose of serving as mailing addresses for people and businesses who have utilised the mileposts for identity. Crossing the Canadian/Alaskan border the posts revert to representing miles once more.

Already there are considerable stretches of Canadian paving particularly at the approaches to the principal townships and this is on the increase. In between I found some extremely rough patches where ice and snow and the permafrost had broken up the road but my chief worry was that of running out of petrol. I carried spare cans but when these were empty my eyes were more for the presence of 'gas' stations than for the scenery. Log cabins and camping sites offered sleeping accommodation at intervals along the way though they are often closed out of season.

At Fort Nelson the Alaska Highway makes a right-angled turn and heads west into the Rockies. Here the foothills are no more than endless uprisings flanking deep river-threaded valleys with the real mountains lurking a long way behind. There is nothing friendly about the Rockies here. Their presence conjurs a kind of sullenness; indeed all along the entire length of the highway the mountains keep their distance as if disdaining the existence of the impertinent road.

But if the mountains do not encourage overtures from man to nature they encourage them from man to man. The absence of all familiar evidences of what we call civilisation, the sheer overwhelming hugeness of the country, and the increasing sense of isolation draw men together in a spirit of camaraderie rarely to be met with on more frequented highways. The number of travellers driving the Highway at any given time is absurdly small in relation to the Highway's length, the logical stopping places being spaced about three hundred miles apart. Thus sight of another human being is cause for not only hand-waving acknowledgement but, where circumstances permit, a union of souls. Driving alone, I was particularly susceptible to the emotions of meeting fellow-travellers and was pleased to offer the occasional lift to Canadian residents en route to the next township or tourists bound for the nearest campsite. I came across cyclists too who were pedalling the full length of the Highway; most of them seemed to have reached the conclusion they had bitten off more

Above left: The former pipeline built to carry oil from Norman Wells to Whitehorse.

Above right: The picturesque Godlin Gorge where we stumbled for two hours along a near perpendicular scree-slope of sharp slate.

Right: A gentler walk along an easier stretch of the Old Canol Road.

Below right: Our camp at abandoned huts in Little Keele Valley.

Below left: David, Byron and Reinhard building a raft to take us across the Twitya River.

Above left: Our felucca *Yournni* being towed up the Nile with Sayed on the right.

Above right: The temple of Karnak at Luxor, the world's largest religious building.

Right: Making our way through the mountain pass of Jbel Bani in Morocco.

Below left: Abdul skinning the gazelle given to us by Libyan troops in the Murzuk Sand Sea.

Below right: A familiar desert scene in Morocco — men drawing water from a well, their camels resting nearby.

Above left: The dappled shape of a woodland walk in the Kulu Valley, Northern India.

Above right: The gentle climb from Dumre along the Marsyandi Valley, Nepal.

Below left: Members of our party walking along the narrow cliff path in the Marsyandi Valley.

Below right: The imposing Atlas mountains along which we travelled by Bedford truck.

Above: The stunning view above Muktinath across to the peaks of Dhaulagiri, Nepal.

Below: The village of Briga, Nepal, with its typical collection of square, flat-topped houses.

Above: The polo match at Naltar, Pakistan.

Below: Dramatic scenery on the Karakoram Highway, Pakistan.

Above: Approximately 950 *karez* or underground canals converge on Turfan in China.

Right: A typical vine-shaded courtyard in China where people retire to eat, talk and sleep.

Below: The dramatic peaks of Mt. McKinley seen from the Alaska Highway.

Above left: The famous 'sign forest' at Watson Lake on the Alaska Highway.

Above right: The entry to the cells at Gestapo Headquarters in Cracow.

Right: The majestic Desert Queen that hauled the Palace on Wheels luxury train in Rajasthan, India.

Below: The colourful reception committee waiting to welcome us to Jaisalmer, Rajasthan.

Above: Members of the Mountain Team making camp at Two Tarn hut on Mount Kenya.

Right: Members of the White Water Team battling with the Tana River.

Below left: Myself walking through the jungle to Kipandi.

Below right: The White Water Team portaging around a waterfall on the Tana River.

than they could chew and were pleased to stop for a chat.

At Mile 456 (Kilometre 734), about sixty miles beyond Summit Lake Pass (at 4,250 feet, the highest point on the Highway), lies Muncho Lake, one of the loveliest mountain lakes in Canada. Enfolded by mountains, its waters of the purest aquamarine and amazing clarity, it lies in a stillness and serenity which today is seldom found in places of great natural beauty. A single fisherman as immovable as a statue was the only human intrusion. I halted to look upon the scene, then crept away as if afraid of sullying it. One day, I fear, when the road is fully paved, the lake will attract commercial interest but at least I am glad that I was privileged to have listened to its as yet unbreached silences.

Beyond Muncho Lake the Liard River — mean, treacherous, dramatic — dominates the landscape and to a marked extent dictates the route of the road. Here the driving is perhaps more demanding than elsewhere on the route, for it follows an in-and-out up-and-down course through countryside of spectacular allure. Rejuvenation of tired cramped limbs can be effected at Liard Hot Springs — pools of water of a constant 100 degrees Fahrenheit.

The actual entry into Yukon Territory is correspondingly undramatic. The Highway crosses an unmarked boundary, bobs back into British Columbia, then forward again into the Yukon. I had also crossed a time-zone at the border, the first of several that came, thick and fast the further north I proceeded.

The Yukon is more than twice the size of Great Britain and much of it is upland plateau cut by deep gorges and wide valleys and marked by mountains that are among the highest and most rugged in North America. From here onwards the land becomes picturesque though tinged with a sombre loneliness. Other motorists sounded their horns and waved as they went by and, at the rare eating houses and snack bars, the staff as well as the transitory clients were, as everywhere else, addicted to much bonhomie and an intimacy that is surprising even for a North American. My gargantuan breakfasts, usually taken at the first 'eating joint' I came to of a morning, invariably turned into social events with a bunch of travellers avidly comparing road conditions and locals interrogating new arrivals.

Six miles inside Yukon lies Watson Lake. For hundreds of miles and kilometres a driver has been counting them to the name on the destination signs and an impression has built up of a great metropolis. But as with other communities, Watson Lake turns out to be hardly a ball of fire. In fact you are out of the place before you realize you were in. Its population is given as 1,167 so you see what I mean. The 'town' has two attractions. One is the famous sign forest started by a home-sick American serviceman working on the construction of the highway in the 1940s. Travellers are still adding signs to the collection — mostly town or village nameboards — from all over the world. The other attraction is the chain of lakes that turns Watson Lake into a centre for fishermen.

The 285-mile run from Watson Lake to Whitehorse I found agreeably restful by comparison with that of the previous day. Here there were long straight stretches of road with few steep gradients. For much of the distance the route is along pleasantly wooded valleys reminiscent of the Scottish Highlands. And it rained too.

Spanning an arm of the Teslin Lake is the Nisutlin Bay Bridge, the longest water span on the Highway, with awe-inspiring views of distant mountains, and, across it, is Teslin situated at the confluence of Nisutlin Bay and Teslin Lake. Again the 'town' is a misnomer but its log cabin homes house the largest native population in Yukon; many are descendents of the Tlingit tribe. Alas, as elsewhere in Canada, there is a problem with regard to the Indian minorities many of whose members live on social security and are more often drunk than sober; I was to see many of them in the few bars I visited to enjoy a pint.

Between Teslin and Whitehorse the Highway is continuously in sight of water with, nearing the Yukon capital, a horizon of the great Alaska Range amongst which can be seen the snow-capped bulk of 20,230-foot Mount McKinley, North America's highest mountain. But perhaps the most exciting moment is the first glimpse of the river — at this point narrow, tranquil, giving no hint of its turbulence a few miles downstream — which more than any other in the north country bears in its name connotations of romance, of suffering, and heroic deeds.

The Yukon is one of the great rivers of the world. It flows for a distance of 2,300 miles between the MacKenzie Mountains in the remote Northwest Territories to pour its muddy waters out of an equally desolate mouth on the Bering Sea.

142

With that first glimpse of the Yukon one is again in touch with history, folklore and legend. Here is the land of Sam McGee and Klondike Kate and gold-hungry miners where great and strange and terrible things happened and mighty deeds were done. For this is the river down which men once swarmed by boat, raft and canoe in the age-old search for El Dorado.

Whitehorse, Yukon's capital, could, for these parts, be classed as a mini-city with a population of around 16,000. I found it to be a most attractive place; not at all the one-horse town I had heard it described. Whitehorse came into being as the northern terminus of the White Pass and Yukon Railway from Alaska's Skagway (see *The Great Railway Adventure*) and it was here that the famed river steamers connected the railhead to Dawson City by way of the Yukon River which runs sedately through the town. The gold rush and the Klondike stampeders have left their mark and twice have turned Whitehorse into a boom town. The stampeders landed here to dry out and repack their supplies after running the infamous Whitehorse Rapids while the gold diggers came to town to either celebrate their luck or, more likely, to drown their sorrows. But the town does not rely solely upon its boisterous past. More respectable now, it boasts one of the most modern hospitals I have seen and a Civic Centre second to none. The old SS *Klondike* paddle steamer and the Log Skyscraper — relics of a bygone age — look out of place in a town fast ridding itself of its Klondike image.

On to Haines Junction over some rough sections of road needing careful driving to the first of two natural features which, even in a land as rich in scenic grandeur as the Yukon, must rate as spectacular in the extreme. The first is Kluane Lake, a blue-green strip of water extending forty miles or more between mountains that are the colour of rusty iron. There were several minor gold rushes in the Kluane Lake country, notably around Burwash Landing near the north end of the lake. Destruction Bay, a settlement a few miles south, memorializes in its name the many miners who are alleged to have lost their lives in the shallow but often storm-hit waters.

The second landscape feature is the St Elias mountain range which includes Mount Logan, Canada's highest peak of just under 20,000 feet. They, together with the Kluane Mountains, parallel the highway, presenting an almost unbroken chain of lofty summits interrupted only by a few wide valleys cut by glacier-fed rivers and streams. Amongst all this jumble of granite is the Kluane National Park, a paradise for trekkers and wilderness-seekers since its many acres are virtually undeveloped and encompass extensive ice fields.

Haines Junction is no more than a grandiose mainstreet with no town and the northern terminus of the Haines Highway to the Alaskan township of Haines situated at the head of the Lynn Canal which, in turn, links it to the coast.

Perhaps the dullest section of the Alaska Highway is that where the road nears the Alaska border. Having cleared Destruction Bay and the Kluane Park the countryside, exhausted after its exciting display of drama and beauty, falls flat on its back. The road snakes over the terrain in an aimless fashion as though it were following the wanderings of a drunken moose. For no obvious reason it develops a rash of 'S' bends, the explanation being that, back in 1942, the road builders were in such a hurry they simply followed the gravel ridges to avoid the marshy ground and swamp which is a feature of the region. To halt at the border is a relief. And an added bonus is that there's someone to talk to.

Canadian Customs and Immigration Authorities are based at Beaver Creek but the actual border with Alaska is a further 19 miles ahead and the fact is straightaway made clear by a refreshing sound of tyres swishing smoothly along on a paved surface. But there's a catch. The permafrost has caused horrific potholes in places which can break the axles of unwary motorists who celebrate the occasions with bursts of acceleration.

The scenery of the road changes not at all with the new territory but with the vanishing of the winter snows the Alaskan woods and meadows produce many varieties of wild flowers, including iris, blue lupin, marigold, larkspur, sweet pea and the tiny forget-me-not, the state's national flower. Along the highway the ever-present fireweed of late summer adds bold strokes of mauve and magenta to the colour of the landscape, contrasting agreeably with the sombre greens of the spruce. The wildlife of these northern climes comprises black and grizzly bears, caribou, moose, red fox, wild buffalo, Dall sheep and mountain goat while the many lakes and river deltas are nesting grounds for a huge variety of water-fowl. Dall sheep are shy creatures and are rarely seen I was told though I was forced to a halt on more than one

144

occasion when a herd blocked the road. Buffaloes, too, roamed the verges and I was to see innumerable moose and caribou.

I had been to Alaska before. It is its remoteness that draws me there again and again. In such regions the inherent 'goodness' of our fellow men (and women) is an attribute honed on compassion as well as survival. As with the other remaining wildernesses of this world, its rare people can be enjoyed and, what's more, they can enjoy you. I remember my first visit. Anchorage, I'd been led to believe, was a city of wooden shacks but I found it to be a plush metropolis of wide modern streets with a drug problem. But if the old frontier conception is missing in Anchorage it is to be found in plenty a little further on. I'd gone north to Nome and flown in little British Islander aircraft across the islands of the Bering Sea to Eskimo communities living in a desolation that is terrible to behold. And I had driven and trekked other 'highways' in the far north; roads that are wilderness arteries by any standards for here, at the top of the world, the arctic scenery is one of the unsung wonders of our earth.

Tok at Mile 1314.2 — we were now back to miles — was a place I knew already. The well-stocked village is on a junction of both the Alaska and Glenn Highways which make it an important communication centre. Based on Tok I had journeyed north along the Klondike Loop Road to join a character by the name of Joe O'Bailie prospecting for gold under the South Forks River near a hamlet rejoicing in the name of Chicken. Together we had searched and sifted but neither of us were to make our fortunes on that occasion. Joe, however, had been there for years and was making a reasonable living from the resisting soil — though I can think of easier ways of earning a buck. For a time he wrote me regularly and the following extract from one of his letters offers a graphic idea of conditions to be found in rural Alaska:

'. . . It's been down to minus 60 and 70 degrees for about two months with warming spells of up to minus 30 degrees from time to time so I was able to walk out of my cabin down to the post office to get my mail. I've not seen *anyone* for four months so it was quite an event. I got two Husky pups just before the road closed for the winter and I'll use them next year to haul my provisions back to the cabin so that I won't have to backpack them up the hill anymore. What a chore that is. I did get stuck out once when (the temperature) went from minus 40 degrees to minus 78 in two hours and I spent the night in a drift keeping a small fire going until about noon the next day when I got hungry enough to make a break for the cabin a mile away. I froze part of my face and nearly froze both hands doing it. This kind of cold can freeze your lungs in seconds to kill you if you're not careful. The worst of the cold I hope is over now that it's the end of January but (the temperature) could still drop again before March. The days have started getting longer too; for a while I only saw three hours of daylight so had to walk back and forth from the digs (work site) in the dark. The trouble is I'm nearly out of provisions so I'll have to get serious about bagging a couple of caribou since, except for an occasional rabbit which are tough as a boot, I'm out of meat. The caribou should be migrating through here any day now but I've spotted some fresh moose tracks so I'm going to try to nail the critter next week. Rice and beans are fine but sure can get monotonous after a while . . . The northern lights are still out, all blue and green; they remind me of a woman's eyes. Sure gets lonely around here and I've even broke my mirror so can't even talk to myself. The pups are good company but they're not much on conversation.'

In a subsequent letter Joe asked me to place a 'lonely gold-digger bachelor in outback Alaska wants to meet suitable girl' type of advert in a magazine. This I did and the response was overwhelming. His last letter to me reads: 'Wow!! I was in agony being alone and now I'm in pain because I'm having a heck of a time making up my mind which one to choose! Dave McCall down at the store took a few pictures of me and I've been sending them to as many of the girls as I can. I feel like a kid in a candy shop.' I've heard nothing from him since.

Not everyone realises that the search for gold continues and strikes are still made if not on the scale of a century ago. Along the Taylor Highway and the Klondike Loop are not only the rotting remains of nineteenth century mines with their unsightly 'tails' — the debris of gold-bearing rock — and rusting dredges but new sites occupied by dedicated men with one eye on the big chance and the other watching out for the income tax man. Some, like Joe, are doing quite nicely; others find it as good a way as any to occupy themselves while playing truant from the mainstream of life.

The last but one community south of Fairbanks is Delta Junction and it is *officially* the end of the Alaska Highway since the remaining distance to Fairbanks is covered by the Richardson Highway. Milepost 1422, an elaborate affair with the United States and Alaskan flags flying above it, proclaims this fact and, if one is required, the nearby visitor's centre will provide gratis a certificate confirming your feat of driving. Beyond the silt-laden Delta River the Alaska Mountains spread over the skyline in snowy grandeur while cool winds from their flanks temper the warmth of the sunniest of days.

North Pole, yes North Pole, (population 500) is the home of many a Fairbanks commuter being just 14 miles from that city. The main business of North Pole is the promotion of Christmas — all through the year. Its post office enthusiastically franks letters and cards especially brought in for its exclusive postmark by travellers worldwide. Santa Claus House, built like a dolls house, is a unique if pricey gift shop and, for laundering there's Santa's Suds. A radio station broadcasts religious programmes all over Alaska and across the top of the world to Greenland and Russia.

Hardly on a par with Anchorage, Fairbanks gives a fair imitation of a city nevertheless with an urban population of 27,000 with another 60,000 in the borough. It is Alaska's second largest town and likes to call itself Capital of the Interior. It is one loaded with contrasts; fancy new hotels, shopping malls and housing projects cheek by jowl with log cabins and creaky timber buildings of circa 1910. Gold, of course, was the reason Fairbanks came into existence and the stampede of 1903 and 1904 brought it the first influx of citizens.

The address of my hotel into which I had pre-booked was given as Fairbanks and my enquiries elicited the fact that it was 'just down the road'. The Alaskan perception of distance is well illustrated when I tell you that it was actually *65* miles 'down the road', though still within the borough boundary of Fairbanks.

My reward at the end of the Alaska Highway? The real pot of gold for me will always be the remote land of Alaska itself, vibrant with the promise of adventure amongst its silent backwoods and eternal mountains that so few are privileged to see. Yet there it lies, just a spin up the road. . .

147

6

On the tracks of the Maharajas

LUXURY RAIL TRAVEL IN
INDIA'S RAJASTHAN

I am not a railway buff but I love trains. This may sound contradictory but what I mean is that I'm not one of that breed of men
who have to know how and why the wheels go round; I'm just
happy that they do. I am, if you like, a railway *travel* buff. On
trains I have ridden many railways of the world and the more
inefficient, antiquated and rural they are the better I like it. The
locomotives don't have to emit smoke but it helps since, so often,
the character of a steam engine is reflected in that of those who
ride its coaches. Likewise a soulless diesel or electric 'unit' can,
all too often, produce an equally soulless train.

In all types of trains I have travelled about the globe and filled
three books with my experiences; I have ridden the Direct Orient
Express to Istanbul, the Taurus to Baghdad, and the Trans-
Siberian to Vladivostok. On all sorts of lines I have ridden
between London and Cairo, Paris and Delhi, and Mombasa and
Kampala. I have suffered in packed third class compartments in
the Indian sub-continent, risked altitude-sickness on trans-
Andean tracks in South America, circuited the Balkans even on
the forbidden trains of Albania, jogged happily the length and
breadth of North America from New York to San Diego and
Alaska to Mexico, marvelled at lineside jungles in Thailand, and
been removed from the despised trains of Cuba. And by the time
you are reading this I'll have added the rail marathon from London, via Outer Mongolia, to Hong-Kong.

With my insatiable appetite for adventure by rail I was unable
to get the sap rising very high when an invitation came to sample
India's prestigious 'Palace on Wheels' that trundles a ponderous
circuit around the state of Rajasthan carrying tourists intent
upon tasting the Maharajan version of rail travel. In Europe the
new Venice-Simplon Orient Express had not excited me much

either, it being — to my mind — no more than a vehicle that panders to the rich — and here was a similar Indian replica of a train doing the same thing. But at least the 'Palace' didn't pretend to be the famed express it wasn't and was headed by steam locomotives. Nor was the cost of riding it so outrageous in spite of a tour programme very much more comprehensive. I decided to give it a whirl.

Up until now it may have been discerned that my journeyings have taken place in an aura of considerable discomfort; even some hardship. However it must be repeated that to experience adventurous travel one does not necessarily have to be a masochist. Adventurous journeying of a, perhaps, more refined kind, can also be found aboard the most luxurious of vehicles as my week riding into nostalgia on the 'Palace on Wheels' during December 1982 will show.

To savour the full delight of riding the Palace on Wheels one has to appreciate that trains in India are not only the lifeline of a nation but are part and parcel of its heritage and manner of living. In my case it was worthwhile to recollect a sobering experience of my first-ever visit to India when, standing compressed within a crush of some 29 sweating, irritable fellow-travellers in a then third class compartment designed for eight, I managed — but only just — to survive a 36-hour journey.

Indian Railways, the second largest railway system in the world, came into being in the afternoon of 16 April 1853 when, to the sound of a 21-gun salute, the first train steamed out of Bori Bunder bound for Thana — a momentous journey of just 23 miles. Since then the network has become the most comprehensive and most used anywhere, and for this, Great Britain is largely responsible since that was where the money, skill and knowledge came to build it. Cynics will claim that the railway was built for internal security reasons, to tighten the hold of the forces of law and order — and there is some truth in this but in opening up the country they effected a revolution. Bombay and Calcutta, Delhi and Madras, were brought into physical contact with one another, a big change from the days when distances were so great as to rule out anything except occasional travel from one end of the country to another. Today the railways are still indispensable; in economic and social life there is nothing that could take their place.

'To travel hopefully is better than to arrive' is the opinion of Robert Louis Stevenson of course and he could have qualified his oft-quoted statement by reference to the product of the Rajasthan Tourist Board who, in conjunction with Indian Railways and the Indian Government Tourist Board, spawned a train of imperialistic delight. To genteely tour the legendary pink, yellow and white cities of Rajasthan offering a visitor a spectacle of India unmatched by any other state in the Union is one thing. To travel between them in a conveyance of such splendour is another. Here without a shadow of a doubt was a double experience for the price of one.

Rajasthan is the obvious state through which to run a maharaja's train. Formerly known as Rajputana, it has become an administrative unit comprising the previously existing princely states. It is a land of rock and desert interspersed with fertile tracts, enchanting lakes and jungle.

From the human angle Rajasthan is a country that is still living in its historic past, despite the changes of the last few years. Home of the Rajputs of ancient lineage, it is the legendary land of chivalry and knightly prowess. Its very name means 'Abode of Kings'. Palace and fort, garden and lake, they speak of love and loyalty, of proud prestige and deeds of derring-do. Rajasthan has a stirring story indeed writ large upon the embattled walls of its cities. Resisting every invader since the time of Harsha in the 7th century the feudal lords and princes of Rajasthan valiantly defended their independence and, in this, they were helped by the British for whom its colourful peoples maintain a high regard.

The long line of dun-coloured coaches that awaited my evening arrival at Delhi's out-of-town Cantonment Station hardly gave the impression of a palace, wheeled or otherwise, and I presumed its colour was supposed to initiate the notion of a golden train. Even though I was only seeing the thing from the draughty platform of an ill-lit station at night the heavy old-fashioned wagons with tightly-closed and barred windows looked more penal than palatial. Resigned to what I concluded was going to be a gimmicky exploitation I allowed myself to be registered, documented and ushered aboard the contraption. My coach, I noticed, was inscribed with the arms of the Jaipur State Railway and I was soon to learn that it had, in fact, borne both the Maharaja of Bikaner (in 1898) and India's present Prime Minister, Mrs

Indira Gandhi. These two worthies, it seemed, had shared the premises with their entourage; I was to have it all to myself.

Mollified a little, I made my tour of inspection in company with the management of the train and my initial misgivings began to abate as the magic of the train worked its charm and permeated my cynicism. In awe I gazed upon the spacious sleeping compartment replete with wardrobe and double bed, plus refinements such as table lamps, fans, and a telephone. The lounge contained a sofa and armchairs of quality brocade, the walls were lined with heavy polished mahogany; not perhaps *quite* so lavishly rich as those of the Venice-Simplon Orient Express but, after all, this was India; not pampered Europe. A well-fitted-out toilet and bathroom and a further two smaller bedrooms completed the suite of rooms, beyond which lay the servants quarters, the domain of two most gracious Rajasthanis attired in crimson and gold tunics and turbans to match, their sole object over the next week of life being to wait upon me hand and foot. Further along the train the restaurant car was a reflection of what I can remember of the one-time Brighton Belle; pink lampshades at each window, the tables agleam with 'Palace'-engraved china and cutlery while the lounge car was plentifully endowed with soft scatter cushions around long low divans and oblong coffee tables of polished carved oak; the whole ménage tastefully encased by the luxuriant folds of curtains aglitter with gold thread. An end section housed a bar and library, each well stocked with its particular requisites. Heading the train a giant steam locomotive wheezed stentoriously, its pistons, boiler and smoke stack reflecting a surfeit of elbow grease and pride of maintenance.

There was a ring of pride too in the voice of the manager of the Palace as he told me that it was Indian Railways who had carried out this major refurbishing project in their own workshops. The rolling stock had been rescued, item by item, from railway sheds and disused sidings at remote railway stations all over India. Saved from the grave but rusted from the monsoons and bleached by the burning sun they were assembled and painstakingly restored to their former glory or rebuilt from a basic framework. Twelve such cars made up the first section but more were being unearthed from the far-flung corners of the sub-continent. And what was more — the lilt of pride now changed to one of challenge — the cost had been less than half a million pounds as against the eleven million of its European rival, the Venice-Simplon Orient.

That the chief power-unit is the steam engine gives the train a vital atmospheric advantage over the V.S.O.E. too though this was not an indulgent concession to the whims of its clients. The simple fact is that more than half the passenger trains of India are steam-hauled anyway and, with the Rajasthan rail circuit a non-mainline route, steam and diesel are the only possible means of locomotion.

As the evening wore on and the European clientele of the train dribbled into the station to be led, wide-eyed, to their respective quarters I fought to come to terms with this latest grade and quality of transportation on which I found myself. In my mind I was attempting to equate an earlier Indian rail journey in company with 29 fellow humans compressed into a stark third-class compartment to one in which I had a whole golden coach of my own, a coach once occupied by a maharaja and a prime-minister to boot. At intervals during the evening I sallied from my private eyrie to survey my fellow mini-maharajas and was even more astounded to learn that not only was the Maharaja of Bikaner's coach the grandest on the train but that, as an invited journalist, I had been accorded the privilege of exclusive occupation. Conceit mingled with my amazement and even before the midnight hour of departure I found myself unable to suppress certain airs and graces totally foreign to my nature. Strolling the platform I gained a perverted satisfaction from watching the well-to-do clients being shepherded into a slightly lesser grade of accommodation to that of my own. And I hardly could spare a glance for the small rabble of low caste Indians for whom the platform was no more than a lodging for the night though my contempt was tempered by the recollection that, once, I too had been one of these shadowy figures and that only by the grace of the lottery of life had I been saved from a permanent situation on an Indian railway station. The world has lived so long with the idea of congested stations and trains that Indian humanity itself has become synonymous with overcrowding.

The clientele assembled, distributed and settled, the call came for dinner. No corridor linked the coaches since the princes and maharajas who rode them had no need of such frivolities; indeed visitations were positively discouraged. Thus progress to and from the dining saloon had to be fitted into the not infrequent stopping schedule though I had been notified that, in my case, I could halt the train at the press of a bell or a word with my coach captain, as the senior of my two flunkies was titled. (With this invitation there came to mind a near-forgotten dream of my younger days — and surely everyone else's — of pulling the communication cord which only an expensive penalty had eclipsed — and here was I being given the chance with no fear of fine or punishment!).

Eating in a stationary dining car makes for a vaguely unreal environment in which to consume a meal for, in company with the temptation of the communication cord, a swaying table and soup in one's lap is part and parcel of rail travel. For this, our first dinner, there was a choice of meat or fish between the usual ancillary items but the paramount attraction of the meal was vested in the assembly of its consumers; the gathering of the clan. Across the soup, the veal cutlets, the halibut and the creme caramel we eyed one another in critical appraisal, pondered upon the type of person who would choose a train for a holiday, and launched into a fever of introduction. Thus, with the coffee and mints, I was able to discern that our numbers included lawyers and doctors, stockbrokers and company directors, a naval captain and a nuclear scientist. That such an upper strata of society should be so strongly represented was surprising only in that it showed who is the most adventurous class — so long as the adventure is padded by comfort and there is the money to embark on it. The coffee and liqueurs concluded we bade one another goodnight and scurried to our respective bedchambers to await the maharajan movement.

The jerk nearly shot me out of bed — but we were away. I lay listening to the sound of wheel on track and the half-forgotten clickety-click which is lost to us in Britain now that we have continuous welded rails. It should have lulled me to sleep but didn't. Instead I found myself rocked and buffeted in a manner that had me wondering if the train would stay on the track. But though sleep was elusive that first night I gained enormous enjoyment since, for me, going to bed on a train heralds the beginning of a potential adventure.

Rajasthan at sunrise was a promise of this adventure with its sounds and sights wrapped in a cool December mist. But the relentless blast of the sun was soon to tear the mist asunder. Not until the unhurried consumption of breakfast in bed or in our private lounges were we invited to leave the train and cast our eyes upon the sights available outside the train.

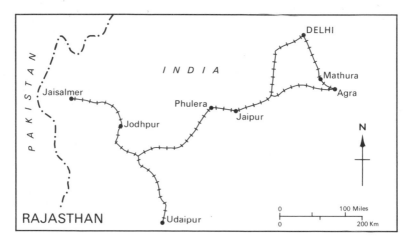

To be pitched suddenly into India is an awesome experience. We had only been on the train for twelve hours but its tranquility and unreality made the transfer back to the world outside the more bewildering. A wonderland of 'fabulous wealth and fabulous poverty, of splendour and rags... the one sole country under the sun that is endowed with an imperishable interest for alien prince and alien peasant, for lettered and ignorant, wise and fool, rich and poor, bond and free, the one land that *all* men desire to see, and having seen once, by even a glimpse, would not give that glimpse for the shows of all the world combined', wrote Mark Twain about India 70 years ago. All at once we were enveloped in noise, smells, incomprehensible chatter and colour. Especially colour. For in Rajasthan it is, more than everywhere else, colour that transcends everything in that first initial curious glance. Together with gaiety it abounds everywhere. Their picturesque costumes reflect the joy by which the people of Rajasthan seek to enliven their existence. The smells are India.

At Jaipur, the 'pink city' built of local rose-pink coloured stone in the 'tone of autumn sunset', as the historical writings put it,

154

we were greeted by a cavalcade of elephants, not pink but vivid nevertheless in glittering head-dress, a band of folk musicians warbling boistrously and the first of seven marigold-garland welcomes from smiling girls of exotic allure. In the station square a luxury coach awaited to turn us 7-day maharajas into mere up-market leathernecks for a tour of the city.

Encircled on all sides — except the south — by rugged hills surmounted by forts, Jaipur is enclosed in battlemented walls. Within them is medieval bedlam. The *Hawa Mahal* — Palace of the Winds — is the landmark of the city though its elaborate, fanciful and pink façade stands amid the high street chaos of clogged roads and rude houses. In the centre of Jaipur is the City Palace — now a museum — more dramatically perched on high. A few miles away, at Amber, came the scheduled elephant ride on which we progressed regally up the hill, musically-escorted, to the deserted Moghul edifice reminding me a little of Dartmoor Prison except for the environment. A lesson on sun-dials at the Jantar Mantar Observatory, tea on a maharajan terrace of a British-designed garden watching a very un-British sunset, and dinner among the floodlit remains of the ruined fort of Nahargarh overlooking the sprawling city brought us wearily back to the peace of our train.

After a more successful night's sleep, my mind and body now attuned to the new motion and environment, in the early morning and by arrangement with my coach captain, I had transferred from the luxurious splendour of the abode of the Maharaja of Bikaner to the sooty glamour of the cab of the train's locomotive called 'Desert Queen'. Here, with my eyes full of smut and a tummy full of sweet oily tea I rediscovered a joy of travel that was in danger of eclipse under the welter of high living. Thus, in the grimy confines between tender and boiler, amongst a cab-full of dials and levers, I was back in a corner of real India and in the company of real Indians, these ones plainly appreciative of my interest in things railway. Here the shudder and shake was not only doubly pronounced but accompanied by the glorious whiff of steam, the searing blast of heat from a roaring flame, the high-pitched scream of the whistle and the sheer exhilaration of riding a mechanical animal vibrating with unleashed power.

It was from the engine crews that I learnt of the importance attached to the Palace on Wheels in Indian railway circles.

Answerable direct to the government it has become the most prestigious train in the country. It takes priority over every other on the tracks of Indian Railways; is the only one double-crewed and its drivers are the most experienced in the business. All along the route crowds turned out to gape at the long winding serpent as well as the un-maharaja-like incumbents who emerged to daily greet the cities of Rajasthan.

All morning I remained with the 'Desert Queen' to return to my abode simply for the purpose of removing the worst of the coal dust from face and hands to join the grand emergence into Udaipur. So, running the gauntlet of the reception committee, we struggled into another sprawling city, this one given a romantic air by the steel-blue waters of a lake. Moated Udaipur, ethereal, unreal, holds island palaces galore that sparkle with pinnacles of coloured glass, of amber and pale jade created by Mahara Udai Singh in the sixteenth century. His palace-fort, massively bastioned and gated, erupts from the crest of a ridge and is the largest such pile in Rajasthan. A less sombre palace takes up the whole of an island in the artifical lake where it serves as a high-class restaurant in which we very adequately lunched on asparagus and venison.

There is something curiously theatrical about an empty train and returning to one in the middle of the night makes for added piquancy. In the waiting silence the presence of long past occupants hovers; the maharajas who travelled in the coaches to state occasions, on hunting parties or to polo matches; the maharanees who made their bridal voyages; vice-regal missions on delicate assignments, the Queen and the Duke of Edinburgh who travelled on one when they stayed with the Maharaja of Jaipur. As the light seeped out of the sky and we climbed aboard our respective coaches the long-slumbering train came to life again though its new occupants are unable to raise the aura of grandeur, the royal grace or proud disdain that surrounded their predecessors. Yet for such a historic vehicle to be only half alive is better, surely, than being dead, the carcases of its component parts rotting in forgotten sidings the length and breadth of India.

That night was, I remember, the idyllic one we remained stationary and there was ample time next morning for shopping and bargaining in Udaipur's warren of bazaars. Here again was a moment, a fragment of the real India intruding into our pseudo-royal progress; the India that is contradictory, confusing, elusive, inexplicable. Streets full of people selling; selling anything — even the unsellable. The town centre of garish signs and toppling buildings was bulging at the seams with the movement of people all intent upon some purposeful errand that held commercial enterprise or so it seemed. Women squatted silently in doorways and children played and laughed in rancid gutters. And pervading everything that smell of India that cannot be described or analysed.

Then we were off again leaving the confusion behind as we puffed importantly over the flat semi-desert where the tiniest of hills drew the eye. I spent the remainder of the day again in the locomotive, this one the 'Fort of Jodhpur', where I was once more regaled with coal-dust and plentiful libations of tea from proud, kindly engine crews who, surely, are the salt of the Indian earth. It was quite a horrendous ride for, as we ground across the steppe, whistling mournfully, we mowed down one water buffalo and two goats that refused to move away quickly enough from 300 tons of train. And at one station we very nearly ran over a mentally-sick woman when her attempted suicide brought the train to a juddering, screeching halt.

Long before the end of the week all the reserve only thinly breached the first evening had broken down and our contingent of guests intermingled, chatted and visited their compatriots in their respective coaches to compare furnishings, experiences and reactions to the trip. The few train buffs were euphoric: they had supped full on steam and all that goes with it. The nostalgic and romantics were gushingly happy. Me? I was content enough, having found my luxury legs.

'Island in the Sand' describes Jaisalmer and, for most of us, it was the most fascinating city of all. A delightfully remote little town it conjures the image of the 'Thousand and One Nights' with its temples, fortresses and, of course, palaces — all constructed of the local yellow stone; a yellow city in a yellow ocean. Our welcome was the sincerest of all prior to our day's excursion to see its labyrinth of strangely-carved houses, handsome façades and elaborate balconies amidst a colourful fairytale population. Once the capital of the Bhati Rajputs, the city stands on a low range of hills surrounded by a three-mile wall. On all sides the desert sweeps into eternity and it was to a distant range of sand dunes at Sam, more Saharan than the Sahara, that we were taken for our scheduled camel ride and to listen to a performance of Jaisalmer musical talents. Dinner was held at a hotel back in the outskirts of town followed by a cultural presentation that included rhythmic offerings from an Indian ex-jailbird sporting the allegedly longest moustache in India.

No palace was to be seen at Bharatpur, our last city in Rajasthan. Instead a bird sanctuary — the Keoladeo Ghana Bird Sanctuary, an ornithologist's paradise. During winter, birds flock here from as far away as Siberia making a remarkable concentration of every feathered creature imaginable that flies and floats. We breakfasted at the lodge and were punted around the reed and island-impregnated lake before moving on by coach into the neighbouring state of Uttar Pradesh. After the magic of Rajasthan, the ghost city of Fatehpur Siki and the forts of Agra were something of an anti-climax. Fatehpur Siki is an imperial city deep-frozen in time. Built at the command of Akbar to become the capital of the Moghul Empire it surpassed even London in size and grandeur before it died for reason of a simple lack of water. Our guide put it more quaintly: 'The water was not very delicious', he explained, referring to the failed reservoir. Akbar was also instrumental in the rise of Agra, the rusty-red sandstone of its forbidding walls surrounding white marble palaces another memorial to that empire. Faded they are now but the glory of the Taj Mahal never diminishes however many times it is seen. It remains the greatest love story ever told; a perfect jewel set by the Jumna river that is a fitting finale to any Indian journey.

I had looked upon it the first time at the end of my other Indian rail journey those years before. Then I had set myself the task of seeing the country the hard way; of experiencing it from the level of the ordinary Indian, utilising third class train carriages and equally over-crowded local buses. With ordinary Indians I slept on station platforms and in hotels that were no more than doss houses, living on local curries supplied for a few pence at wayside stalls. The exercise had taught me much about India and lost me the best part of two stone in weight; a tough education which has added to my appreciation of the modest comforts offered me on my many subsequent visits.

The memory certainly added spice to my present journey now nearing its end. I had become inured to the insulation from the grit and grime of the 'real' India, the pretence that kept us from making contact with 'real' Indians, the illusion of grandeur that we had not earned or inherited. We had observed rather than become part of the country but then this is the very essence of a journey on the Palace on Wheels; a dream with no real substance.

A last night in our golden coaches and we were rolling towards Delhi from whence we came. The countryside was agricultural, full of buffalo and sugar cane and it had ceased to interest us. Dinner was in the restaurant car; a choice of Indian or vaguely European dishes and most of us had had our fill of curry. I spent the last morning hours in the cab of the 'Desert Queen' re-learning the rules of an old-fashioned semaphore signalling procedure from the crew. We were an hour late but it didn't matter. Back at Delhi Cantonment there were no garlands. We were maharajas no more.

7

Smoke Channel

CLANDESTINE TRAVEL IN WARTIME EUROPE

I am aware I may be cheating a little by bringing clandestine travel into the scope of this book since anyone wishing to follow my example or footsteps would have to await the unlikely circumstances presented by a hot war. The best on offer at the present time are those arising from a *cold* one, though here, I hasten to point out, I am not encouraging would-be Don Quixotes to go tilting at communist windmills. That I have done just this in my time — and undergone prolonged incarceration in a political jail for my pains — was entirely due to circumstances prevailing in the bad old Stalinist days of the 1950s — but I'm not going into that here.

We homo sapiens are a rum lot. We might not realize it but, just below the thin crust of what is looked upon as civilised behaviour, lies a suppressed desire to steal, rob, insult, maim, even kill in certain circumstances. In fact, for many of our fellow men and women, these cravings break to the surface all too frequently as our daily newspapers make only too plain.

During a hot war these savage urges can, to a controlled extent, be legitimately released and, in the eyes of one's own countrymen, the perpetrator is respected the more for it though he or she can expect short shrift from the other side if caught. To a far lesser degree, breaking some of the unjust laws imposed by totalitarian regimes might bring heavy-handed reprisal from the authorities concerned but, to one's own more tolerant society, the act is looked upon as anything but criminal.

With these reflections in mind allow me to tell of an instance from my own experiences as a soldier-captive in World War Two with Nazi-occupied central Europe as the backdrop.

Never in all my life had I felt such triumph. It was autumn 1944 and I was but 20 at the time but, looking back over the decades of my life, this was one of the few great moments that shine the brightest. Together with a Scottish companion I had cut my way out of a strongly-guarded POW camp in the bleak Silesian plain of what is now western Poland and, with the deed accomplished, we had spared a few exquisite moments to look back, from the *outside*, at the brightly-illuminated compounds.

Gordon Primrose of the Gordon Highlanders and myself, a then NCO of the Dorset Regiment, had been captured on different dates, in different battles and in different parts of Normandy. My own termination of liberty occurred on July 10, the day the city of Caen fell to the British 21st Army. My regiment and division, indeed the whole army group, had been fighting village by village to this end for weeks; ever since the break-out from the beachhead following the landing. The utter savagery of the struggle made a sickening indictment of man's ability to inflict inhumanity upon his fellow men and when my SS captor said, 'For you, Tommy, the war is over' I did, just for a moment, see a vision of *Shangri-la* that was, alas, to disintegrate into yet worse savagery and terror — as well as, for me, excitement and the most original of journeying.

Not that those awful days of travel between the battle lines in France to our final working camp in Silesia constituted a journey I want to remember. It was by rail; fifty or sixty of us to a '40 hommes ou 8 cheval'-type closed wagon with the RAF and USAF bombing, rocketing and machine-gunning the hell out of us by day and by night. And in between these attentions the Germans fed us salt beef and denied us water so that the weaker of us went mad with thirst. After brief sojourns in transit camps here and there, the lives of Gordon and I became entwined at the dismal coal-mining town of Zabrze (then called Hindenburg, more pronounceably, by the Germans) where our travels, such as they were, fizzled to an end.

I am not sure whether it was an utter detestation of coal-mining under slave conditions or the sudden cessation of travel that prompted the escape attempt. Today, in more mature years, I like to think that patriotism came into it though more likely this was mixed with the simple desire to go home. Whatever it was our plans were carefully laid and carried out with the unwitting co-operation of the RAF whose bomber fleets passed over nightly at intervals so regular that one could set a watch by them.

Their scheduled arrival doused the camp perimeter lights and the source of power to the searchlights which had a disconcerting habit of sweeping the camp, abruptly illuminating anything that moved after prisoners had supposedly been locked inside their barrack blocks. And with the passing of the bombers on their way and on their way back we had time to put into effect our nefarious plans. These involved cutting (with stolen wire-cutters) through the first barbed wire fence, prising apart — using simple pulley and cord apparatus — the rolls of concertina wire coiled between the first and second apron fences, cutting through this second apron and finally scaling the third cable-mesh fence to drop out of sight amongst an allotment of brussel sprouts. Everything, miraculously, went according to plan except that the lights came on a fraction too early, catching us atop the third fence. But no one spotted us as we dived for cover amongst a vegetable for which I have since acquired a high regard.

The moments of basking in our new-found freedom were brief in the extreme, the urge to put distance between our former captors and ourselves becoming the stronger emotion. The new urge caused us to fall into a hidden slit trench, fortunately unoccupied, belonging to an anti-aircraft battery whose guns, thudding vigorously, we had heard so often as we lay in bed listening delightedly to the passing bombers. And from the trench we blundered, in the dark, into the guns themselves with gutteral commands to 'halt! halt!' ringing in our ears as we fled away at a tangent. Any instant we expected the crack and whine of bullets but nothing happened as we hared across an open meadow in a direction we hoped would preclude further surprises. God was plainly on our side that night.

For what was left of it we spent it lying, compressed together for warmth, in a wood. Rain began to fall and, subconsciously, I burrowed beneath Gordon in an attempt to keep dry; a movement that was all too successful to judge from my damp colleague's wrath as the grey dawn revealed the situation. We wore the khaki battledress in which we had been taken prisoner but had covered the tell-tale uniform with our less provocative working clothes. Unfortunately both tunic and trousers displayed a big yellow 'K' (for Kriegsgefangener, or Prisoner of War) ineradicable and conspicuous, even though we wore them inside out to reduce the brilliance of the stencil. Plainly a change of attire was an urgent priority. We also carried a small store of the more durable items saved from the few Red Cross parcels that had filtered through to the camp and which we hoped to supplement with more basic fodder scrounged or stolen from field or farm. Our planned direction of escape was vaguely east towards Warsaw via Cracow which was roughly south-east from our present position. Beyond Warsaw lay the Red Army and it was alleged to be closing in on the Polish capital. To be honest, our Russian allies were not a first choice of liberating agent but with the British and American lines many hundreds of miles away to the west we had little choice. The Hindenburg camp was of comparatively recent origin so could boast of no escape organisation that could provide the likes of us with natty civilian outfits, forged passes, compasses, maps and the complete escaper's box of tricks. Only officers and gentlemen in oflags — POW camps for commissioned ranks — could indulge in such luxuries, not being required to spend their time in hard labour for the greater glory of the Third Reich. Thus we were no more than ourselves; plainly British soldiers on the run with but our own resourcefulness and luck to see us through. Our small trump card was the unlikelihood of immediate pursuit. Not only had we taken the trouble to conceal the breaks in the wire but had arranged for delaying tactics on the morning roll call (and here I must record our gratitude to my fellow inmates of Camp E902 who stood for many hours on a cold wet autumn morning confounding the commandant's count).

Came the moment we felt obliged to enter upon a life of crime and in this Gordon set a far less conscious-stricken example than I. The farmhouse of our initial attentions lay conveniently close to the wood, was remote and we were able to observe the occupants departing for work in the surrounding fields. A chained dog was barking incesssantly which suited our purpose admirably since its bark of real alarm would be masked. Ignoring it we sauntered into the yard with an air — we hoped — of casual labourers looking for a job. Reaching the door we found it unlocked so pushed inside to stand uncertainly in an untidy kitchen-cum-living room, mercifully devoid of occupants except for a cat that fled, spitting, out of another doorway. As if he had done it all before Gordon scooped up several jackets and sundry garments that lay across an ancient sewing machine while I contented myself with a loaf of bread from the table. My companion then swooped on a peaked cap from a hook behind the door and I'm sure, if I hadn't stopped him, he'd have made a sortie into the nether regions of the house in search of the silver. Clasping our loot we withdrew back to our refuge, the barking resuming its less strident tempo.

Sharing the spoils between us and discarding a woman's apron that had come with the bundle we arrayed ourselves in our new attire with, I regret to declare, some levity. Our working clothes went the way of the apron and I ruefully thought of the heavy fine authority would impose should we be recaptured. Gordon retained the cap — an item that is almost *de rigeur* in industrial Silesia — insisting that my blonde hair was Germanic anyway and gradually we were transformed into something akin to Silesian gentlemen of leisure. Additionally fortified by hunks of bread with Red Cross marmalade — but no tea in case smoke from a fire drew unwelcome visitors — we issued forth in search of liberation.

The events of the previous evening had graphically proved to us the folly of moving by night. Hence we put a mythical Plan B into operation, resolving to make our way using minor roads and tracks or open fields so long as we could maintain the right direction. We did hold a map of sorts; a sketch provided by a sympathetic miner, indicating a line of towns through or near which we would have to pass en route to Cracow. At the time of these events Silesia was part of Germany and populated by a Silesian peoples who did not seem to know whose side they were on. Despised by the Germans, hated by the Poles they were in a most unhappy situation and, from our point of view, none were to be trusted. Once on true Polish territory help, if needed, would be at hand; in the meantime everyone was to be classed as enemy.

Over the flat landscape towns and villages were easy to pick out, their gaunt pithead shafts proclaiming their trade. We felt obliged to enter one town if only for the purpose of finding out where we were and this we proceeded to do but not without some trepidation. The place selected was of depressing uniformity; rows of workers' houses, some dingy shops and a hopeless church. Had the name of it, shown on a yellow sign at the approaches, meant anything to us we well may have by-passed its centre but it told us nothing so we kept resolutely on into the shabby streets intent upon locating a signpost or indicator board offering better advice. The exercise was not wasted for, at the main intersection a plethora of signs made most helpful reading, emphatically recommending Chrzanow, well on the road to Cracow, and marked on our sketch map. Our bravado proved something else too. Nobody but nobody took the slightest notice of us though I was uncomfortably aware of my own bare head and resolved to rectify the omission at the earliest opportunity. Passing a crowded beerhouse, a gaggle of German soldiers ejected onto the pavement in front of us. One of them, a corporal, asked for a light for his cigarette and Gordon unhesitatingly obliged, babbling happily away in Gaelic to which the soldier turned not a hair. With Europe awash with uprooted nationalities *any* language with the possible exception of English passed muster even if not understood. On the spur of the moment I nipped into the smoke-filled tap room, nicked the shoddiest cap from the coat rack and returned outside well-pleased with myself. I then had to restrain Gordon from going in for a beer, not only on account of the pilfered headgear but also because of our shortage of funds. By smuggling Red Cross cigarettes down the mine we had managed to raise a stock of Reichsmarks but these I was not going to allow Gordon to squander. Acquiring more money by theft was not going to be as simple as rummaging around people's kitchens for the odd loaf of bread; cash was usually locked away, its acquisition a very different ball game. And bank robbery had such a pursuit-raising quality about it.

Heartened by our reception — or lack of it — from the good citizens we made our way along the road to Chrzanow, leaving the depressing streets with undisguised relief. The trouble was that we were the wrong side of a region headed by the town of Katowice — later to be known as Stalingrad — which consisted of a host of smaller, ugly mining and steel communities through which we would have to make our way. The British equivalent of the area is, I suppose, the Black Country, and, in Germany, the Ruhr.

We left the road as soon as we were clear of houses. It was a well-used artery and in spite of the lack of interest experienced in town it only needed a nosy minion of authority to enquire after our health and papers and that would be our lot. The alternative of walking parallel but away from the road resulted in tiring, frustrating progress, detouring around fences, farms and bunches of workers in the fields. In making just such a detour to avoid some houses Gordon stumbled into some barbed wire and tore his trousers from the thigh to below the knee. We hastily tied the corners of the tear together with string and slogged on seething with hatred for the Silesian farmer who filled his ditches with barbed wire. Needle and thread were beyond our resources but we chalked them up on our list of requirements to be 'borrowed'.

On the bank of a stream we bathed our feet in cold, rust-coloured water. Long-unaccustomed walking had produced blisters on our heels and worn holes in our socks but the water treatment cooled the throbbing and raised morale a little.

While so engaged a bunch of soldiers and girls with bicycles suddenly appeared, laughing and chatting. We had not realized that a sunken lane lay behind the hedgerow beyond the ditch and it was along this that they had come. Their appearance was a shock but we stood our ground, continuing our ablutions, our hearts in our mouths. The girls waved, the soldiers scowled and they all moved on. Quickly we replaced our boots reprimanding ourselves for carelessness.

'Bicycles!' I exclaimed a propos of nothing. Gordon glanced at me blankly, holding his torn trousers. 'Cycling's faster than walking', I went on cryptically and he got the message. Another item we added to our shopping list.

The road became erratic, running straight for miles and then taking a corkscrew route to serve half a dozen villages. Sometimes we found ourselves on the road itself and fell to the temptation of its smooth firm surface but the sound of approaching vehicles would send us scurrying into the fields again. At the edge of one such field we came upon the hot embers of a fire in which we baked potatoes gathered from a clamp. This was the only time we found food and the means of cooking it in the same place.

The autumn dusk arrived all too early and we cast about for shelter for the night. A barn held more attraction than the depths of a wood; it could offer both a roof and the warmth of hay or straw, and within an hour we found one. It was locked and heavily barred but a window at the rear surrendered to our onslaught. We crawled inside, located a stack of soft clover-scented

166

hay and staked our claims. Our eyes, adjusting to the darkness, took in the contents of the building: a derelict tractor, several carts, some harness, a pile of bricks and various agricultural implements — but no bicycles. Through cracks in the brick and timber walls we studied a neighbouring house noticing the thin plume of smoke issuing from its chimney.

'Hope they choke on their sauerkraut!' was Gordon's bitter comment and I could not but agree. Potatoes, bread and marmalade keep body and soul together but make for uninspiring eating.

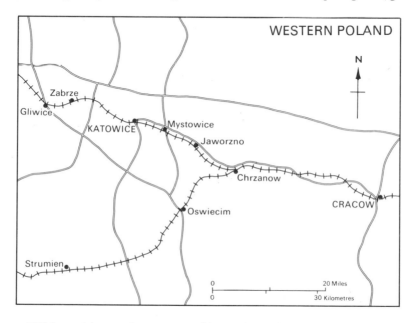

With nothing to do we turned in early and slept extremely well after an initial bout of scratching resulting from the attentions of the insect life. But these were a lot less unpleasant than the lice and bed-bugs that had been the bane of our lives back at camp. We awoke early, partly from hunger but also from the noise of a horse and cart outside the barn. We lay listening uneasily to rough unintelligible voices, ready to dive deeper for cover at the first signs of the barn door being opened until the unmistakable sounds of the cart being driven away released us from tension.

The morning light filtering through the crevices feebly illuminated more of the barn's interior. Now we could see two stalls, one obviously once used for a horse, the other as a store containing a heap of roots. Selecting two swedes, yellow and unhealthy-looking, we cut each into portions to make them more appetising but they proved coarse and fibrous, and raised a thirst we were unable to assuage. Disgusted, we flung the bits away.

Another scrutiny of the house revealed no signs of life except for the wisp of smoke so we prepared ourselves for another forced entry. Aware that bold confrontation paid dividends we made straight for the back door, gently pushed it open an inch or two, and listened. All was quiet; not even a dog barked. The muddy yard and few outhouses gave no indication of being occupied by man or beast so, encouraged, we stole into another kitchen. Straightaway Gordon noticed a pair of trousers on the back of a hardback chair and I homed in on a bread-bin containing most of a loaf and half a cake which I bundled into a sack brought along for the purpose. Gordon was rummaging through a handbag when voices and approaching footsteps sounded from the other door to send us into inglorious retreat, Gordon flaunting trousers and handbag. We sped across the yard keeping to the lee of a windowless wall in an effort to avoid detection. A copse of trees drew around us.

Assured of no pursuit or overtures of rage we made a roundabout return to the barn there to retrieve our few other worldly possessions and Gordon to climb into his new trousers. They were far too large but by liberal application of string at the waist and the turning up of the legs the garment passed muster. There were even a few coins in the pockets. A search of the handbag produced the equivalent of £6 in German currency and a collection of woman's knick-knacks of no use to us. We buried the torn trousers and the handbag in the hay and, munching bread and cake, left our night's refuge for the last time. Once again a spasm of guilt assailed me but not for long. Plainly I was becoming inured to this life of crime.

There was not a stir in the crystal stillness as we climbed down a slope, broke through a hedge, and came back to the road to descend with it into a shallow valley. Two men appeared before we could take evasive action so we continued walking, mumbling a reply to their greeting. We felt their eyes boring into our backs as we marched on not daring to turn our own heads. The thought came to me that perhaps one of them recognised his trousers.

168

That second day we made better progress in spite of blisters and stiff calf-muscles but our general weakness from months of semi-starvation and neglect was plainly telling. Pauses for rests became more frequent and, as the day wore on, we found ourselves being increasingly light-headed and careless. Too tired to care, we walked straight through villages instead of detouring around them. Some mounds by the roadside, which we thought at first to be armoured cars, turned out to be potato clamps so we dug several out, putting them in the sack with the idea of risking a fire that evening. The only unguarded bicycle we saw was propped outside a shop. We could have stolen it, but what use was one between the two of us?

The town of Mystowice we trudged straight through without a care and were surprised at its size. We felt far safer in the big industrial centres and far more anonymous than was the case in villages where strangers — even legitimate ones — were objects of scrutiny. A town centre signpost indicated Oswiecim as '21 kilometres', another arm 'Chrzanow 24 kilometres' and it was only because we had designated Chrzanow as a landmark — it being astride the road to Cracow — that we chose the more easterly road. At that time we were not to know that the German version of Oswiecim was Auschwitz.

Soldiers and members of the *Volksturm* (Home Guard) were among the dowdy civilians in the streets but none appeared to be on duty. We remained in dread of the sudden materialisation of a patrol or road block where identity papers would be needed. But our luck held. Silesia being under German authority had no strong reasons for imagining its population to be anything but pro-Nazi. Crossing the border into a not entirely subdued Poland proper could produce mixed blessings; the hand of friendship as well as the arm of repression. A thought tore at me. Would the border be guarded or merely submerged into the great stronghold of Occupied Europe?

A lone barn provided a third night's bed; this one rotting and stagnant and far from any human habitation. The straw was musty and smelt of manure but was dry, so dry in fact we utilised some as fuel for a fire, filling the place with smoke. Straw makes a poor heat source so we dined that evening on luke-warm potatoes as hard as unripe apples.

The ensuing days were ones of pain and grief. We had no idea where the border lay; if indeed there *was* a border, but firmly stuck to our course slowly, oh so slowly, reducing those kilometres to Chrzanow. Looking back from the pedestal of my older but fitter age, it occurs to me how ridiculous it was that we should have taken so long to cover so short a distance. It is equally hard to recollect the effects of our physical condition; how it caused bouts of nausea and vomitting whenever we ate something that disagreed with stomachs that had been ill-treated for a year. We didn't like the look of Jaworzno so tried to go round the sizeable town only to get lost in allotments and hostile suburbs. Twice we were chased out of gardens and on one occassion had to make a real run for it when Gordon, hunger getting the better of his judgement, lunged at a skinny chicken. Barns continued to provide shelter — the single plus-element of that excruciating walk — and in only one of these barns were we in danger of being caught. This was when a couple of men invaded our privacy to haul out a farm implement stored beneath the stack of hay on which we lay, not having even had time to bury ourselves in the stuff. Our further efforts to steal were lamentably futile. The shops in towns held so little that there was hardly a thing worth stealing and, so far as I can remember, our haul from shop-lifting amounted to no more than a couple of pears and a tin of spam that tasted like dog-meat and probably was. We did at last catch a chicken, the unfortunate bird's squawkings being drowned by a dog's barking. That evening we lit a fire amongst trees and toasted the limbs, one by one, on the flames but the smoke drew a couple of boys to the fireside. Their curiosity became too belligerent for our peace of mind so we finally had to stamp out the flames and move on, stuffing half-cooked drumsticks into our pockets.

We could see Chrzanow long before we reached it; the villages and townships becoming fewer and spread further apart. Cracow, we judged, would be at least another 30 miles — 45 kilometres — and Warsaw God-knows how many hundred eastwards after that. But we could think of nothing after Cracow. There we would be in real Poland and in a land where people universally hated Germans. Anything could happen once we were there.

All our minds could contemplate was the pain of walking another 30 miles. We evolved great longings for not only a decent meal, but a modicum of comfort; a soft bed, a hot bath, a warm fireside — all so unattainable, a forgotten condition that we once took for granted.

I think it was about this time that the 'train plan' was born. We had discussed the idea during the planning stages of the escape but had discarded it as too risky. But we had not delved so deeply into the concept of *freight* train travel; secreting ourselves away in a railway truck where no questions would be asked or papers demanded. However this form of transit was fraught with difficulties, complications and dangers too but, out here in the sticks getting nowhere and weaker all the time, the prospects appeared less daunting. Stowed warmly away in our bed of hay on the sixth night, we discussed the matter at length and agreed to have a go.

Chrzanow, we knew, was on a railway and the line was part of a network that served Cracow. What we'd have to look for was a stretch of track that fitted all the circumstances of the situation. The spot where we would have to lie in wait for a train going in the right direction would have to be suitably remote, the geography of the terrain raising a gradient and need for a curve of the line, both to slow the train and foil vigilance from those already aboard it. Freight trains, we were assured, carried armed guards at the rear and there was, of course, the engine crew at the front. It was imperative that these occupants were ignorant of what we were proposing to do in the middle.

It was raining steadily when we left the old barn. The last hunk of bread and a fill of rain-water deluging out of a broken down-pipe was an apology for breakfast; all we could raise now that our reserves of food — marmalade, raisins and cheese — had been exhausted. With no beating about the bush we took the road directly into Chrzanow, intent upon locating the railway station, maybe investigating its rail yards if it had any, and following the line out of town. Our stomachs rumbled audibly as we tramped the pot-holed tarmac but our spirits had risen with the prospect of new action and likely interesting developments. Intricately-designed lamp standards accompanied us into a maze of awakening streets.

Whether Chrzanow was classed as a border town or not we had no means of knowing but nevertheless we watched carefully for any sign of a checkpost. Given warning, we could steer away into a side road or stop to gaze into a shop window appraising the situation from the reflection in the glass as they do in the movies. Without it our unsynchronised reactions would be a giveaway. People, muffled against the cold mist that heralded winter, scuttled along pavements made uneven by subsidence. A policeman directed desultory traffic at an intersection and a horse-drawn wagon full of soldiers clattered over ill-laid cobbles.

Suddenly I caught sight of a man from the camp; a German sergeant we had christened 'Snotty Nose'. He was on the pavement coming towards us and it was too late to take evasive action. I whispered urgently to Gordon. We bent our heads, pulled our caps lower and tried to melt into a knot of women. The danger past, Gordon declared the man not to be 'Snotty Nose' but, if so, then he must have a double. Chrzanow straightaway became a place of ill-omen and sinister alert.

We located the station with no difficulty. It was quite a large one for the size of town and I knew why. Chrzanow was a rail junction where four lines met, only one of which linked with Cracow. We would have to be careful to follow the right set of tracks. The freight yards adjoined the station but the entrance was manned by a member of the Worker's Militia so we dropped the idea of snooping around for a train. Even had we been able to understand the despatch cards clipped to the wagonsides there remained a four-to-one chance of the chosen train taking the wrong route.

Following the railway out of town offered no great problems. The bifurcation of the lines must have occurred on the west side of the station, we surmised, having walked for some miles with the double track keeping firmly to a single route. Disinclined to walk the trackside path itself we kept the railway in view from the Cracow-bound road though this too had become too much of a main artery for comfort.

Both road and rail entered a spruce forest and, losing sight of the tracks, we moved through the trees to stand upon the line. With nobody in sight in either direction we felt bold enough to walk alongside the rails yet close enough to the trees to make a run for it if necessary. In this manner we made heartening progress, the only interruption being an oncoming two-coach passenger train which sent us helter-skelter for cover.

From a bank we watched it rattle by, noting its speed which was much too fast. Continuing, we located a curve in the line and rested here for two hours to await the passage of another train — a second but longer passenger train moving towards Cracow — but, again, it moved at too great a speed for the purpose we had in mind.

For most of the day we continued along the tracks resting up at likely points to gain information from passing trains — both passenger and freight — but only as the trees were thinning by late afternoon did we come upon a curve sharp enough to offer hope of providing the circumstances for which we were looking.

The rain had ceased but the undergrowth was wet and soggy with a steady litany of drips from sodden trees. We were in a clearing; the line of spruce and fir had moved back to leave the railway naked of cover. The spot was far from perfect but would have to do; hunger and exhaustion was making walking difficult again as well as affecting our judgement. We waited, crouched in a hollow.

A heavy goods train rumbled into view and we dashed for the trees again, aware that the dusk was not enough to conceal us in the open. An overworked locomotive engulfed in a sweat of steam headed a long line of heavy-duty wagons that rattled and jerked against each other as if the driver was applying his air-brakes. We could see the driver and his mate leaning out of the cab and we surmised that some obstruction ahead was causing a speed restriction. The speed of the train was just right now but the thing was going the wrong way damn it. I cursed our luck but then it came to me that the obstruction — if there was one — might work for trains coming from the opposite direction; those that had already been slowed but had not yet had time to get up speed. But why hadn't the earlier trains been affected? The problem was beyond me. We watched the brake van disappear into the distance but could discern no occupants.

Night descended rapidly but the darkness was not complete when the sound of a train from the other direction lured us from cover. A headlamp pushed a yellow antenna ahead of another large locomotive, its stack belching spark-injected brown smoke. We waited a few seconds to allow the engine to pass, then sprinted for the track, confident that the darkness would be intense enough to hide our running figures. Crouching close against the passing wagons, we watched for hand holds, not even sparing a glance at what the wagons contained. So close now, the rattle of the train had turned to a steady roar and the dark mass hung above, with iron wheels below, cruel and menacing.

I started running again, trying to watch for signal cables and for hand-holds at the same time. Behind me I heard Gordon pounding at my heels, swearing with the exertion. A lever caught my eye and I lunged at it, clutching the cold metal and holding on. It dragged me along the balast and I felt a terible fear that my legs might become enmeshed in those grinding wheels. Trying to swing them outwards into the air my other hand fastened upon another protrusion. My feet dropped again, the toes of my boots bumping along the line but with two hands firmly anchored I was able to draw myself upwards though the effort took every ounce of strength I could muster. A red mist curtained my eyes as I fought to raise my body to the side of the wagon, my right foot searching desperately for a toe-hold above the wheels. And then it was all over as, with a final struggle, I reached the couplings between two wagons.

Gordon was already atop the high sides and now worked his way round to join me. 'Thank Christ for that!' was his breathless comment. We turned our attention to the interior of the truck and were dismayed to find it empty; just a few coal-begrimed sacks on the floor surrounded by four cold, damp walls.

Attempting to stand upright we explored our new domain. There were enough sacks to cover us in the event of a cursory examination by railway staff but a load of pit-props would have provided a better hide. We shook out some of the damp bags and gingerly sat down to await events. The train rolled on making no effort to pick up speed.

It was pitch dark now; only the sparks from the locomotive made dancing illumination up ahead but we could see that the countryside was clear of trees. By climbing the walls of the truck we observed our progress but it told us nothing of where we were going. Chinks of light from houses occasionally slashed the night.

Hardly three miles had gone by when the train drew to a halt. No town showed but we covered ourselves in sacks in case of a search. Maybe some one had spotted us climbing aboard? We listened to the wheezing of the engine and the sound of a shouted exchange followed by a prolonged banshee whistle. Then the train moved again — *but in the opposite direction.*

I glanced at Gordon. He glanced at me. We flung the sacks aside in a gesture of exasperation, our white faces smeared with coal dust. The train rolled on, still quite slowly and we debated whether or not to bale out. But following the hassle of boarding, the inability to believe that our efforts may have been in vain, ensured we stayed put. Maybe they were shunting the trucks onto another line? Perhaps there was a junction this side of Chrzanow after all? By the time we had exhausted the unlikely possibilities our minds had been made up for us when the train picked up speed, blocking any attempt to leave.

A glow in the sky indicated a return to Chrzanow so we took cover once more but the train never slackened pace for an instant as we rattled across a complex of points and crossovers, roared through the station and out into the darkness again. The cold night air whipped our faces as we clung to the high walls of our prison. Which line had we taken? The question had arisen with Chrzanow passed for going at this pace we could be back in the Katowice industrial region, even Hindenburg itself within the hour. We might as well drop off at the gates of the camp and give ourselves up. At least we might get something to eat. Bleak despair engulfed us.

An hour passed and the train sped on but no urban lights or pit workings showed — and we were familiar enough with industrial night scenes offered by the region. Maybe we *had* taken another line? We blundered through one biggish town but though aglow with lights it was alone in the dark countryside. Then all was darkness again.

It must have been in the very early hours when we began to slow with a ponderous deliberation. Still there was no industry just as there were no stars or moon in the sky. The faint outline of houses drew nearer the tracks and we discovered that we were entering a centre of some description. We waited, clutching wet sacks, uncertain what action to take.

With a final hiss of steam we drew to a halt in a small siding. A few early morning workers were about their business; faint figures whistling in the darkness. Furtively we clambered out of the wagon and dropped to the ground. Ensuring nobody was near we ran to the fence that bordered the tracks.

A small road led away from the village and we took it. Strangers at large in villages at such a time could only be viewed with the highest suspicion. No barn offered us its roof so we lay down, shivering and apprehensive, on a bed formed of stalks and twigs in a patch of undergrowth. That we slept a few hours was a measure of our exhaustion.

It was the cold that awoke us. Dawn showed only as a bruise in the sky. Jumping about to restore a sluggish circulation we surveyed the methods available to us of retracing our steps for plainly we had allowed ourselves to be transported deeper into enemy territory. The very fact that a train had brought us this far raised the possibility that a train might be induced to take us back. And to make sure we knew where we were going on this occasion a *passenger* train offered a much more positive means of doing so. Walking was out of the question; we were fast starving to death, and jumping non-public transport vehicles was getting us only from the frying pan into the fire. We now had adequate funds and presumably the nearby village boasted a station. Neither of us liked the idea of loitering around such establishments — anathema to escaped prisoners — but we concluded a small one like this would be unlikely to raise all that number of nasties. Another method of escape discarded at the planning stage had, all of a sudden, become infinitely appealing.

As the new day dawned so we went to work sprucing ourselves up; scrubbing our coal-streaked faces and the more visible portions of our anatomies with the help of none-too-clean and very cold water from roadside puddles. We also did what we could to repair the ravages to our clothing. If we were going to travel in style we would have to look and act a little more like human beings, that was for sure. Over and over again we repeated to ourselves the German phrase we would have to use at the station ticket office: 'Eine fahrkarte erster klasse nach Krakau, bitte' — 'A first class ticket to Cracow, please' — and the reason we chose to travel first class was not only because we found 'erster' easier to say than the German equivalents to 'second' or 'third'. As first class ticket-holders we hoped to raise a little more respect from any minion to whom we might be subjected and, at the same time, have less nosy fellow travellers around with nothing to do but stare at our deficiencies. A weak sun was pushing through rain clouds when we deemed the station to be open for business.

The establishment was very much in existence a little way out of the village and we entered it in company with several other

176

members of the commuting public, timing it just right so that, while they lined up at the ticket office, we had time to steal a glance at a wall timetable. And joy of joys, there *was* a service to Cracow.

At the ticket window Gordon, clearing his throat, spoke the magic formula and received a hard look from a teutonic lady behind the grill with the little white card. Swiftly I added 'Ich auch' — 'I too' — and the deed was done. We even got change from the total sum of our monies tendered. On the platform a train indicator announced the next service as the *'Personenzug* to Strumien' though where Strumien was we had not the faintest idea. But the place was obviously the destination of everyone in the station except for us which would lead to the very loitering on its platform we had hoped to avoid. Their train duly arrived, scooped up the clients and left us alone with our misgivings. To hide our nervousness we stalked around the little station and so came upon the stall that sold frankfurter-type sausages and packets of biscuits. Before I could stop him, Gordon had purchased half the stock.

Rarely has food given such pleasure. The sausages may have been horse or dog meat, the biscuits cardboard but they filled a yearning gap. We sat and muched away, oblivious of any eyes that may have been fastened upon us in disbelief.

An hour and a half went by before the train we wanted came in, a two-coach affair, seemingly so popular on this line. Only half of one of the coaches was reserved for first class ticket holders and in one of the four empty compartments we settled ourselves, side by side, nearest the corridor and facing the engine.

The train creaked into motion, gathered speed and bounded joyfully along the single track that spiralled gently about a dead flat countryside that, by little stretch of the imagination, could have been Essex; small fields and woods and rural villages. Only the onion domes of the churches spoilt the illusion. Gordon began to laugh slightly hysterically and I felt strangely light-headed as well.

The door slid open and we stopped laughing. The ticket inspector stood in the opening staring at us questioningly. His 'Fahrkarte, bitte' was laced with sarcasm and impending wrath. Germans are more class-conscious than we British are and to be caught in a higher grade of compartment than a ticket shows constitutes a grave offence. The man was short and tubby but authoritative and he was plainly taken aback when we produced the appropriate tickets. He slammed the door and moved on, shaking his head.

There were a number of halts at tiny wayside stations mostly out of sight of the community they served. Few people joined the train and none invaded our portion of the coach. We stopped for a longer period at a larger, busier station. Its name was Oswiecim and, except that we remembered it was astride a road we hadn't taken a few days earlier, it held no significance. People — soldiers among them — joined the train in more numbers but, again, we were left in peace.

The ticket inspector padded down the corridor at intervals, glaring disapprovingly through the glass but taking no further action. We bowled on, rocking from side to side.

Another prolonged halt occurred at Chrzanow, back on the main line, and here our luck faded. Two officers — a naval lieutenant and a *Wehremacht* captain — entered, stowed their briefcases on the rack and sat down on the opposite seat. We feined sleep for all we were worth.

I felt the newcomers' eyes resting upon us, sizing us up and taking in our unsuitable and none-too-clean apparel. It was a hard penetrating gaze, loaded with query and, though I shifted my position thus proclaiming a doze rather than deep slumber, I felt myself weakening. Just for a second I opened my eyes and was caught. The smiling captain obviously wanted to talk.

He nodded in a friendly fashion and, in German, enquired politely of our nationality. We were ready for this one so I mumbled 'Ungarish', a nationality we had agreed to 'borrow' for such an occasion, its choice governed by the unlikelihood of anyone speaking or understanding Hungarian. Gordon entered the exchange and I hoped, in his enthusiasm, he wasn't going to air his Gaelic. The two officers were handsome young fellows putting me in mind of fresh-faced American university students. Young they may have been but their medal ribbons indicated considerable experience of action, some on the Russian front.

'Ah, I have never been to Budapest, more's the pity. A lovely city I understand', observed the captain and I felt obliged to offer a morsel or two of information about the place. At that time of my life I had never been to the Hungarian capital but the chap seemed well content with my description of Bristol. Gordon joined in, his

178

yardstick being Glasgow. Our German was atrocious and words of English kept intruding.

The navy entered the conversation. 'What do you do?' I heard the word 'arbeit' so caught on. 'We work in a hospital', I said quickly before Gordon could come up with something sardonic like 'trapeze artist'. 'In Krakau?'. I nodded, hoping he wasn't going to ask *which* hospital. We'd only hit upon that occupation because it was comfortably vague, smelt of useful war work and 'krankenhaus' and 'lazaret' — 'hospital' — were words we both knew. I tried explaining that we had been working on a farm in the country over the weekend but got bogged down with lack of the right words and also because I couldn't remember whether or not it *had* been a weekend.

Gordon fortuitously interrupted. 'Fahren sie nach Krakau?'. The two men nodded and mentioned some barracks or office or other of which we'd never heard but pretended we had.

Our pretence of sleep had ensured we'd missed the spot on the line we had made our ill-fated boarding of the freight train but judged the city to be close. At all costs we'd have to leave the train before the station which would be a big one — a *hauptbahnhof* — lousy with police, Gestapo, military police and other horrors. I stared out of the window attempting to pick out tell-tale signs of an imminent urban conurbation but the flat terrain remained obstinately rural.

The captain rose to his feet, took down his brief case and sat down again. The lieutenant smirked as if he knew what his companion was about to do. The captain opened the case with a snapping of catches and held up a bunch of black grapes in the manner of a conjurer producing a rabbit from a top hat. Obviously grapes were a rarity in wartime Greater Germany and they certainly were for us. Breaking the bunch into four he distributed the fruit to everyone.

'Vielen Danke', gushed Gordon and I with unfettered enthusiasm, wondering what the two would think if they knew they were giving comfort to the enemy. Gordon began wolfing his portion down, stalks, pips and all so I kicked him gently, trying to indicate that he should eat in a manner befitting a first-class ticket holder.

'Funf minuten nach Krakau', vouchsafed the lieutenant thereby supplying the answer to what we wanted to know. Outside, the countryside began to sprout a rash of houses.

179

I mumbled something about being late for an appointment and therefore in a hurry, rose from my seat and, with Gordon, slid open the door. 'Vielen danke und auf wiedersehen', we enthused, flashing our erstwhile companions our brightest smiles. We moved to the exit at the head of the coach, hoping nobody else would be in a hurry to leave.

The corridor was still empty giving us a clear and unobserved run to make an unorthodox departure which we proposed to effect as soon as the speed of the train permitted it. We retained a wary eye for the approach of the ticket inspector but that individual was nowhere to be seen.

The brakes came on with a squeal and we felt the slowing motion of the train. I lent out of the window and unfastened the door. Our eyes now were only for a convenient landing pad. At any moment passengers would commence issuing from their compartments.

I climbed down onto the outside step, hanging onto the hand rail and trying to hold the door from swinging too far open. Gordon was right behind me. I saw a heap of clinker and coal ash — the spot where locomotives had their boilers raked out — coming up. 'Here we go!' I whispered.

I landed with a crunch on the heap, Gordon virtually on top of me and, together, we rolled away from the moving train. Hardly had we risen to our feet when a voice shouted at us, more in a tone of enquiry than anger. Ignoring it we moved off fast in the opposite direction to dodge behind a line of trucks and from its cover took stock of our surroundings.

It appeared we had landed ourselves in the middle of a military freight depot with soldiers loading flat trucks with lorries and crated machinery. The voice had come from a squad of men at work a short distance away who were taking no further notice. There seemed to be only one entrance to the depot and it was swarming with soldiers. A high timber wall made of old railway sleepers enclosed the yard, the scaling of which, while not impossible, would be in full view not only of the soldiers but from anyone at the windows of the houses overlooking it. We made our way to a derelict wagon quite close to the wall, its roof half caved-in; a perfect refuge in which to lay up until nightfall or departure of the working parties; whichever came first.

We waited all day. More troops arrived; cheerful fellows in

180

overalls, and a convoy of further lorries. A group of youngsters took time off for a smoke very close to our hideaway, forcing us to remain very quiet indeed. With nightfall, powerful arc lamps were switched on and the work continued under artificial light. Cramped, cold, hungry and bored we saw visions of being confined for days on end.

It must have been after midnight when work finally ceased. The troops marched off, the gate slammed shut and the arc lamps were switched off leaving a softer illumination from lattice steel standards. An unfamiliar silence crept over the yard; only the low reverberation of the city confounded it.

Stiffly we moved to the wall, helped each other over it and jumped down the other side onto a road. Not a car, not a soul was to be seen and the windows of the houses were no more than blind eyes on the street. Even for so late an hour the emptiness was uncanny.

Proceeding cautiously along the pavement, trying to lessen the thump of our hob-nailed boots, we made our way towards the city centre not quite certain as to what we were going to do. A delicious smell of baking assailed our nostrils, deflecting us into a dark alley.

In it we could just make out a bakery and the smell issued from a vent above the locked door. I played with the idea of knocking, revealing our identities and asking outright for food for we were now in true Poland. But Gordon had other ideas.

Some of yesterday's bread was displayed behind a glass frame that formed an adjustable window. Picking up a metal hinge lying on the ground, Gordon went to work in an attempt to prize it open. In this endeavour he was only too successful, the whole frame falling outwards with a tremendous crash of breaking glass. We each grabbed a loaf, turned back into the street and ran.

It was just our luck that a military foot patrol should choose that moment to materialise from around the corner. Even had the four steel-helmeted soldiers not heard the crash, the sight of two ruffians, loaves of bread in their hands sprinting for dear life along the middle of the road, told its own story. We were ordered in no uncertain manner to 'Halt oder wir schiessen!'. Swiftly we came to heel to stare into the barrels of three rifles and a Schmeiser.

Neither our combined deviousness or recently-acquired cunning could be enough to extract us from this one. There was little point in trying for we could fight no more. Resignedly we raised our arms.

The soldiers, upon learning what we were, became exceedingly friendly. 'You were lucky', they told us, 'we have strict orders to shoot on sight anyone who breaks the curfew.' The *curfew*. We'd clean overlooked it.

An indignant baker appeared on the scene, having discovered the damage to his property. A big florid Pole wearing a white flour-dusted apron he took in the situation at a glance and invited all six of us back to his bakery.

And there we were plied with all the fresh bread we could cram into our stomachs and what it did to our respective digestive systems I dread to think. Even the soldiers encouraged us and we were to learn the reason.

The sergeant, looking ashamed, proceeded to inform us that he had orders to hand curfew-breakers over to the Gestapo and there was absolutely nothing he could do to alter the situation. He spoke a little English and was so sincere with his apologies I felt almost sorry for the man.

Our pockets stuffed with steaming bread we were marched away to finally reach the centre of Poland's third city. Thus we gained our initial objective — if not in quite the manner we had hoped. As we tramped the cobbled streets of the lovely old town I ruefully appraised the sum of our accomplishments. It had taken ten days and more than 150 miles to cover 50 miles towards liberation; no cause for much pride there. And the fact we had been at large for all that time with no papers or evasion aids was no more than the luck of the devil. But not all was negative. Hadn't we successfully avoided ten days of slave labour down our hated coalmine? That alone had been worth the trouble.

It was still night when we were escorted through a side door of a large imposing structure near the main square. A black-uniformed Gestapo clerk glared at us with no smile, signed a receipt and dismissed our escort. The soldiers scurried down the steps without a word as if all the hounds of hell were at their heels.

I would have given a lot to have followed them. For Gordon and me the fun was over. Now came the account.

The remainder of my wartime experiences are outside the confines of this book but I feel duty-bound to tidy up the loose ends.

Systematically beaten and burnt (by cigarette ends) as the result of Gestapo interrogatory methods over many days we were finally sent to Stalag VIIIB at Teschen on the Czech-Polish border to which camp we resolutely insisted we had escaped from. And it says little for teutonic efficiency when I disclose that it took the Germans three weeks to discover our *real* camp and return us to Hindenburg. Christmas in solitary confinement on bread and water was no great hardship and early in 1945 came the general evacuation of all camps east of the Oder that lay in the path of the Russian advance. Those months on this 'death march' were the most terrible of my life as millions of people — captives and captors — floundered westwards during a Polish winter of unparalleled harshness. But I managed to survive this greatest enforced migration in history spewing its tide of human misery across the Silesian plains and on into Czechoslovakia and Saxony. Stumbling over snow-bound roads thick with frozen corpses I was to witness scenes that have never erased from my mind as I lived through a vacuum of despair and hideous cruelty.

In Czechoslovakia I escaped again, was sheltered and fed by Czech patriots and then betrayed by a village Judas. Later, in Bavaria, I escaped a third time, this time successfully to reach the American lines to finish the war as a half-track gunner in their Third Army.

8

Taming the Tana

EXPEDITIONARY TRAVEL IN
EAST AFRICA

Perhaps the ultimate in adventure travel is to be experienced through participation in an expedition, with Black Africa, surely, as the continent offering the most exciting territory. There are, of course, many commercial companies offering such expeditions to anyone wanting them; indeed some of the journeys described in this book are of that type. But the purest form of expeditioning is that where there is an *aim*, both in the realm of exploration and research, the results of which benefit mankind in general and the peoples through whose territory the expedition passes in particular.

My participation in the Polytechnic of Central London-sponsored Tana River Expedition of 1976 was a watershed in my life. In the following account I have concentrated upon the more adventurous occurrences of that project rather than the all-important research tasks that were the reason for it.

The basic aim in this case was simply to put a 25-man Anglo-Kenyan expedition consisting of scientists and their support teams into the field for the purpose of carrying out a three-month ecological and medical survey of the middle and lower reaches of the Tana river with the concurrent adventure phases of the expedition consisting of climbing Mount Kenya, finding the source of the river and navigating its upper white water sections. For the ecological and medical tasks involved we had the full backing of the Kenyan government whose plans to construct a series of dams on the Tana were well advanced. The end result of this construction was to provide large-scale irrigation benefits for the peoples living in the regions through which the river flowed but since the artery was a suspected faunal barrier between people and animals more information about the habits of the river's denizens and of those who depended upon its waters was needed by the Tana River Development Board, the Fisheries Department, the Health Authorities and other interested bodies. Additionally, the museums of Nairobi and London were anxious to obtain rare specimens of flora and fauna which such investigations might discover.

Such lofty considerations made an ample springboard for an adventure off which we were not slow to throw ourselves with enthusiasm.

There is an almost legendary affinity between the British and the great deserts and jungles of Africa. 'Doctor Livingstone, I presume' are words that epitomise the British love of inflicting discomfort upon themselves in the interests of exploration, of discovery, experience and conquest. The inhabitants of these regions suffer simply because they happen to live there. But Peter Fleming spoke for the majority when he said that the trouble about such journeys nowadays is that they are easy to make but difficult to justify. Only a few places remain untrampled and they are those that are inaccessible on wheels.

With the spread of the package tour and development of ever-faster, ever-larger aircraft the days of the explorer are numbered so the cynics tell us. And with most of the challenges of geography overcome by intrepid pioneers there is a certain amount of frustration creeping into the deliberations of the would-be explorer as he glowers perplexedly at the globe now singularly devoid of all that red which Doctor Livingstone and his kith went to such pains to daub. Thus it is becoming a case, not so much of being first up or over a feature of this earth but of ways to negotiate it in an original manner.

But though the fields of conquest may have diminished, the same need not be said about those of investigation. Here the choice widens dramatically. Though there are many regions of the world that have been traversed by intrepid pioneers few of them have halted long enough to scratch beneath the surface.

So when I was invited to join the Tana River Expedition I saw myself as the new member of a band of investigators rather than explorers. My emotions were more of profound interest than surging excitement for simple conquest will ever remain the headier potion. It was brought home to me by my contemporaries that middle age not only hardens the arteries but also one's ways, ideas and outlook. I was unable to do anything about the arteries but I thought I could shake up the other items. Suddenly Black Africa became a desirable place to go.

But where and what was this Tana? The first book I looked up told me it was a lake in Ethiopia. Then I discovered it to be a river in Kenya; in fact the *longest* river in Kenya. A wild, inhospitable, disease-ridden river which cheered me up no end. Then someone I met in my local who had lived some years in Nairobi said 'Oh yes, he knew the Tana — he'd crossed it once on a ferry', and my dreams of discovering a 'lost river' vanished. I dug deeper and learnt that the Tana was six hundred, eight hundred, one thousand miles long but definitely one thousand if every bend was taken into account. And we, paddling down the river in boats, would most emphatically be taking every bend into account. I was also given to understand that sections of its lower route had been traversed by canoe and that eighty years before, the paddle-driven *SS Kenia* reached Kora in the first and last attempt to navigate a vessel upstream. Appropriately Kora was to become the site of the expedition's first base camp but its fame has to do with none of these events. As everyone in Kenya knows, George Adamson lives below the large rock projection on the flat scrubland with his legendary lions — those that were portrayed in the books and films *Born Free* and *Living Free.*

In the realms of science and economics the Tana can produce more down-to-earth promises than the more glamorous efforts of single-minded canoeists and rehabilitated lions. A hundred years ago the two Denhard brothers undertook the first scientific expedition on the river. In 1892 an expedition under Captain Dundas assessed the possibility of it being the main artery of inland communication, with Kipini the future port of Kenya. An interesting speculation this for it was a railway that lost Mombasa a capitalship and it could have been a river that neutralised its port. Half-hearted exploration continued sporadically for many years but the very inhospitability of the climate, vegetation, insects and wild game damped enthusiasm.

However, the Tana, winding through the barren Northern Frontier District and attended by its riverine forest, was not to be ignored in spite of the miserable welcome afforded the pioneers. Like a spoilt child it cried out for attention and its potential as a hydro-electric power and irrigation source was noted. Today the river is part of a vital and large-scale redevelopment programme. Dams have already been built on the upper reaches and others are raising their concrete heads while irrigation schemes are underway at various places along the lower Tana. But with progress comes destruction for, as is so often the case, the two walk hand in hand.

Progress cannot, nor wants to be halted particularly in a parched and desolate land. The Tana River Development Authority was resourceful enough to concern itself with making sure that human, water, animal, land and other resources should be utilised to the best possible advantage. Yet there had been very little accumulation of ecological data on account of the very inhospitability that deflected proposed development in the late nineteenth century. So here, on an unsympathetic river, as has been made clear earlier, were rewarding tasks to be performed that, if it does not sound too grandiose, could benefit mankind. An adventurous river too that sprouts in a 17,000-foot mountain, frolics youthfully amidst untamed rapids and courses maturely through animal-infested territory remote from civilisation.

Thus the challenge, the lynchpin of any expedition.

Preparation for a three-month scientific expedition is no overnight accomplishment. The volume of work involved in putting some two dozen adventurers and scientists into a foreign field has to be seen to be believed. The leader was Nigel de Northop Winser, then a 24-year-old student at the Polytechnic of Central London (the main sponsor), and for his years a man with considerable expeditionary experience tucked beneath his belt. Bearded, hairy, afflicted with a slight limp his formidable appearance contradicted a charm and gentle force of character emerging from a heart and not just simple expediency. The limp was a legacy of polio which severely restricted his prowess on the playing field and, to a boy, such matters assume gargantuan importance. A resident of the country for eleven years his eyes were fastened upon Kenya from the very start. The remote Tana, he noted, could offer both adventure and worthwhile investigation and he began to pick his team for this, his most ambitious exploratory undertaking, early in 1974.

There are, as yet, no Trade Union restrictions for explorers, so although each new member of the team was chosen for his or her specialist knowledge and ability in a particular realm, each was also expected to 'muck in' with the carrying out of tasks outside it. As the designated 'Chronicler of the Expedition' I suppose I was flattered that somebody thought I could write but in addition to the supplying of pre-departure features to the news media I found myself deeply enmeshed in the world of sponsorship, publicity and public relations. Also joining the team were mammalogists, ornithologists, entomologists, zoologists and an immunologist each with his or her individual topic to investigate. And though the oldest of these scientists was under thirty and therefore hardly of the absent-minded professor school there had to be a back-up organisation and adventure squad to provide a logistic tale and a touch of glamour. Which is how the British Army came into the scheme of things. And with Kenya a Commonwealth country the British Army and Royal Air Force were able to maintain a modest training 'presence' there thus presenting us with the chance of obtaining transport, basic rations and considerable amounts of non-scientific equipment in exchange for the hardly debital cost of accepting a number of military personnel as members of the expedition.

At the outset the expedition group were to be divided into three main teams: the Mountain Team, the White Water Team and the Scientific Team, each with their supporting elements. In several cases, so far as the Mountain and White Water Teams were concerned, some members were in both which meant that events and coverage of the river had to be carried out in chronological order. But the idea of negotiating the Tana from source to mouth remained, in everyone's mind, a feat to be accomplished. While the Scientific Team based at Kora, a halfway point along the river, carried out its initial investigatory tasks the adventure squad of the Mountain Team were to make their way to 17,085-foot Mount Kenya in the heart of the country there to trace the source of the Tana and, while so doing, ascend the highest peak if for no other reason than it being there. The tracing of the Tana's source, on the other hand, offered a suitable if inconsequential introduction to a three-month association with the river that was to continue with a subsequent negotiation of its rapids above Kora.

Not unnaturally it was the army that predominated in the adventure side of the project and the two non-scientific teams were headed by experts in their specific fields. Captain Harley Nott, Royal Engineers, 28-year old son of a brigadier, had amassed considerable climbing experience on various military-supported expeditions so qualified for leadership of the Mountain Team. To Captain Paul Turner, 26, of the Queen's Own Hussars, went command of the White Water Team, his membership of the famous 1974 Zaire River Expedition under Colonel John Blashford Snell making him an obvious choice. The Scientific Team came under the direct supervision of Nigel.

As chronicler of the expedition I had acquired the privilege of being able to participate in all its varied activities. Thus not only was I to be afforded the opportunity of participating in the Mount Kenya ascent as well as the subsequent white water negotiation of the Tana but also of seeing something of what the scientists were up to at Kora. I was thus in the unique position of being an observer to the expedition's multiple aims and achievements prior to the intended link-up of its members for the voyage down the Middle and Lower Tana and the research projects along its banks. For this multiple undertaking I prepared myself as best I could.

Thus the year drew past its halfway mark and two dozen investigators stood poised to go. Some were old hands at the expedition business; others, like myself, were not. An assorted bunch indeed to descend upon an obscure East African river.

By joining the Mountain Team I had, so far as the initial period of the expedition was concerned, forfeited my chance to go places untrodden by tourist feet. Mount Kenya, beyond all doubt, is 'wild and exciting' but it is also a national park. However, one saving grace was that we would be on the mountain out of season and so would avoid the majority of the trekking tourists who manage to reach the lower altitudes.

Tourist. The word had developed a hollow ring since I had joined the expedition. It was pure conceit of course. On my more gruelling treks about the world I am a 'traveller'. Now, surely, I had attained the purest form of transit by accepting the accolade of 'explorer'. But I was reminded of a quote from Gerald Durrel. 'Expeditions', he says, 'are for commerce, curiosity and fun and in that order.' Put like that it brings exploration almost into the nine-to-five syndrome. In this instance commerce had, for us, little part to play in the expedition. Curiosity and fun most certainly. And satisfying a curiosity surely *is* fun.

My companions of the team made an interesting study. I was to know them all a lot better later but only in a minor capacity did I have to revise my opinions. Harley Nott, tall, fluent, very much the ladies' man was a born leader. Though considerably older I stood slightly in awe of him. He had married a very pretty girl hardly a week before we had left Nairobi. In some ways Robert Williamson bore similar characteristics. The same age and rank, equally fluent, equally handsome, he was also intelligent and a fine organiser. Yet he could take a back seat without loss of grace. He was doing so now, in fact, as deputy leader of the expedition and a senior captain to Harley because he was aware that his climbing experience was less. But nobody is perfect and Robert could make himself utterly objectionable at times with and without reason. The third member of the team was Doctor John Richardson. If anyone could be described as a link between the military and the 'mere civilians' it was John for, as a member of the Territorial Army with the rank of major, he *was* midway between the two. Together with his wife, Suzie, he had been on the British Trans-Americas Expedition while his education and abilities had left him with twenty-two letters after his name to which he was in the progress of adding another four.

I was to be thrown together with John Richardson more than with anyone else during the course of the expedition. Another efficient organiser he was a calming and knowledgeable influence while his beaming face atop the inevitable pipe was as much comfort to some as the fact that he was a doctor. Both he and I had the task of supporting the trio of climbers in their endeavours.

The third climber was Richard Matthews. Nothing at all military about Richard and, at 23, he was the youngest member of the team. While he had limited climbing experience and had been on a previous expedition he must have felt at a disadvantage against his older military co-climbers but, if so, he never showed it. His expedition tasks were numerous and included photography, public relations, climbing and captaincy of the second boat in the White Water Team. He coped valiantly with them all which speaks volumes for his spirit.

It is almost impossible to do justice to the serene splendour of

THE TANA RIVER EXPEDITION

the mountain that was to become our constant companion for all of two weeks. It is set where no mountain has a right to be and the twin peaks of Bation and Nelion shine white above the glistening glaciers. A belt of ever-drifting snow, like weft on a loom of mist, spread downward to the region of giant groundsel and lobelias and, lower still, to forests of strange gnarled trees, the home of elephant and leopard. To add delight to this ethereal sight the sun shone warmly offering an impression of an enormous plateau; a soaring land of milk and honey. And to the Kikuyu peoples, of course, it was more for was not Mount Kenya a sacred treasure, more precious than all the gold in Christendom?

191

Most of the highest peaks, including the eroded plugs of Batian (17,058 feet) and Nelion (17,022 feet), are hard rock cores exposed by the erosion of the volcanic crater. At the mountain's prime, perhaps a million years ago, the peaks stood at nearer 19,000 feet but erosion, mainly glacial, has reduced both its height and volume very considerably. The existing twelve glaciers are all that remain of an extensive ice sheet which once covered much of the area above 10,000 feet. This ice sheet began to decrease about 15,000 years ago, a process that continued until only 150 years ago when the glaciers could have been smaller than they are even today. But the renewed advance of the ice occurred over fifty years to be succeeded by a further general retreat which is continuing to the present day.

Our approach to the mountain was by way of the Naro Moru route via a road that turned into a track at the entrance to the Mount Kenya National Park. The track wound through the girth of forest the mountain wears like a kilt with a tartan composed of European Elder bearing large flat clusters of white-pink flowers that turn to purple fruits together with tall cedars and yellow wood 'podos', many with massive twisted trunks. Palm and bamboo form distinct crescents at certain altitudes with sporans of dense Alchemilla and curious 'old man's beard' hanging phantom-like from outstretched limbs. Within this fertile jungle are buffalo, black rhinoceros, leopard, antelope and elephant. We watched for a fleeting glimpse of movement within the skein of trees that was, for some of us, our first contact with wild forest.

As we rose from the warm savannah country and the plains below spread away into the haze of distance the temperature fell and belts of cloud, dark and angry, spat raindrops at us. The track had turned to mud and the Landrover slid from side to side with Harley fighting with the wheel. We crossed Percival's Bridge then climbed more steeply to a bog at 9,000 feet that defied further ascent the easy way. Parking the vehicle with its bonnet pushed into a bamboo thicket, we struggled into our rucksacks and tottered up the last 500 feet from 'swamp corner' to the meteorological station at a nice round 10,000 feet.

Seven porters were awaiting us. They were smiling fellows, garrulous and swarthed in old British Army greatcoats. Harley called an 'Orders Group', gave out his instructions for the morning and we called it a day.

192

Leaving shortly after dawn we made reasonable progress, under lightened loads, along a steep and winding track. Out of the forest a region of open parkland, studded with small trees bearing leaf rosettes at the tip of their branches, led to a further floral zone, clearly defined and entirely distinctive. It was also where the bog proper started. This lay in open country, the texture of the marshy ground being governed by rainfall. Weeks of the stuff ensured us a treat. The 'Vertical Bog', as the area is known, had become an inclined sea of clinging, spongey mud producing the toughest and most exhausting climbing.

Gradually we squelched our way to the false summit of a crest with the fitness of the army telling its own story. Harley and Robert were nearly a mile ahead at the trig point with an altitude-stricken Richard, escorted by John, far behind. We rested at the marker but cold and a lowering cloud drove us on. An expanse of tussock grass marked the beginning of the alpine zone and an oblique descent from 13,000 feet into the Teleki valley brought us to the Naro Moru river, boulder-strewn and icy cold, which some of us failed to vault.

The Teleki refuge hut provided excuse for a prolonged rest and inside we found a half-frozen young man who had reached his limit. Half indignant, half encouraged by his amazement that anyone so ancient as I had got so far, I pushed on before my aching limbs could stiffen though it was shortage of breath that imposed the greatest burden. In this manner we all staggered into Mackinders Camp, three lines of two-men permanently-erected bivouacs plus a couple of mess tents.

We dined, hardly royally, on stew and hard-tack biscuits, courtesy of the British Army, and I perceived the fare had not changed one iota since my own military days. The night was cold with flurries of snow as we lay listening to the curious high-pitched chattering of the hyrax, a small guinea-pig like creature whose closest relative is, unbelievably, the elephant. They had been scrounging food from us the moment we set up camp, taking tit-bits from our hands and refusing to be frightened away. But it was the altitude of 13,700 feet and its effect that reduced my sleep to a minimum.

The trio of the highest summits of the mountain drenched in dawn sunshine made a sight worthy of the effort to reach Mackinder's, the orange hues striking diamonds out of the frozen snow. Bation and Nelion looked, to me, the more dramatic in the knowledge that they were the private domain of experienced climbers only; not for the likes of stumbling amateurs such as myself. Gazing at them in awe I was reminded of the Kikuyu legend whereby their God Mogai, maker and distributor of the universe, created Kere-Nyaga — 'Mountain of Brightness' — as a sign of his miracles and as a resting place for himself. Mogai took the man Kikuyu, founder of the race, onto the top of the mountain and showed him the beautiful land he had created for him. Before dismissing him, he told Kikuyu that whenever he needed help, he must hold up his hand towards the mountain and he, Mogai, would come to his aid. Surreptitiously I raised my own hand half expecting something to happen, but a cloud abruptly masked the summit and the magic was gone.

To reach Lake Höhnel meant a stiff climb up and over the southern wall of the Teleki valley. At the top the wall was crowned by age-worn pinnacles of the strangest shapes. The highest was Point Joseph.

Below, at 13,500 feet was the emerald green tarn, its polished surface calm and unruffled. And, beyond, all Africa lay at our feet.

We descended to the water's edge and took a considerable number of photographs, particularly of small streams emerging into the tarn from the bowels of the mountain, one of which we knew to be the source of the Tana although it was impossible to discern exactly which one.

Atop Point Joseph again we paused to gaze for the last time at the lonely tarn. Harley was thoughtful. 'You know, there were buffalo droppings on the shore', he remarked. The others too had noticed them. Thirteen thousand feet is high for buffalo but not for the elephant who, moving with extreme delicacy, is a fine climber. Hannibal knew what he was doing when he chose elephants with which to cross the Alps.

Back at Mackinders Camp the afternoon sun was warm enough for basking and for drying wet boots but the moment it dropped behind the hill the cold gripped us. Such were our appetites there was good-natured squabbling over who deserved the more popular but limited tinned steak and kidney puddings for supper. The spaghetti, too, produced problems, its length and springiness not being an ultra-suitable raw material with which to stuff a pressure cooker.

Yet another early morning start saw us on the way to Top Hut, at 15,720 feet, and a steep uphill grind that had me gasping for air every dozen steps. It was our prelude to the conquest of Lenana, at 16,300 feet, the third highest peak. Top Hut was composed of three compartments, each sparsely furnished with a few bunks and a lot of debris. We made ourselves as comfortable as possible but, with no water, had to collect fragments of ice hacked from the nearby Lewis Glacier. Ensconsed in the other compartments were a party of Germans and a party of Japanese; all the ingredients necessary, vouchsafed Robert, to recommence the Second World War. In the event everything was extremely amiable, even sociable, for, while we were busy 'cooking' our ice cubes we received a visit, first from the Swiss Ambassador and his wife, and then the renowned American climber, Phil Snyder, and his girl friend Caroline. Our climbers crowded around Phil Snyder leaving me to talk with Caroline. She was shivering with cold, inadequately shod and looking rather miserable. I gave her half a bar of army-issue chocolate, and a handful of Spangles which cheered her up a little. She said she was also American and lived in both New York and in Massachusetts. She knew Brighton and neighbouring Glyndbourne — she often came with her mother — and thought the British were as quaint as their Spangles. We chatted desultorily until the party broke up with the dusk, and when our beloved pressure cooker, in an excess of enthusiasm, blew jets of boiling soup around the room. Only later did I discover that Caroline was the daughter of the late President Kennedy.

The night was nothing if not chaotic. Hardly had we fallen asleep after an interlude in which everyone was assailed by altitude sickness, when Harley's alarm clock shrilled and we all had to struggle stiffly back out of our cocoons. It wasn't until we were all dressed and ready to go that we discovered that the clock had gone off two hours early. It was still barely light when we set out for Lenana.

With steps in the hard snow made by previous climbers the ascent was not difficult. I suffer very slightly from vertigo so kept my eyes straight ahead for most of the time. One missed step and I would be sliding helplessly down the slope towards the crevasses in the Lewis Glacier and the idea of my refrigerated corpse emerging down the mountain in the twenty-second century did not appeal. Poor John suffered far worse but pluckily stuck it out to the rocky crags of the summit.

The cold was bitter at the top; the view the stuff of poetry. That we had to fumble about taking pictures of a sponsor's bottle of hooch bordered upon blasphemy though we looked forward to drinking its contents later.

We made a roped descent; a more perilous business than uphill progress but the bottle came down most of the way on its own. The rope, suddenly tautening, ejected it from my anorak pocket and we had to watch in anguish as it rolled to the edge of the glacier to lodge in an indent of snow. Its rescue was the most difficult feat of the entire day's work.

The base from which the military climb of Bation and Nelion was to be attempted was Two Tarn Hut and it was to become our home for more than a week. Standing at an altitude of 14,750 feet it is no Hilton. A corrugated iron shack something on the lines of a World War Two Anderson air raid shelter it leaked, had tattered plastic sheeting in lieu of window panes and was infested by a particularly fearless brand of small rat. But there was water. One of the two tarns lay beside the hut, its icy water, grey and lifeless, providing a minimum of attraction.

Already the hut held two occupants whereupon arose the problem of accommodating seven bodies into a space designed for five. A raised shelf represented the sleeping quarters; some four tattered foam rubber pads the beds (the fifth had ceased to exist). Everything was dirty and muck-strewn so we made our first task that of a major spring-clean.

The two additional bodies belonged to Alistair, an English dentist, and Ram, a bearded American. They settled in with us amicably and donated some fresh tomatoes and vegetables as well as bread which added a touch of luxury to our tinned creations. Both our new companions were working the wanderlust out of their systems and had been on the road in many countries for months. What they thought of our semi-military group I was to learn from Ram's personal diary an entry of which started thus: 'Coming up Mount K, freelance as usual, meet an ultra-organised Brit army group eating weird nosh that comes out of small cans'.

If the night was cold we never felt it. Not only did we wear everything except our boots but, compressed together, the heat generated was considerable. And it was as well we had our boots to hand since they made useful missiles against the rats that were soon scurrying towards us across the floor seeking food.

In spite of steadily deteriorating weather conditions Harley was determined to accomplish the ultimate climb and straight-away instigated a series of practice ascents. These went on for several days culminating in the attempted scaling of the huge, unfriendly-looking pyramid of rock that loomed above us from across the tarn. Some 16,100 feet high, Point Piggott is fourth in the Mount Kenya hierarchy and a very different kettle of fish to Lenana.

Accordingly we rose early the morning of the climb, everyone bustling about in preparation for getting two pairs of climbers onto Piggott. Because of Harley's insistance upon ropework in pairs an even number of climbers were to undertake the deed. These were to be himself and Robert, and since Richard was deemed too inexperienced, Alistair and Ram whose disapproval of our lifestyle was not strong enough to prevent them sharing Piggott with us.

The morning was fine and clear. As the four climbers, muffled, goggled and swathed in ropes, ice-axes and crampons, strode off round the tarn I felt not the slightest envy. Instead I felt singularly depressed. For John, Richard and I the waiting had to continue. This was far from the Africa I had dreamt about for so long.

Throughout the morning we were able to catch glimpses of the quartet as they made slow progress up the granite walls of Piggott. The sunshine failed to last; we hardly expected it to. A pattern of weather had emerged with the best of it invariably at the beginning of the day. John read and re-read his medical journals, of which he had brought an endless supply, and Richard polished and repolished his camera lenses; activities occasionally interrupted by dismembered voices from a mist-enshrouded distance. A couple of rats were put to flight and innumerable pots of tea or coffee made on our temperamental petrol cooker, the lighting of which had become an exercise in Russian roulette.

At midday we were joined by the Top Hut trio of Japanese. The social whirl on Mount Kenya revolves in a somewhat repetitive cycle and we began to wonder how the amenities of Two Tarn Hut could be stretched to embrace the Germans as well,

197

having resigned ourselves to the prospect of a further three occupants in the communal bed. Our Japanese friends straight-away went to work on the mass production of some special chapatis, full of herbs and tantalising smells, the operation ending with a bowing session as they sat cross-legged on the floor and invited us to join their orgy. Two Tarn Hut had become a Mount Kenya equivalent of the Teahouse of the August Moon.

But there was nothing either Japanese or African about what was happening outside. A thin fall of snow had turned into a full-scale blizzard with low cloud obscuring not only Piggott but even the far shore of the tarn. And as dusk brought an ugly dark-ness to the sombre scene what began as a nagging worry devel-oped into a crisis.

We held a council of war to decide upon the actions we would take in an emergency already upon us. None of us had read the mountaineers' book of rules or that relating to mountain rescue but we assumed that a policy of 'staying put' was the only one that could apply. For a climber, torchless, up a mountain to attempt descent in darkness would be folly. And what could the most sophisticated rescue service do at night even if it were able to be contacted? I offered to descend to Mackinders Rangers Station at first light next day while John and Richard, with emer-gency medical supplies, would try to reach the trapped climbers. In the meantime we decided to go out and attempt to make some sort of contact.

Togged up in every item of clothing we could lay our hands on, the three of us approached as near as we could to the base of Piggott. The Japanese group, though understanding little English, realised what the problem was and had joined us. And there, by the side of that evil little lake, we waved torches and attempted to make some form of contact by light and voice, shouting until we were hoarse.

One by one we cupped our hands and yelled futile questions. 'ARE YOU OK?' 'DO YOU REQUIRE HELP?' 'IS ANYONE HURT?'. At first our words were whipped away by the howling gale but by moving to the windward side of the tarn we eventu-ally succeeded in getting a message across the void. Faintly, sometimes inaudibly, came words that might have been a ploy of the wind or trick of our ears but, by constant repetition, resolved themselves into the basic answers to the questions. 'ARE YOU

OK?' 'NO'. 'DO YOU REQUIRE HELP?' 'YES'. 'IS ANY-ONE HURT?' 'NO'. If nothing else the replies showed that our four friends were still alive though whether they could remain so through the coming hours was another matter.

The night was the longest I can remember. Guiltily we ate their supper of onion soup and overcooked spaghetti which one of the Japanese men had tenderly prepared nearly incinerating himself in the process. And in bed, warm but unhappy, we lay listening to the wind wherein, through a freak of accoustics, offered fragments of ghostlike voices that, in our tortured minds, were pleas for help. In the window the tiny flame of the candle epitomised our hopes and frightened away the rats.

Excerpt from Robert's diary: 16.30. Finally freed the rope and prepared for a further descent which might have brought us back onto our original route. I feel certain that we are destined to spend the night on the mountain. A dismal and rather frightening prospect. This last abseil brought Harley and me down to a small ledge a hundred feet below Alistair and Ram. Here disaster struck. The two of us, in fast fading light, are unable to flick (the rope) within reach of the two above. 19.15. We all realise now we are here for the night. Harley made a brave but futile effort to climb in almost total darkness. Alistair and Ram began shouting that something had to be done (for), with justification, they rate their chances of surviving the night as slim. It dawns on me that from being a five hour training climb we are now involved in a possible life and death situation. Thoughts of exposure, frostbite, hypothermia etc spring to mind. Alistair and Ram are convinced they cannot survive the night belayed, as they are, on a small ledge with virtually no room to move. But I know it is suicidal to attempt to climb in the dark. Harley and I occupy a narrow sloping ledge (of which) the only protection consists of the end of the rope and an ice axe with a sling. The ledge allows only for two narrow footsteps which means we are not able to do more to keep warm than move on the spot. We (don) every available garment and discuss ways of staying alive. Sleep is out of the question and we will have to keep up constant movement to prevent frost-bite. We must also shout to the two above periodically to maintain their morale. Probably we overrated the severity of the conditions but the low cloud ensures the temperature is not sinking much below freezing. But I am worried about Alistair and Ram because of their lighter clothing and more exposed position. After three hours we shall know if we have a chance of emerging relatively unscathed. Harley and I do all we can to remain awake, telling each other stories and executing shadow punches at our rucksacks. The (shouts) from John, Christopher and Richard from below are a good morale booster. Hope they heard our replies. Alistair keeps repeating that his leg is dead. 02.30. The hours seem interminable and it is increasingly hard to remain awake. Our stories, jokes and songs are becoming less effective and we must look pretty ridiculous standing bolt upright side by side solemnly asking each other if we are awake. 04.00. Dawn is suffusing the mountain. Thank God. It has also begun to snow hard little pellets of ice. Harley has donned his crampons and is inching his way up towards the ledge above. Through a break in the cloud I can see a candle burning in the window of Two Tarn Hut. . . '

The alarm clock trilled at four in the morning though we were all awake anyway. Two Tarn Hut blossomed into a hive of activity as its British and Japanese occupiers donned climbing boots, overtrousers and duvets with enthusiastic deliberation. At last we could do something.

It was dark outside but snow fell only intermittently. The wind too had dropped. With John and Richard making ready to scale the base of Piggott I made my stumbling way up and over the crest of the ridge intent upon descending to Mackinders the moment the dawn light allowed it. One of the Japanese men came with me. We carried torches though the whiteness of the snow muted the darkness. But the snow was also a hindrance as it concealed the holes between the slippery rocks of the 900-foot escarpment which meant beginning the descent on our hindquarters and sliding, skidding and jumping down the scree. Breaking a leg or ankle was my greatest concern but I was quite unprepared for the tumble I took when, in the treacherous light, I mistook a shadow for a solid rock and took a header into space. Rolling over and over, all the breath knocked out of my body, I ended up against a boulder, my head pushed into a pocket of snow. My companion, hearing the commotion but seeing nothing, kept calling 'Mister Porty, Mister Porty, are you all right?' in a worried falsetto. I assured him that I was, surprised indeed that I hadn't broken my neck and we continued together to the bottom of the valley. Here bog was the only impediment its veneer of ice fragmenting as we floundered through and cold water sluiced around the inside of our boots. A track led us to the low timber building that housed the rescue services, its slender radio antennae gently waving in the morning air, and we completed the journey, some two hours after we had set out, on all fours, crawling up to the door in a state of complete exhaustion.

Within very few minutes a squad of African rangers, equipped with walkie talkies, were leaping up the escarpment like scalded cats. We followed in our own time which was dead slow. My task was done.

It was broad daylight when I regained the ridge. Snow was falling again and cloud once more wrapped the silent peaks in their damp embrace. The only occupant of the hut was one of the Japanese engaged upon the preparation of a mammoth breakfast in celebration for what we all hoped would be a deliverance. From the direction of the rocky bulwarks of Piggott came the buzz and crackle of voices.

Halting a moment to regain breath I made my way along the edge of the tarn to join the would-be rescuers. Low cloud precluded any possibility of a helicopter lift-off but John and Richard, together with an excited Itsui, the third Jap, had managed to attain a point from which they had re-established communication with the climbers. The replies they were getting to their shouted questions were reassuring. The lower sections of Piggott had become an ants' nest of muffled figures and before long the four weary survivors were being carried towards the hut.

A swift examination by John revealed no serious damage and, within the hour, all of us were consuming vast helpings of soup, tea and porridge. One by one the African rangers left and life in Two Tarn Hut reverted to normal. With no source of heat available we went to bed; the climbers to sleep, the rest of us to thaw out our frozen feet.

True climbers are not easily beaten. That Harley and Robert, Alistair and Ram could so easily have joined the victims of previous accidents whose mute graves overlook the Lewis Glacier made no impact upon them. Within hours of waking they were discussing the final onslaught. But the weather remained fickle to the last. A gap in the clouds, the parting of rags of mist, showed the face of Bation, glistening with frozen, treacherous snow.

The fact that the peaks would not be in a fit state for climbing even were the weather to improve had to be taken into account. There and then Harley reluctantly declared the intention to evacuate the mountain. Time, likewise, was not on our side and the expedition needed our services in lower and warmer climes.

Without porters our loads were of gargantuan proportions as we wound down the great fortress of Mount Kenya. Each rucksack with its attached impedimenta could not have weighed less than seventy pounds which, unevenly distributed about our frames, had the most disturbing effect on balance. Every time anyone fell he had to be helped to his feet from a position to which he was anchored to the ground.

What had been snow above 14,000 feet was rain below it and the Teleki valley was awash. Sometimes up to our calves in water the 'Vertical Bog' was a nightmare even though the gradient, this time, was down. Over to our left the infant Tana made less burdensome progress on its way off the mountain.

To each his own pace. The five of us were spread over a mile or more which meant fighting our own battles. I keeled over a dozen times to find myself gazing at the sky in the manner of an upturned beetle. But, like the beetle, I found ways of righting myself — especially when it was a bog in which I was lying. In this manner we came to the jungle belt through which we marched on legs of lead. A flock of parakeets in a tree watched my erratic progress then took off in a multiple screech of maniacal laughter. And round the hundredth corner was our Landrover.

In a real bed that night I totted up the score. We had failed in the bid to conquer Mount Kenya. Instead we had lived with and experienced the ruthless spawning ground of the river to which we had come so far to explore. And there is nothing like beginning at the beginning.

For me the ascent of Mount Kenya had been something of a diversion. Lake Höhnel had shown me a birth of a great river and I was eager to pick up the thread of this new life.

The Tana is put to work, like many of its peoples, at an early age. When still a child meandering through Kikuyu country it becomes, unromantically, a drainage source for the mud and straw villages along the way. From the base of the virgin forest clothing the shoulders of the mountain we followed it on foot as best we could, the scenery changing to sparse trees and brown bush that choked all efforts by other plants to grow. The lush grass banks gave way to sand, soft and powdery. Like an old beggar woman the countryside grew poorer and poorer as if it had donned an old coat while the young face of the Tana transformed to one deeply lined with dried-out streams and pimples of rock to disfigure it still further. Even as I looked at it in its youthful dotage at Sagana Bridge I had sorrow in my heart.

The water was dark, dank and bubbled with infection. Here and there it increased pace and made small clattering noises while rushing over ledges of rock as if objecting to the country around it. But out beyond Sagana, the noisy little township through which beautifully ancient steam locomotives haul ramshackle wagons along the freight-only line to Nanyuki, the Tana kicks itself free of its torment and roams, idyllically, amongst the lonely bushland.

Sprawling candelabra cactus rose spiky from the red earth embankments and then, out beyond Kinderuma, we were back in the bush and among the baobab trees. Huge fat trunks with a few squiggles of bare branches coming out at the top they look like upsidedown brussels sprout plants with their roots at the top. Soft bark and warm pink tones offered an illusion of melting wax running down the side of a bottle.

For the Tana its freedom and wild abandon through the embryo bush is short-lived. At Kinderuma a dam complex deflects it into slavery. The Tana seems to understand and emerges from this indignity a different river. Gone is the placid stream following a meandering, useless course through a thick bush that scorns it. Now a sullen waterway, dark with anger and a force to be reckoned with, it drives into a harsh territory of solid rock. Sandy banks become chasms, mudflats are transformed to barriers of boulders and quiet ripples build into restless waves flaked with the spittle of madness. The battle of water against rock begins and the Tana lowers its head for the charge.

Naturally, we had a team for it. Except for Paul Turner, the White Water squad was, if anything, as green as were its predecessors of the mountain. But we were an enthusiastic bunch blithely ignorant of what we were in for. Here was a last adventure before we joined the scientists; a last madness before the routine of investigation.

To negotiate the rapids of the Middle Tana we had two 13-foot Avon Adventurer inflatables, *Adamson* and *Thesiger,* each holding a crew of four. The lead boat was *Adamson* commanded by team leader Paul Turner. With him was Harley, Marcus Keane and myself. *Thesiger's* complement was Richard (captain), Robert, Peter Gilfillan and Derek Bromhill. *Thesiger* was the photographic boat and had been rigged out with a Meccano-like frame to which various cameras could be fixed to record for posterity the deeds of daring we were hopefully to perform.

A word about the unintroduced members of the Team. Captain Paul Turner, if he had not chosen the army, would, to my mind, have made a fine diplomat. In the ensuing days he was to pour oil in liberal quantity on the troubled waters of a rebellious team. He was quiet-spoken, thoughtful and behaved in a manner well in advance of his 26 years. Though born in Germany he was undeniably British and was 'something in advertising' before becoming a soldier. Derek Bromhall arrived late to the expedition and hardly had he flown into Nairobi when he was whipped off to record the doings of the second adventure team. For Derek was our documentary film-maker and not only had he his own skin to look after but several thousand pounds worth of delicate equipment. Staffordshire-born, 47 years of age, a Ph.D., his life to date was the most varied of all of us. His love of underwater photography obviously triumphed over all else and blossomed into the general field of documentary photography from where he suddenly struck out for the highly insecure life as a freelance.

Taking time off from the Scientific Team to accompany us was Andrew Mitchell, a native of Jersey, who had packed into his young life more than most people three times his age. His interests ranged over wildlife conservation, sailing, surfing, skiing, skin-diving, photography and exploration. Though, at the time, it was half-hidden by an unruly mass of hair and a beard his face was alive with character. The zoologist of the expedition, his tasks were sometimes to overlap with those of others in the Scientific Team but the hippo and crocodile count was exclusively his baby.

The remaining two members were classed as 'attached personnel' of the expedition and they resided in Kenya. Peter Gilfillan, a photographer of some standing, became assistant to Derek. Resourceful and knowledgeable he was a good person to have around in an emergency. So too was young Marcus Keane who 'bribed' his way into the expedition by offering his Toyota Land Cruiser for our exclusive use.

In addition to the complement of the boats we had a vehicle support group. This was composed of Andrew Mitchell and Peter Tilbury, the latter also living in Kenya; in fact for a time his home formed our Nairobi base camp from where he and his wife, Ann, were twin towers of strength in the administrative field. Plump and ever-beaming, Peter looked and acted like a man who enjoyed life to the full.

We had chosen as our start point a bend in the Tana close to a hill called Kaumuthai and below Kamburu Bridge. These were the only landmarks for miles around though, nearby, was a tiny village of *manyattas* — little thatched huts on stilts to guard against flooding. All around was the bush, formidable in its sense of eternity. Through this our well-laden vehicle fought its way until we came to the cross on our map designated as the start point. Here we were welcomed by the dismissive shriek of the 'go-away bird'; its real name I cannot recall. Ignoring its request we prepared our overnight camp and inflated the boats. The river was as tranquil as a mill-stream though a faint roar downstream heralded fun to come. Lying under the stars that night I pondered anew what I had let myself in for *this* time.

We were up with the sunrise loading the boats and lashing everything down. Into *Adamson* went all our personal kit doubly sealed into thick plastic bags, cooking gear and rations for three days, an Evinrude outboard engine, a five-gallon drum of petrol, the .303 rifle wrapped in plastic and an assortment of canvas baler buckets, bellows, paddles, life-jackets and crash-helmets all tied to the boat with lengths of cord. *Thesiger*, being the film boat, was less heavily laden and though Paul had stipulated a 0900 hours start it was nearer eleven before his motley crew of cantankerous individuals untangled themselves from various unaccustomed tasks. Paul himself hardly shone his brightest when he accidentally slashed his own inflatable with a penknife while cutting a length of cord.

Once false start for the benefit of the cine mogul, Derek, and we were away gently bobbing down-river in a strong current. High banks hemmed us in and the water was dark and petulant. All being well we would meet up with Andrew and Peter two days hence and some forty miles on, an inspired piece of over-optimism as ever I have come across. They, as well as us, were equipped with military transmitters — a fact that did little to increase my confidence.

Some five hundred yards, an island, and we came upon the first obstacle; not a big one by subsequent standards but memorable because it was our first. Paul Turner, looking very professional, stood up in the boat to survey the thundering water ahead. The current gripped us but we veered to the island to give our captain a prolonged view.

'No problem. It's quite a small one', he muttered then rapped out his commands: 'We'll take the middle tongue keeping the prow to the front and avoiding that rock on the left. When I say "paddle" paddle hard on the right to midstream, then straight for it.' He signalled *Thesiger* to follow suit when we were through.

Gazing wide-eyed at the frenzy of water below what looked like a reasonable imitation of the Aswan Dam my enthusiasm for white water negotiation began to drain away very swiftly indeed. We swung into midstream and the tug of the current was irreversible.

I glanced at Paul anxiously. 'Aren't we supposed to wear those?' I enquired indicating crash helmets and life jackets adorning the inflated walls of the boat.

He bit his lip. 'Good point', he replied. 'Of course we should. I forgot, but it's too late now. HOLD ON!'

The prow approached the slipway of water known in white water parlance as a 'tongue'. Though I was sitting in the stern I could see the yawning drop and cauldron of spray. I held my breath, anchored my feet firmly beneath the thwart and fixed my eyes on calm water beyond the maelstrom wishing to hell we were there.

The boat up-ended, fell and was jostled madly as we entered the cataract.

'PADDLE!' screamed Paul and we were galvanised into action. The boat all but disappeared under the foam to emerge with all on board yelling like dervishes.

Now it was *Thesiger's* turn. We beached our craft on a sand-spit, started baling out the water that swished about the rubber floor, then turned to watch how our colleagues fared.

They and their boat took the obstacle with illogical ease.

'That's the advantage of a light load', observed Paul drily and I realized that I was in the wrong boat. Congratulated by our captain for our performance, being told that we were in full command of our vessel was news to me.

Continuing downstream we made good progress before the ominous sound of angry water had us staring uneasily ahead. On both banks of the river the iniquitous bush was devoid of pity.

Paul repeated his Nelson act, standing to assess the turmoil of the next obstacle. Encouraged by our alleged expertise he was not to be deflected by a mere cataract. 'We'll take it', he decided. 'Don lifejackets and helmets. It's bigger than the last one.'

He wasn't kidding either. The edge of the fall hid what lay beneath it but the cloud of spray told its own story. Ahead, the storm of water tumbled through dragon's teeth of rocks to seethe joyously round a curve. Somewhere in the bush a go-away bird squawked at us and, this time, I'd have been most happy to oblige.

We approached the new hazard with caution, resisting as best we could the tug of the current. Some yards from the point of no return we halted, anchoring the boat by clinging to an overhead branch of a tree. Paul's eyes scanned the course he proposed to take.

'We'll make it the right-hand tongue keeping left of that rock on the edge. At the bottom that boulder, bang in our path, will have to be avoided. We'll go to the right of it and down that chute over there.' He sounded as if he were designating a route for a ball on a devil's pin-table.

At least we started in the correct manner and hurtled, prow first, down the chosen tongue. In the swirl of water we struck a submerged rock, then another which buffeted us from beneath and knocked us off course so that we were moving crabwise.

'PADDLE LEFT!' screamed Paul which had Harley and me scooping at the water for all we were worth.

'I MEAN RIGHT!' corrected our gallant captain as we turned full circle.

To help the others Harley and I back-paddled frantically but to little avail. The boat gyrated, smashed into rocks, shook itself free of one cauldron and flung itself joyfully into another. My feet, fiercely implanted under the rubber thwart, alone held me from being flung overboard as wave after wave washed over us.

There was no let-up. First the prow reared, then the stern. I was not a little amazed to count three heads still in place as we emerged from one wave that came unaccountably from the opposite direction.

Abruptly the storm subsided and, looking over my shoulder, I perceived *Thesiger* under fire and saw the black neoprene of their underside as the craft stood on end like some torpedoed destroyer on its deathdive.

With both boats through and their crews none the worse for the ordeal we could raise no energy to cheer though exhilaration still edged our laughter. And to come through a battering like that *is* exhilarating make no mistake. We beached both boats and baled out for all we were worth. Cargoes were floating about in the trapped water like flotsam from a shipwreck.

For the next couple of hours we were content to let the current carry us. A few hills craned upward from the flat bush and we attempted, with no success, to pinpoint our position. A couple of straightforward rapids we shot with little fuss for they were now mere playthings.

According to our combined calculations we totalled fifteen miles that first day, but *Thesiger* lagged far behind, her photographically-minded crew indulging in close-ups of strange storks and long-legged beasties. Reasonably satisfied with progress and none too keen to acquaint ourselves with the source of another ominous thundering that emanated from around the next bend we beached on an island and prepared camp, first attempting to raise the support group on the radio without success.

That the island belonged to a colony of crocodiles was clear the moment of our arrival. Several long scaly forms slid reluctantly into the river from the warm sand. And they were not the only tenants. Before realizing it we had floated right over a group of hippos who had taken to the water upon seeing us coming. Now, indignant at our acquisition of what was plainly regarded as their pad, they proceeded to blow raspberries at us as we spread our damp sleeping bags to catch the last warmth of the sun.

Over a fire we cooked a scanty supper from our rations which, because of the load factor, were reduced to a minimum. Long after the meal we kept the logs ablaze to hold at bay the former occupiers of the island and, round the dancing flames, we lay to sleep in troughs of scooped-out sand.

We estimated a further twenty-five miles to the rendezvous so an early start was deemed essential. We knew we were behind schedule and we had no idea what horrors may lie in wait. We washed hastily to a reveille of hippo snorts and endeavoured to improve upon the previous day's boat-packing time.

The thunder up front materialised into another set of rapids different only in that they were preceded by a widening of the river indicating a stretch of shallows. A maze of tree-covered islands were drawn across our path. It was a case of getting out and pushing for, even crewless, our flat-bottomed vessels struck the stone-strewn bed. The operation was made the more difficult by virtue of the unevenness of the bed whereby one leg could be thigh-deep in water, the other unable to locate any footing whatsoever which made the going highly erratic. At times it became necessary to lift the boats, cargo and all, out of the water which all made good action stuff for Derek filming our struggling, cursing figures from a comfortable bank.

Back in deeper water the trees increased to jungle proportions with lush greenery liberally hung with thick creeper overflowing both shores. More islands — these ones bare of trees — appeared and from one we reconnoitred the rapids beyond.

With Derek grimacing behind his shoulder-supported camera we took off into the grasping current. 'Keep away from the rock!' reiterated Paul but such was the pressure that we smashed right into the one and only huge boulder for miles, spun sideways and floated backwards towards the portion of the fall we had wanted to avoid at all costs. *Adamson* tipped forward on its stern, went over the edge with us clinging onto anything to hand, and flopped squarely into the massive turbulence. Water gushed everywhere hiding everything from view and, coming to the surface, the boat was flung onwards to collide violently with rock after rock; those you could see and those you couldn't. Then silence, joyful silence.

Swiftly we regained our lost control, pointing the boat in the right direction. But we were surging forward too quickly for comfort and found ourselves being inexorably born towards a second cataract. And there was simply nothing we could do about it. A worried Paul surveyed the approaching maelstrom and, in a voice weary with resignation, said: 'We're committed chaps. That left-hand tongue's the only way.'

In we went again to be assaulted, buffetted, swept against rocks and overwhelmed with water by a terrible force. Once we were shot clean into the air and our 70-pound engine and heavy petrol drum were, for a fragment of time, suspended in space. All too easily their descent could have broken a leg or smashed an arm.

Free of the river's fury we beached the battered craft and set to making it shipshape once more. We kept an anxious eye open for *Thesiger* but there was nothing we could do to warn her of the second rapid.

Her crew were surprisingly chirpy when they reached us. Much of it was relief and the reason quickly became apparent. Richard had been thrown bodily out of the boat and the current had taken him ahead of his pulverised vessel. He had climbed a rock island and, as the boat swept by, had simply thrown himself back into it.

A subsequent set of rapids rejected our advances. It was uncanny to find ourselves deflected up a *cul-de-sac* even though the current seemed to want to take us to the lip of the turbulence. We fought the side motion but to no avail so, hoping the subsidiary route would return us eventually to the main course, we ceased resisting. But then a particularly unnegotiable waterfall came into view which sent us hurriedly to the shore.

There was only one thing to be done and that was return the way we had come. But easier said than done since the current was irreversible. We clambered ashore, tied ropes to the boat and slowly, painfully — trying to avoid the many obstacles — hauled it in the opposite direction. *Thesiger,* meanwhile, had caught onto our predicament, and had wisely tied up at the junction and waited. Her crew were not allowed to rest for long however and soon they too were roped into the big haul.

So began 'The Day of the Portages'. The dictionary defines the word 'portage' as 'the act of carrying; a journey over which boats have to be dragged or carried overland'. In this instance our actions were to cover the definition in its widest sense.

The rapids that spurned us were found to be utterly impassable since the savage rocks at the bottom of a considerable fall would have torn us to pieces. Thus the two boats had to be unloaded, the cargoes and vessel itself manhandled over cliffs of granite, and reloaded further down river. The operation took four and a half back-breaking hours under a burning sun and it was all we could do to crawl back into the boats praying for a few hundred yards of peacefully-flowing water to restore our sanity.

How the Tana must have laughed. Just around the next bend appeared one of those fantails where the water divided into a series of channels; a kind of delta. All roads lead to Rome, they say, but all these rivulets led to twenty-foot and more waterfalls. We investigated every avenue, some of us risking the strong current to swim to the islands offering better vantage points. But there was no way through.

So, another portage. This one sent us staggering over a plateau of stone and down an almost vertical face into ruffled water the far side of the mainstream fall. Transporting a double-skinned Adventurer inflatable thus — plus all its appendages and cargo — is no light undertaking even when utilising the services of four persons, not least through a difficulty in synchronising one's direction, balance and the placing of feet in a leg-breaking environment. But the deed was accomplished with no casualties and everything again packed and stowed away. *Thesiger*, as always, lagged in this respect and the first flash of resentment came to the surface when our crew were requested to go to their aid. Fatigue was wearing us down; draining the milk of human kindness. It was easy to forget that photographic equipment is not so simple to stow safely away and that a multitude of fiddling tasks are necessary. Paul played judge-advocate in his wisdom, soothing frayed tempers.

Our reckoning of having put but five miles behind us that second day was an optimistic one. We were but halfway to the rendezvous, could field two punch-drunk crews and, if we spun things out, held rations for just one more day. It was a thoughtful bunch of white water sailors who hauled their boats onto the mudflats and prepared camp that nightfall. Everything in my 'waterproof' bag was wet and had to be draped around the camp fire — and sleeping bags are the devil to dry.

211

A small but adequate crocodile slid into the water as we came ashore awakening recollections of another menace. Strange how the mind cancels out one danger when confronted by another. We sat and discussed the day's events not without some acrimony and resolved to undergo no further unreconnoitred rapid-shooting even if the pre-shooting survey further sacrificed precious time. And time too was running out and — God forbid — the next day was Friday the thirteenth.

It couldn't have been anything else. If the day before was the 'Day of the Portage', today was going to be the 'Day of Disasters'. The first morning portage had already sapped our strength and frayed our nerves when *Adamson* was pinned against a huge rock and overwhelmed in mid-cauldron. We were too occupied with saving our own skins to warn *Thesiger* against taking the same course and, sure enough, down she came, tossing and twisting in the maw of the tempest. Walls of stone restricted the channel to a deep and powerful conveyor belt of water and, really, there was no alternative route. *Thesiger* performed a repetition of our gyrations and we watched, horrified, as, in spite of the wild paddling of her crew, the craft smashed sickeningly into the self-same rock to disappear beneath a mountain of water.

Derek and Peter were, literally, swept out of the overwhelmed boat but held grimly onto the outboard life ropes. We managed to throw them a line and another to Robert and Richard — their own was already floating away downstream — who secured the craft and began throwing its cargo ashore. When Derek discovered that an expensive piece of his equipment had gone to the bottom, he had to be physically restrained from following suit.

Right from the start it had been Friday the thirteenth with a vengeance. Hardly had we risen from our sleeping bags when our eyes had fallen on a straggling line of near-naked tribesmen moving stealthily along the opposite bank of the river. They were armed with bows and arrows. Were they poachers or *shifta*, the sullen Somali brotherhood whose presence spelt trouble? Either way their arrows would have been dipped in deadly poison. If they had seen us they made no sign. There were at least forty in the party outmanning us by five to one. My eyes had strayed to the rifle but no attack developed. A little later Peter, on a foraging mission, came upon their poacher's cache of food — mostly barrels of honey. The resourceful Peter was anxious to annex a few items but there is a law of the bush that stipulates that nothing shall be taken in such circumstances unless something can be left in its place. And we had nothing worthwhile to offer in exchange.

The portage that followed the swamping of *Adamson* was quite the worst of the lot. Two more, one hefty rapid and three medium ones and it was well into the third afternoon. 'We'll pull up round the next bend for lunch', announced Paul sounding like a host humouring his weekend house-party guests. But even two and a half biscuits and a squeeze of jam have a certain attraction when there's nothing else.

Hardly refreshed we in *Adamson* led off as usual but with a tinge of nervousness for we were suspicious of a current that saved the effort of paddling. Everyone was desperately tired. Terror coupled to the physical drain of portaging had warped our powers of rational thought. We were in the new rapids almost at once — or had I fallen asleep in the meantime? — and creamy water was tossing us unmercifully. Paul must have investigated the new peril for I heard him say it looked worse than it probably was.

The tongue was a steep one and very fast so that we lost control at the bottom and shipped a lot of water. Like automatons we acted upon Paul's staccato instructions but the boat refused to respond. A house-high wall of water hit us, knocked the prow round in a complete circle and threw everyone into the middle of the boat in a whirl of arms and paddles. Hardly had we recovered our positions when we rammed a submerged rock, slewed round and lay in the trough at the mercy of a towering reverse wave.

We all saw it; guessed what it could do to us and edged down into the flooded boat. For a fleeting moment I saw *Adamson* as if it were another craft, prow uppermost, vertical in the air. I clung to a rope but the force of water tore it away. I performed what seemed to be a double somersault and felt myself being sucked down into the depths gently revolving as I went. Everything went quiet, the water turned from brown to grey and there was a great peace. I experienced no panic. Instead I was able to assess the situation and wonder at the ease of the process of drowning. I remember thinking of my notes; I always thought of my notes in moments of crisis for they were the tools of my trade; the reason

213

I was on the expedition. Richard had his cameras, Derek had his movie apparatus; I had my notes. A rushing in my ears produced a new sensation but I could not tell if I was descending or ascending. I was wearing a life jacket so presumably it was upwards but maybe the suction of the whirlpool was greater than the buoyancy of my jacket? My thoughts were clogging, my brain clouding up. Sleep. That's what it was. Drowning was no more than going to sleep.

My potential slumber was rudely shattered. Suddenly I was at the surface amongst the confusion of wild water. I came to life and struck out for a mass of rock that was the shore. The current fought me, whirling me downstream but I was desperate now and I wanted to live. I missed the clump of rocks, made for another and hauled myself out of the water.

I looked around. Paul was already ashore and running towards me. Far downstream I perceived that Harley and Marcus had beached the boat and were struggling to turn it right-side up. It took me some time to regain my breath and rejoin the others.

The miracle was that we had lost very little. A gym shoe, a belt and a few personal belongings; that was all. But, alas, *Adamson* was badly ripped. I retrieved my notes from their bone-dry cubby hole which also contained the batteries for our useless radio only to discover that the acid had spilt onto the paper so that it had disintegrated into nothing. In this game you just can't win.

Nineteen miles down river Peter Tilbury and Andrew Mitchell lay in the shadow of the Toyota. Three days they had waited; or two and a half days to be strictly accurate for it had taken them many hours of track and bush driving to get themselves into position at the spot they were now. Until last night the waiting had been no more than a boring chore and the fact that no word had come through on the radio was, initially, of no great concern. After all, distance and hills would make communication difficult. But today the silent radio and empty river aroused nagging fears. Peter checked and re-checked the set, transmitting Paul's call sign again and again. The third day dragged on towards its end and the misgivings grew. Below them, the river smiled, peaceful and innocent. The banks shimmered in the heat and constant scanning of the water played tricks with the eyes. Dusk clothed the low, bush-clad hills in a cloak of a menacing darkness.

Back in Nairobi the rear link would be expecting a report. Peter gave it another ten minutes, searched the chortling, phosphorescent river one last time and raised base camp on the radiotelephone to spell out two words: 'Disaster Action.'

With *Adamson* damaged beyond repair and an onward route dominated by the impassable Kiambere Gorge, a deep cleft with perpendicular walls through which the Tana hurled itself, we found ourselves stranded, foodless, in the remote bush. Straightaway we divided ourselves into scavenging parties. Marcus and I were designated an area of search upstream, Harley and Peter Gilfillin were to cover a downstream location. None of us had slept well, the sand of our encampment being inhabited by unsociable stinging ants bolstered by a sprinkling of baby scorpions. But for breakfast we had fish drawn from the Tana by hook and line which formed part of our survival kit. So much for the prophets of doom amongst us.

Marcus and I carried, between us, a compass, knives, money, water and a powerful catapult. I noted the path we took alongside the river could only have been made by man or beast. Occasionally Marcus let fly with his catapult at some inoffensive bird but without effect and we had put a mile between us and the camp when we came upon our first fellow creature. There, poling himself across the river in a little square box of a boat, was a tusslehaired African. Even while we watched three more appeared on the bank seemingly waiting to be transported to the opposite shore. We hesitated a moment; the three were Wakamba hunters and they too carried poison arrows. Shrugging away an instinctive caution we approached the group waving a greeting.

They stared at us blankly. Marcus spoke to them in Swahili and they responded with nervous grins, ceasing to finger their bows. Yes, there was a village a mile or two away the other side of the river. Yes, there were provisions and a shop in the village.

The Wakamba made a picturesque trio. Small men, they had fierce faces, were jet black and their skin shone with vigour. Their bare feet were balls of hard cracked skin tougher than the leather of any sandal. While we were talking another man approached. He was attired in western dress and belonged to a different tribe for he possessed none of the striking attributes of his fellows. But he was going to the village across the river and would be happy to accompany us there.

We negotiated a party-rate with the ferryman and, squatting — hardly daring to breathe for fear of upsetting the boat — crossed to the north bank. Up river a couple of hippos sported, blowing thin plumes of spray into the air.

The 'mile or two' was at least five, mostly uphill and at a killing pace. A network of paths criss-crossed the thorny bush and, had we been alone, heaven knows where we would have got to.

Our guide was the local Christian lay reader. He spent his time touring the villages imparting the word of God in addition to selling more earthly wares from which he made his living. Everyone knew him in the village we eventually attained and he solemnly introduced us to the elders of the community congregated in the communal char house.

The name of the village was Katheni. The 'centre' consisted of a single row of mud and wattle huts including a 'bush supermarket' secured by a heavily-padlocked door around which any child could have crawled since the walls consisted of no more than a few sticks. The inhabitants of Katheni were immensely curious about us and flocked to the char house to watch us consume mug after mug of hot sweet tea. The village was surrounded by a thorn stockade or *boma* embracing about three acres of bush and in the far corner I could see more dwellings.

Over a charcoal fire the hindquarters of a goat were roasted and, joined by His Reverence, we ate hungrily. During these pleasant proceedings Marcus bargained for supplies and arranged for delivery to the encampment. Then Harley and Peter appeared on the scene having fetched up in the only village for miles in similar manner as ourselves. Whilst explaining the arrangements the sound of a low-flying aeroplane brought everyone out into the open.

Diving out of a vivid blue sky came a light Beaver monoplane, its pilot and passenger staring down at the village. We waved our arms wildly and, skimming low over the huts, the aircraft performed a circuit returning to drop a weighted message. Overcoming their alarm a score of villagers tore after the missile and brought it back to us in open-eyed wonderment. The piece of paper read: 'If unable to reach you by 1500 tomorrow will return to drop food. Others informed. Nigel.'

216

Having aircraft looking out for us increased both our stature in the eyes of the villagers and the price of the goods we were buying. I was now being addressed as *Msee*, the translation of which is roughly 'elderly and respected' and I was henceforth thrust into the bargaining committee. Only old men wear beards among the tribes of Africa, 'old' being anything over forty. My beard was by now a startling ginger, more bristly than flowing, but a distinct improvement on the stubby chin that had started the expedition. By adding ten years to my age I managed to wield a sobering influence over the more zealous merchants and so kept the expenses within bounds. The bargaining committee was composed of a wizened little man with a multi-coloured woollen tea cosy for a hat, a younger, more efficacious character sporting a Dunlop sports cap and a woman of indeterminate age whose bulbous breasts kept bursting out of a torn blouse to romp amongst the potatoes she was trying to sell at an exorbitant price.

Loaded with flour, sugar, tinned milk, potatoes and the promise of bulk delivery to follow we returned the way we had come. His Reverence bowed politely, elicited a promise that we would attend his Christian 'teach-in' upon our return and smoothed our path with a gravely recited 'Peace go with you my brothers'.

Back in camp everyone had indulged in a surfeit of fish which the pressure cooker had turned into a brand of *bouillabaisse*, so our offering of flour and potatoes was hardly received with the enthusiasm of starving men.

Andrew was, later, to tell me the lurid details of the rescue mission. Though only nineteen miles up river as the crow flies, to approach our encampment involved a gruelling drive of a hundred and fifty. Like knights of old the two members of the vehicle support group had hurled themselves to the rescue. No damsel in distress could have asked for more. Nothing stopped them. The thicker the bush the noisier was the plunging through, the wider the ditches the more shattering the gear changes. On the river we had attempted to avoid all obstacles. On that drive all obstacles were simply overcome...

From the middle-Tana our next assignment was at Kora where we would join the scientists at their base camp. But first one more diversion. It was at Kora Rapids, a dozen miles above the camp, where the river, emerging from youth adulthood, was to lay down its challenge to avenge the ignominious defeat we had suffered at its hands. We just *had* to win this time.

Kora Rapids had never been shot before. They were considered extremely dangerous and it was easy to see why. Less than thirty feet wide the river had, over the centuries, forced its way through a plateau of solid rock. Now, concentrated waters lunged, at horrifying speed, into the deep gash they had made. The river had dropped perceptibly, some thirty to forty feet, forming a series of waterfalls amongst the grotesque shapes of rock. The turmoil of water fell over itself as it plunged downwards and onwards to the distance where the banks softened and opened out once more as if to pacify the uncontrollable anger. Driftwood, bleached and scarred, lay trapped against granite pillars or swaying gently in pools and crevices.

This awful cataract lay astride our path, its very presence a provocation. Nothing could survive in that tumult but as we gazed in awe each of us bent incredulous minds to the possibilities of conquest. We set up a camp overlooking the lower, quieter section of the gorge at a spot shaded by trees, and for a whole day made a close study of the obstacle. The water was treacherously low, revealing a hefty rock that would kill any crew foolhardy enough to be swept into it.

Next morning we shot the growling torrents to the very edge of the big falls as if to steel ourselves for an ordeal we knew was coming. Again we inspected the eye of the cyclone against a background of restlessness and indecision.

To test for hidden treachery Paul ordered the damaged *Adamson* to be put, empty, through the fall with Harley and Andrew below with a lifeline across the gorge with which to salvage it. The boat came through, riding the storm like a thoroughbred even missing the lethal rock of its own accord. Paul thereupon nominated his crew, taking into consideration skill, experience and, of course, acceptance of the risks involved. Joining him in *Thesiger* went Robert and Peter Gilfillan. Only a three-man team was to make the shoot.

As if determined to better *Adamson*, *Thesiger* sped like an avenger for the tongue, dropped down the first chute, gave a rock a glancing blow and, out of control, was lost in the maelstrom.

Crash-helmeted heads and orange, life-jacketed torsoes emerged momentarily into view as the boat swept on, safely passing the larger rock to plunge down the further step nearly overturning in the process. Encased in a spume of foam Peter was lifted bodily overboard but grimly hung to the exterior line, his life dependent on the hold, and from which he managed, with tenaciousness bred by fear, to pull himself back. And then it was all over with the crew whooping with relief and victory as *Thesiger* glided into smooth waters, a record broken.

On the fourth day we continued downstream to Kora camp closing the twelve-mile gap and rejoining the main body of the expedition. The tasks of the White Water Team were at an end. Against a sunset, a memory of which Kora has bequeathed us for evermore, and a chattering of baboons we toasted, with a secretly-held bottle of sponsored scotch, our success, our failures and our endeavours, and offered silent gratitude for our deliverance.

In retrospect I am inclined to dispute the assertion, stoutly maintained by the Scientific Team and its supporting elements, that Kora was not the best camp of all. Of course I am not a fit subject to judge since I was there only a few days against the three weeks of the others. On the other hand, coming from the cold of the mountains and discomfort of the rapids to the idyllic sanity of Kora I had every reason to praise its amenities, which, without doubt, were the finest of the six main camps to be established between Kora and the mouth of the river. Later camps were of no more than a week's duration which gave less time for improvement.

The Scientists had left Nairobi the same time as we of the Mountain Team. They had taken two days of hard driving to reach the site spending a night at the town of Garissa, on the Tana. They had stayed in the only hotel which, apparently, was the local whore shop. A party developed and beer flowed copiously to celebrate the end of the beginning. Reports there onwards became somewhat vague and my informers reticent. Only one, rather diffidently, came out with a story of waking up in the morning to find a black lady beside him in the big old-fashioned double bed. They bade each other a polite 'good morning' and promptly returned to sleep. At least that was one man's story and the teller shall remain nameless. Later I was to spend some time in Garissa so could appreciate the fact that hotel accommodation was, indeed, limited.

If there was a village called Kora I never saw it. There was Kora Rock, an immense granite boil on the face of the flat bush country that made a landmark for twenty miles in all directions. But for most of us Kora camp was an introduction to the real Africa. Situated in the remote Northern Province it marked the Tana's halfway point at which our scientific survey began. In all respects, Kora was ideal. As both a terminal and a terminus it indicated the end of the Tana's youthful tantrums and the beginning of a more serene adult progress through the life-giving riverine forests.

Lions, elephants, rhinos, basilisks and unicorns dwell in East Africa, according to historians of medieval times, intermingling fact and legend. The Queen of Sheba was an Ethiopian ancestress of the late Emperor. King Solomon's mines, supplying the queen's mythical wealth, were said to lie in its snow-capped Mountains of the Moon. Dotted around the endless territory were giants and pygmies and incredibly rich African potentates. East Africa was an altogether wondrous land.

Today it still is. Granted no unicorn has yet appeared on hunters' trophy lists, neither has anyone been known lately to have come face to face with a basilisk and been instantly transformed into granite. But all the other creatures that have excited travellers since Ptolemy compiled his famous map are there. Alas, some are on the verge of extinction thanks to the poachers' greed but many become wise to man's hostility and manage to survive. It is just that, outside the game parks, one has to go and find them.

So Kora, for most of us, earned the distinction of being the place where we actually saw our first wild animals. By the time the eight of us from the White Water Team and Mountain Team had rejoined our colleagues at Kora the others had seen their first *real* land animals and were becoming almost blasé about it. To see wild animals outside of a zoo for the first time is an experience not to be missed.

To the scientists Kora will be remembered as the camp where it all started. Animals were more numerous and exciting further down river but the magic of living in the African wild and seeing strange creatures gave the place a special significance. Yet it was utterly unreal and ethereal; a landmark not only for the expedition itself but in our lives. From Kora onwards the civilized world seemed not only non-existent but nearly impossible to envisage. Life's usual mundane preoccupations had been completely replaced by the most sensitive attention to noises and movement. We too had become creatures of awareness, attentiveness, quietness and not a little fear.

En route from the Kora Rapids to Kora we of the White Water Team made improbable guests of the Adamsons at their ever-open straw-thatched home. Yet the Adamsons must be equally improbable: George and Terence living alone with their lions and their guinea fowl, with beady-eyed chameleons darting about the furniture. A younger man, Tony Fitzjohn, helped George with his tasks and we dutifully did the rounds to be rewarded by sight of two wild lion cubs. Offspring of the famous Elsa they may have been and wild into the bargain, but the necessity of seeing them fed behind a fence robbed the moment of its magic. George had little to say to anyone. More accustomed to royalty flying in by helicopter he seemed slightly taken aback by our unscheduled arrival via a dirt-encrusted lorry and one of his brother's roads. Terence, on the other hand, enjoyed us. A small battered, weathered man, with nervous mannerisms, he has been farmer, prospector, professional hunter, road, dam and bridge builder, soldier, water-diviner and hotel owner throughout his years. His roads are as legendary in Kenya as George's lions are to the world. We drank copious cups of tea, expressed the hope we would see them both at our camp, and left.

At Kora camp we received a spirited welcome from Nigel and the scientists. The tents had been erected on a spit of sand where the Tana curves to such an extent as to make a virtual island of the site. So low was the water that the causeway was dry but I was assured that, whenever the upstream dam allowed it, the river rose high enough to permit a trickle to creep in behind us. Within the taped boundary four 6-person bivouacs and a marquee (which doubled as mess tent and laboratory) were lined up with military precision though, such was the warmth that most of the inmates slept outside. A generator provided electric light and, tastefully hidden by jungle foliage, were the hessian screens of the camp bathroom and toilet. To round off the complete Boy Scout's outfit there rose, from the centre of little England in a foreign field, a flagpole bearing the expedition's pennant of a hippo's head against a green background.

Everyone wore the minimum of clothing and was abnormally tanned. Mary, Alison, Gail and Mona, the four ladies of the expedition, sported a natty line in bikinis which contradicted the air of complete absorbency in which they went about their chores and tasks.

My first night with the scientists I was invited by Andrew Mitchell, now back in his role as zoologist, to partake of a night observation walk. We left as soon as it was dark taking with us a pair of image intensifiers loaned to the expedition by the manufacturers and the Ministry of Defence. These expensive items of equipment were originally developed for military purposes to assist vision at night without the use of artificial light. The telescope-like instruments gather all available light from the moon and stars to which the human eye is insensitive and transforms it into light images that the eye can see. These images are projected onto a phosphorous screen in the form of a greeny glowing picture the power source being no more than ordinary Mercury 1.5 volt batteries.

We also carried head torches, ordinary torches but with the bulb and reflector attached to the forehead by a harness. With these probing the dark ahead we moved off parallel to the trees towards the further extremity of our 'island'. But on this, my first night observation sortie, nothing, absolutely nothing, came into our straining vision unless you count tiny spiders' eyes, like glow-worms, twinkling from beneath small rocks in the wet sand. But at least I got a whiff of stalking the African wilderness by night and it was exciting, heady stuff. Every noise was laced with menace, every shadow edged with terror. The lights of the camp were never more welcome and crossing the boundary tape was akin to returning to the barbed wire coils of our own lines after a wartime patrol into enemy territory.

I lay awake in my sleeping bag gazing at a sky ablaze with a myriad stars. Is it only for Africa that the heavens can produce such magnificence? And when I settled down to sleep I found myself listening to the unexplained noises of the living jungle so that, when I slept, my dreams were but a continuation of those wonders of the darkness. In the small hours I awoke to make my way surreptitiously to relieve myself and nearly jumped out of my skin when our African *askari* (guard) crept up to flash his torch upon me. But if the African night is a period of mysticism so is the African dawn. Never would I have believed that light could fashion so much beauty anywhere on earth. It was the birth of the very first day; a radiance and a richness streaming over golden sand and ethereal trees that shimmered as molten wire.

Gradually the camp came alive. The *askaris* had kept the fire alight and the duty cooks distributed mugs of tea. It was a case of first come first served in the 'bathroom', which looked out upon the river. The Tana looked peaceful and inviting in the early morning but, as with Africa in general, things are not always what they seem. At Kora the water was not badly contaminated though we were instructed to have as little physical contact with it as possible. Later, even our washing water taken from it, had to be treated which offered virtually a full-time job for one of the support members.

Breakfast was a feast. Cereal with dried or condensed milk, fried bacon roll and as much tea or coffee as one wanted. Following this everyone moved off to execute their various missions. It was a bit like 'going to the office'. Had there been a railway station nearby I'm damned if we wouldn't have become commuters. Instead it was a short walk to the jungle or the laboratory tent. I felt as if I ought to clock in somewhere.

Local inhabitants were few and far between for we were in an area devoid of any static communities. What other humans there were consisted of roving Somalis — like the ones we had glimpsed earlier — and for days on end we were to see these scowling nomads, with their endless herds of camels and goats grazing their way past the camp. It was difficult to say whether these hard-looking men, devoid of the happy smile of the Kenyan, were those of the province or whether they were part of the 'peaceful invasion' then taking place from neighbouring Somalia. Many may have been *shifta* — a kind of bandit/guerrilla — for this north-east corner of Kenya had long been a breeding ground of strife. Inter-tribal banditry was rife and terrorism, arising from and aggravated by political tension between Somalia, Somaliland and the Kenyan government, a constant threat. Whether these surly men with their herds of beasts were *shifta,* disguised soldiers or simply homeless Somalia citizens 'encouraged' by a government to occupy their former land, nobody could say but many possessed guns barely concealed beneath their dress. We watched them pass uneasily for they went their way as enemy and spurned the gestures of friendship we made.

But this sinister intrusion failed to damp the enthusiasm of the scientists and their helpers. I began to pry into the doings of the young investigators and to accompany them on their business in the forests. At first I was somewhat nonplussed. Taken individually the tasks appeared insignificant; almost childish in their simplicity. How could the collection, examination and occasional dissection of a little furry creature or pretty butterfly help mankind to delve into the complex and massive problems of the development and harnessing of a great river?

I watched Gail, our one and only lady scientist, lay out her traps — small wooden boxes with spring-lids that caught their prey unharmed — on the, to me, invisible runs of the tiny mammals of the forest. And in the morning I would accompany Lorio, our African taxidermist and skinner, to collect the catches and reset the traps. Frequently we caught nothing but every now and again we would return triumphant with a brand of rat or squirrel. And I well remember the excitement at the capture of a civet cat, a long-bodied, wiry-coated animal as large as a medium-sized dog but with a very unsociable bent. Some of the smaller mammals were put to sleep to become specimens for dissection or for preservation for Nairobi Museum and the British Natural History Museum in London. Others were held simply for observation and photography, then released.

The butterflies caught were not so lucky. Tony Pittaway, 23-year old Bachelor of Science, was our entomologist and he lived in his own world of butterflies, moths, insects, bugs and creepy-crawlies. Rapid-speaking, tall and bronzed he was an aloof figure preferring the intimate company of his bugs to close human companionship. During the three weeks at Kora he collected over seventy different butterflies, including a number exclusive to the Tana.

His methods of capture were by the use of a slightly larger butterfly net to the one I remember wielding as a boy, a fine net stretched between trees across what he considered to be nocturnal and daytime 'flight paths', and special net traps baited by a smelly concoction of fermented banana soaked in Guinness. Butterflies by day; moths by night and the nocturnal wanderings of many a flying insect ended in a plastic cone containing an ultra-violet light bulb.

Through Tony's narrative I learnt more about butterflies and moths than I ever thought possible. He talked of butterfly migrations, million upon million arriving from some source unknown and travelling to an equally mysterious destination. And in the sun-pierced jungle I could clearly discern how the ancestral development of the butterfly and the moth led back through a million years, how their patterns had reason as well as beauty. At night as I watched moths being drawn to our jungle lantern a latent dread of nocturnal predators turned to a sensation akin to horror as a rabble of moths became an enormous, amorphous super-organisation piled up in fluttering droves, pressed against the lantern glass, manacled by the unreasoning drawing power of light. It came to me that what the sun, moon and stars cannot do, is performed by a single 100-watt bulb.

One particularly colourful specimen fell on its side, its wings stretched far up and the body curved into an unpleasant hairy caterpillar, or so it appeared. Upon the insect a trance had settled which neither shaking nor dropping disturbed. If I were a hungry bird or lizard I should having nothing to do with such an unpleasant object, and this is exactly what this unconsciously-induced display was trying to effect. We humans are not so clever or our eyes so unconfused. We see a butterfly and marvel at the beauty of its wings but shudder at the caterpillar whose metamorphic body lies between those wings.

The wonders of the lowly insect world became apparent to me likewise. Many a bug was similar to those of Britain but bigger and this included the bite or sting in the tail. Here at Kora I saw scorpions, big brown and black specimens crawling in the sand, loathsome but fascinating. Here too were wasps that were not wasps, beetles that were moths, centipedes as big as slow-worms, moths with wings rolled tight as maps. And here too, all but invisible, were craneflies dancing up and down on bended knees for no reason that my poor brain could fathom.

Birds of the forest and the river came into Sandy Evans'

domain. Sandy, at 22, was the youngest of the expedition members, but his knowledge of ornithology was considerable. An inveterate smoker and a lover of rugby as well as the bawdy songs its players are inclined to render, he would go around reciting dubious limericks. His thirst for adventure was partly quenched by his curiosity about birds and animals and, on the bird side, he had an ally in Kenneth Campbell who joined the expedition from his Nairobi home towards the end of our Kora tenure. A serious young man his sojourn with us was to rub the raw edges off him as it did off no other member to the same extent.

The catching of birds was effected by mist nets erected at strategic points in the jungle and sometimes by the more dramatic method emanating from the barrel of a gun. Besides the .303 we did possess an aged small-bore shotgun and a .22 rifle both on loan from the Nairobi Museum. In both cases ammunition was severely limited. While in the jungle or on the river we also carried pyrotechnical devices known as 'thunderflashes' which, when ignited by striker and thrown, explode with considerable violence. However it was the mist net that claimed the bulk of our winged specimens — especially bats — and these were collected at dawn and dusk by Joseph, our second dark-skinned taxidermist and skinner, from which a selection were dissected or preserved for study.

Many geographical authors have referred to the Tana as a faunal barrier. This we hoped to prove or disprove. Quite plainly the river was the largest single factor contributing to the presence and survival of the various tribes we would be meeting on our journey along its tortuous course. The communities living on its banks obviously depended heavily upon its waters for much of their livelihood. Just how much we had to learn. Much of the old nomadic way of life is being abandoned; even the tribes whose way of life had rested on the need of constant movement. It was not adopted by choice in the first place but by necessity. They are nomadic because of the grazing facilities available to their animals. But the Tana provided a good reason for not indulging in constant moving and, as a result, tribal villages along the lower Tana were growing and becoming more permanent. Here at remote Kora there were only the nomad Somalis and *their* movement was, ominously, more for strategic reasons than any other.

Yet, both man and beast of Tana country were approaching the crossroads. Already we had noted the daily change in the level of

226

the water as the upstream dams controlled or released its flow. Almost it was like a tidal river yet Kora was hundreds of miles from the nearest sea. But what was happening at Kinderuma (where the initial dams were) would, over the next decade, be repeated in the Hola area down-river for the Lower Tana Hydro-electric Scheme, Kenya's most ambitious infrastructure project. The long-term venture is costing millions and will not only spread the benefits of electricity to much of the country in general but also a water supply currently dependent upon a highly unreliable source. At the time of the expedition Kenya was importing power from the Own Falls power station in Uganda which had put a political lever into the hands of the despots who then ruled that country. The Tana River scheme seemed likely to make Kenya self-sufficient not only for existing needs but also for industrial expansion. This alone might not have made the project worthwhile — self-defficiency can be bought at too high a price. But the fact that the Tana also flows through a large area, then pure semi-desert, lacking only water to become highly fertile since the soil itself is known to be good, gave a new dimension to the programme. Opportunity there was; vast opportunity but nothing in this world is quite what it seems and progress can also bring destruction in its wake. The lives and ways of the Tana people, the big game that can provide new injections of funds from increased tourism, the river itself. Little was known about the mud-brown Tana but knowledge stems from small beginnings. Hence the examination, in life and sometimes death, of little furry creatures and pretty butterflies which signalled the start of our much-needed survey. Our mission, in fact, was that of bringing tiny chinks of light where before there was only darkness; small beginnings where there had been next to nothing.

My third afternoon I sat idly on the river bank ostensibly writing my notes but, in reality, reflecting upon a twelve-foot crocodile basking on a rock. After the drama of the mountain and the rapids I found the knowledgeable doings of the scientists difficult to get excited about. Like our soldiers they belonged to an exclusive club and I was, again, an outsider and one who didn't know a bug from a beetle, a croc from an alligator. Their exclusive findings were all being written down in an exclusive language that all seemed very inconclusive to me. Scientific team leader Raj Patel sat in his canvas laboratory, lord of a paraphernalia of microscopes, text books, unpleasant-looking instruments and small, opened-up bodies of fur and feather. Small himself, his dark Asian face with its sharp eyes and neat beard gave him a distinguished air.

Even in the jungle our sponsorship undertakings crept up on us. The last day at Kora, in between the striking of camp and the loading of the boats and vehicles, we had to perform before Richard's cameras a variety of poses holding aloft a plethora of branded goods donated by our sponsors. Already our Bedford lorry, two Landrovers and the inflatable dinghies were sandwichboards of stickers. The hippos and crocs we were likely to encounter on our impending voyage would remain in no doubt as to whose oil, petrol and washing powder we were using.

The shallowness of the river was to have a disappointing effect on one of our more flamboyant crafts, the jet boat. There had been rumblings of discord about allowing what, at first, seemed a noisy gimmick, to perform within our earnest endeavour. But its usefulness as a reconnaissance boat was vigorously expounded by its owner, Ralph Brown, a senior employee of the Hamilton Jet Boat Company of New Zealand. At 50 Ralph was the second oldest of the expedition personnel. He was a Californian but had homes around the world. His was a lifetime of boats and water and methods by which each could take advantage of the other. His craggy bronzed face, invariably wreathed in smiles, made him something of a rock of dependability. His wife, Mona, made the perfect foil. She was Swedish, blonde, could speak four languages and was, more importantly, a delightful and warm-hearted person who never looked put out, fatigued or unkempt whatever disaster was to have the rest of us in turmoil. In the face of such multiple attributes the opposers of the jet boat surrendered unconditionally.

The craft itself was its own undoing. The shallow, muddy waters of the Tana and its sandy bed were contributory factors in addition to a number of technical malfunctions. Yet there were to be times when the vessel spluttered into life and went tearing along in a plume of spray.

While Ralph and Mona wrestled with the intricacies of the reticent jet boat, preparations for the voyage went ahead. The scientists had their own apparatus and stores to pack away so the bulk of the striking of camp fell to Mary Garner and Alison Izatt. The former was expedition secretary, treasurer, welfare officer, nurse and supervisor of water treatment. Another New Zealander, Mary's itchy feet had taken her to much of the world including a spell of nursing in the Vietnam war. Her cheerful good nature was, just occasionally, broken by short spells of depression which she diagnosed as culture shock. Another SRN and New Zealander was Alison, this one dabbling in modelling, film acting, public relations, interpreting and translating though her numerous tasks on the expedition touched on few of these accomplishments. One of the most decorative amongst us, teased unmercifully, never quite managing to convey the tough explorer image, her good nature too was put to an extraordinary test.

It was Nigel who gave us the pre-departure briefing and outlined the possible hazards — natural, human and animal — likely to be met. We were reminded to be alert for *shifta* and to keep our rifle and its ammunition dry, protected and out of sight. The main animal menace was the crocodile and the likely danger-point the river's edge. Hippo could also be a threat as some of us knew already. The danger here could stem from either land or water for, though timid creatures, they lunge for deep water at the approach of alien beings while, on land, their runs are strictly for the passage of their own kind. In both cases a human being in the path would suffer grievously. The river itself held less spectacular pitfalls, that of the disease, bilharzia, being the nastiest. Already we were banned from pleasure swimming though the risks were minimal at least until beyond Garissa, the first major human habitation.

As the tents fell and the scientists' chests were loaded onto the Bedford there was a distinct feeling in the air akin to the last day of the holiday. Three weeks at Kora and the team had established themselves in this tranquil place more than it cared to admit. Moving off into the unknown produced something of a threat. In the remains of the laboratory Raj was supervising the packing of books and I thumbed through the *Kora Animal Book*, a notebook full of entries in different handwriting giving dates and details of birds and animals seen in the vicinity of camp. 'Fish Eagle, Bateleur Eagle, Baboons, Vervet Monkeys, Warthogs, Water Buck, Hippo, Albino Bushbuck, Mamba, Sykes Monkey, Crocodiles, Impala, Spotted Genet, Dik Dik, Jackal, Lesser Kudu, Camels,

Gerenuk, African Hare, Civet Cat, Wildebeest, Giraffe, Osprey, Bohor Reedbuck, Monitor Lizard, Steinbok, Galagos and Goats'. Not perhaps the most thrilling bunch of animals that Africa could produce but not bad for an introduction.

Yet the security of Kora was, in some ways, a false one. The Somali threat remained. That very evening an ill cow was despatched by a lion just a hundred yards from the site. Chum van Someren, the eminent ornithologist from Nairobi, and George and Terence Adamson, attending our farewell 'Mess-Tin Dinner', spoke of the risks. 'They now know your habits. It's time to move on', they declared, inserting a serious note into the festivities.

Our boats were a 15-foot Avon Professional and two 12-foot Redshanks as well as the lame jet boat to be crewed by hand by Ralph and Mona. My boat was initially *East Midlander,* one of the Redshanks, captained by John Richardson with Alison as my fellow crewman. With the jet boat as 'pathfinder', the Professional *Habari* (Swahili for 'greeting') was to follow and carry the bulk of the scientists under Sandy Evans. *Charity,* the other Redshank, was to take up the rear of the procession. We were given a lesson in boat drill and methods of communication between boats and told that the only method of relieving oneself en route was to stick whatever extremity we chose to use over the side.

The vehicle support party, composed of driver, Lance Corporal Andy Winspere, Raj and Tony, were to meet us at Saka, a village some fifty miles downstream.

As darkness fell I sat listening to the gargling of playful hippos on the evening air. The camp fire was poked into a cheerful blaze. This now became our sole source of illumination for luxuries like generators and oil lamps had been packed away. I felt at ease with the world. Tomorrow perhaps I would at last find out what exploring was all about.

The merging of the 'adventurists' with the scientists for the long voyage down the middle and lower Tana could be described as the high water mark of the expedition. It was a moment when individual talents could be utilised for the benefit of the expedition as a whole and not simply for one small section of it. Henceforth 'the team' meant all two dozen of us, not just a group of five or eight. Yet there were those of the 'adventurists' who prophecied an anticlimax upon reversion to the role of explorer, a notion to which the army chiefly subscribed. On the other side of the coin one or two of the scientists were beginning to chaff at the bit, finding three static weeks of Kora, sometimes devoid of the subjects of their survey, quite long enough to be hanging around while others were performing feats of daring. Only Andrew had managed a stint with the drama-makers and, though not all the scientists were cast in this mould, there were others for whom adventure held undeniable attraction. As the four vessels making the flotilla that caught the slow current out of Kora we all wallowed in pleasurable anticipation.

Our departure from Kora was effected to a degree by the dictates of the documentary camera and, with a cast of strictly non-actors, was something of a slapstick performance. Crews wielded paddles and punting poles to which they were completely unaccustomed with an air of having done it all their lives even though some of the boats promptly vanished into thick prickly undergrowth to transform stiff upper lips into squeals of pain.

In my boat John was the only crew member with any poling expertise at all which was just as well since it compensated for the fact that my paddling was stronger than that of Alison. The Tana was the colour of Windsor soup and much debris — mainly fallen trees — muddied the edges. It swept round eternal corners in wide curves with a certain grandeur, dimpling and gurgling in its shallow sections leaving the deeper channels to surge ponderously forward. The current was not strong; nothing like that of the upper middle reaches, yet it provided enough impetus to allow occasional respites from paddling.

For the scientists, moving down a river was a new and exciting experience after the restrictive activities of Kora. To sit and watch the lush banks go by, knowing that sooner or later a panorama of fascinating wild-life would appear on nature's wide screen rivetted our eyes to every tree and clump of undergrowth. The birdlife immediately caught our attention as a vividly coloured Malachite Kingfisher, a small enamelled statuette, came to life to catch a fish from the river's surface. Standing in the water a great white egret, whiter-looking than a swan — with its compact plumage and sleek, torpedo-smooth body — minced with appalling deliberateness after frogs and minnows. In the tangled creepers tiny bee-eaters perched close together, darting straight upwards to snatch a moth or bug.

The bush had drawn closer to the river again and that the waterway offered life as well as death was emphasized by the sight of buck coming down to its edges to drink. They made a beautiful sight; so gentle and delicate, yet so aware of the close proximity of predators.

With the jet boat leading the way and locating the most advantageous currents and channels we advanced upon the first hippo herd in the full knowledge of their presence. Previously we of the White Water Team had sallied over and past them before we knew they were there which makes all the difference to one's peace of mind. Now came a clash of opinion. The scientists, congregated in the big inflatable, wanted to get as near as possible to observe and film the animals. Not so the others who were quite prepared to live and let live.

We could see their low foreheads and protruding eyes above the water level some distance away so had ample warning. We proceeded quietly and the beasts, assured we constituted no great threat, continued their cavorting until, one by one, their heads submerged. Being ignorant of the ways of hippo we imagined them to be approaching in the manner of hostile submarines and this fallacy was given impetus by the optical illusion created by a twig sticking out of the moving river and creating a furrow of water, a tiny bow wave seemingly approaching the boat. Only when we were well beyond the group did the heads re-appear, their eyes again upon us in curiosity and distrust.

The hippopotamus — *kiboko* in Swahili, meaning 'Horse of the River' — is actually a member of the even-toed pig family. To sustain their two or more tons they require a nightly forty-five kilos of grass and they live for an average of thirty years. With huge tusks and jaws these stumpy-legged pink-grey leviathans can outrun a man and kill lions and crocodiles.

All large but shallow rivers possess a deep-flowing channel and these have a distressing habit of following the outer curve of every bend which precludes even the possibility of cutting any corners. Gradually we developed a sixth sense as to where the deep channel flowed and in this Sandy Evans was to become a master. Faint ripples on the surface usually proclaimed shallows to be avoided though the wind not only blew us off course but ruffled the water's surface to deceive our eyes and senses.

Grounding produced a drill which became second nature to us. Our flat-bottomed craft displaced very few inches of water but

232

considerably more when loaded with three or more humans and a great deal of cargo. Thus it hardly needed the captain's order of 'All out' for the crew to be over the side, pushing or pulling the boat to deeper water. At first some of us wore no shoes but the Tana had some nasty sharp surprises for tender feet.

It was surprising, too, how soon we came to terms with the crocodile menace. Yet the threat still mesmerised us. It remained our secret fear mainly on account of the experiences of previous Tana explorers, and possibly because it represented the chief danger in the minds of our families and friends. Crocodiles are despised animals, yet their very unpleasantness is respected. Heavily armoured, they are accountable for more human deaths than any other animal in spite of their shyness. Once frightened they stay submerged for hours and the ones we saw were, more often than not, those asleep in the sun or feeding at night. As soon as they saw us they would slip into the water very silently, a mere ripple in an ever-widening circle betraying their entry.

But it was the hippo that constituted our chief concern those first days. Their concentrations became more and more numerous and to bypass them we sometimes had to press close against the bank, our inexperienced boat-handling projecting us painfully among thick foliage plentifully endowed with thorns.

We estimated a good twenty miles of progress that first day and, as dusk fell, made camp beside the river on a plateau of sandy shore. Away from any likely sand 'platform' so beloved of the basking crocodile, we were, nevertheless, conscious of being on a hippo track which resulted in us choosing to sleep close against a tree trunk to reduce the possibility of being trampled on in the night. The chores of making overnight camp were to be repeated over and over again as we made our way down the river. Usually we divided ourselves into parties to carry out such tasks as wood-collection, firemaking and the preparation of food following the general unloading of the boats. Sandy invariably chose to sleep in the bottom of an inflatable both as a measure to discourage theft by marauding Africans and, more to the point, because it made a softer pad.

Noises at night included the grunts and whine of lions. Often they were very close though rarely did we see them. There were occasions when one's hair felt as if it was standing on end when an unidentified squeal or shriek rent the silence — though a later familiarity or knowledge of the source of the noise provided an immunity to alarm. In the Lower Tana we were to use mosquito netting which offered a sense of security that was a complete illusion.

Hardly had we moved off from our first overnight camp when we saw our first buffalo on the opposite bank. Enormous, head down, he stood preparing to drink. Come upon unexpectedly, buffalo are supposed to be dangerous for they have alert, sharp senses and are exceedingly cunning. At the time I was not aware of the fact that buffalo are regarded as the cruellest of all big game animals and this big bull gave no indication of it by running off into the forest, together with his unseen mates.

The river scenery changed little though every corner produced a new view of it. All manner of winged things we saw those early days until familiarity began to dull our interest. Here on the Tana the variety was bewildering. Some were ugly like the vulture and the marabou stork; some were tiny and brilliantly coloured like the sunbirds; and some were predatory like the hawks and eagles. Ken's bird records of those first days alone gave the cold facts: Water Thicknee, Grey Heron, Hardada Hybis, African Darta, Egyptian Goose, Grey-headed Kingfisher, Fish Eagle, Wood Sandpiper, Spurwing Plover, Pied Kingfisher, Malachite Kingfisher, Open-billed Stork, Yellow-billed Stork, Great White Eaglet, Little Eaglet, Common Sandpiper, Tawney Eagle, African Kite, Sacred Ibis, Wahlburg Eagle, Hooded Vulture, Gabar Goshawk, Woolley-necked Stork, Marabou Stork, Hammer Cup, Pale Chanting Goshawk, Ruppell Griffin Vulture, Woodford Owl.

Our second afternoon we had a close encounter with a crocodile. I was dangling my legs in the water (against orders) while John was gently poling when quite close to my left foot I saw a twelve-footer gliding along just ahead of the boat. Alison gave a lady-like gasp, John nearly dropped his pole and we all watched hypnotised as the reptile swung round, bared his teeth at us and dived. Only then did I remember to withdraw my feet from the water.

It was intended that we met up with our vehicle support group below Sarka and pitch the second base camp nearby. However this failed to happen owing to the fact that the vehicles were unable to reach the river. But here we were back among people. The village was a big one by African tribal standards so we landed to investigate the possibility of purchasing fresh food. Word gets around quickly in such places — particularly of the arrival of strangers —

and there was good reason in this instance. The village had been raided by *shifta* who not only had destroyed many of the houses but murdered the inmates as well. In the event the one and only shop could produce no provisions but it was good for a prolonged chat with the elders who used it as a council chamber. Backed by a hundred or so of his citizens even more naked than we were the rotund litte chief unloaded onto us large quantities of cigarettes and matches and offered a lurid account of the *shifta* raid.

The general layout of the village was typical of others we were to see over the next few days. We entered through one of the openings in the hedge of at least six feet thick, made of two fences of saplings driven into the ground, the space between being filled in with brush. Right across the entrance lay a frame of branches which were dragged over the opening at night to wall in both villagers and cattle. The herds were out with their herdsmen so that the *boma* was nearly deserted. Here the dwellings were finely constructed; plastered with dried dung on the inside, then a stuffing of grass and, on the outside, upright sticks bound close together with some kind of tough grass. The roofs — also of dung — were dry and firm, like thick felt.

On our way back to the river I glimpsed in the distance another 'convoy' of Somali nomads making their slow relentless way south. I could guess what the citizens of Sarka thought of these hostile wanderers. I should not have been surprised to see, on this twilight, sinister path, a line of slaves yoked neck-to-neck, driven on by Arabs and Somalis with whips and long muzzle-loaders. Surely a scene of Africa as Livingstone saw it.

The ferry crossing, which offered the reason for the existence of Sarka, was marked on the map though no vehicle-carrying craft existed. Here, as the long, heavy, expertly-manipulated dugout canoes criss-crossed the river, was a popular meeting place for those men of the village with nothing to do. Women were here too in considerable numbers, attractive, often striking in their colourful *kangas,* as they scrubbed and beat their loads of washing in the murky Tana.

Amongst the crowd were Raj, Patel and Andy and we drew in to the bank to learn of their inability to locate a base campsite. Nigel decided to continue downstream even if this meant another day's journey. In the event it meant two.

It was the hippos that gave us a fright the third day out when, without warning, *East Midlander* sailed right into the midst of a herd and, worse, into the classically wrong situation of between the young and the parents.

'Paddle like hell', growled John suddenly aware of the danger.

I hardly needed the warning and plunged the blade back and forth through the water for all I was worth. But Alison, paralysed with fright, made no such move with the result that we simply went round in a circle. John was occupied removing the igniter from a thunderflash and so was unable to correct the manoeuvre with his pole.

Low squeaks of terror emerged from Alison but my grated, 'For Christ's sake *do* something, woman,' sent her paddle back into the water and we swung the other way.

All this must have been very confusing to one papa hippo who abruptly lunged at us, making a beeline for the boat to disappear beneath the water just before he reached us. I raised my paddle with the vague idea of giving him a crack about the ears should he appear at the side of the boat but nothing happened. Considerably shaken, we made faster progress than we had all day but not before a couple of baby hippos, hearing the commotion, leaped into the water from the bank at the spot where our boat had been but seconds before.

The land-based game provided more secure observation. Baboons screamed and barked at us from the bank and hyenas wailed like sirens. Tiny dik diks shyly stared out of huge mouse eyes ringed in white. We spotted warthog too, cropping grass and digging for roots with their villainous tusks and later were to rescue one from a hole into which it had fallen; not an easy job since they are vicious when cornered.

Herds of waterbuck watched us inquisitively before bounding off into the trees frightening a group of tailcoated Maribou storks, solemn and pompous on the ground but so graceful in flight. With them were sharp-faced vultures peering from their huddled witch capes.

The trees were alive with Sykes monkeys leaping spectacularly from branch to branch and, while we lunched frugally on biscuits and fish paste, wildebeest approached a watering place in docile line. These substantial animals appeared to have no orderly system of drinking, yet, when finished, they retired hastily but calmly. Gazelles, too, we saw on the same errand.

Two more nights — five in all — were to pass before we came in sight of the red marker denoting the presence of the vehicle support party and the site of another base camp with its promise of the little additional comforts of semi-permanency. But its main attraction for me lay in the prospect of a whole week of relative languor and an alternative from the incessant propelling of boats. The place was Mulanjo.

Raj, Andy and Tony had done us proud. The tents, erected and ready for occupation, lay as an oasis beneath a cluster of trees, and best of all, a substantial stew stood steaming on a trestle table. Riches indeed.

Most of us spurned the tents for comfort does not have to mean all that civilisation has to offer. Would we be denied the sights before our eyes. By the time dawn came to the forest in a blaze of scarlet and gold most of the nocturnal animals had retreated to holes in trees and caves and the diurnal animals taken over. There was a great echoing burst of bird-song and, in the morning dew, the cicadas started zithering experimentally with long pauses as if aware that they were out of tune. Then the forest promptly rang with its more characteristic noise — the wild exuberant cries of the baboons.

These dawns were, to me, one of Africa's greatest gifts and could only, sometimes, be equalled by an African dusk. 'Kora dawns' we called them for the eastward sky at Kora was bare of foliage. In other respects Mulanjo was very similar to Kora and camp life at Mulanjo was to start where it had terminated at Kora.

Though the tiny, straggling village of Mulanjo was but a mile into the bush and a few of its more inquisitive souls came to visit us daily, the pattern of observation of tribal life and customs never took coherent shape at our second base camp. Thirty miles downstream was Garissa, a town on the east bank of the river with a road bridge to boot, one of the very few on the Tana. Not until below Garissa would our enquiring minds delve into the ways of the Tana peoples. From the point of view of wildlife Mulanjo was, perhaps, a slight improvement upon Kora. To the visitors' book of animals we were able to add a sighting of elephants by Joseph, a lion by Alison and John as well as impala, an anteater, terrapins and a puff adder.

If Ralph and Mona had something of a roving commission with

their jet boat at base camps even more so did John Axford and his Tana Pox Team. In fact we saw little of John, Sue Hall and Gilbert Wangabe, their African assistant, during the subsequent section of the expedition since it was from Mulanjo that the trio set out on their medical survey.

I am not going to attempt to pretend I have more than the sketchiest idea of what Tana Pox and the other nectar-borne diseases the team had come to investigate are all about. For a long time even the basic facts of the oddly-titled Tana Pox escaped me for it was an infection about which nobody seemed to have heard. And not surprisingly perhaps, since it was one that had not fully materialised though the logic of going for a cure before it reached infamous proportions was to be applauded. Ours was not the first survey of its kind. In 1971 one was carried out to establish the levels of this Smallpox-like virus remaining in the population of the Tana after a small outbreak in 1969. It was noted that the disease was confined to the Pokomo tribe. Now John and his helpers, lavishly equipped with white-painted Landrover supplied by the Kenyan Ministry of Health were all set to descend upon the local Pokomo population whose river villages are spread between Garissa and Garsen to take blood samples and to ascertain to what extent the disease has been prevalent since 1971. Malaria, filariasis, cholera and other horrors are present in the area, with malaria endemic throughout the Tana Basin so John, notwithstanding additional ailments and woes his survey would assuredly uncover, had his hands full.

John projected more of a playboy than a doctor image. Twenty-three years of age, already a B.Sc., he was now taking his Ph.D. in immunology though he did not seem, at the time, certain where his future lay. His hobbies of parachuting and yachting intensified the playboy image as did his ability to be not around when there was manual work to be done. However, there was no doubting a high intelligence level and he did his job well.

His associate was Sue Hall, SRN. About John's age she had worked in both America and Switzerland and was a proficient cook. A gentle girl she was always ready to help with anything and it wasn't only for her culinary expertise that I wished we could have seen more of her on the expedition proper. She seemed to do a lot of the donkey work on the Tana Pox survey.

Gilbert Wangabe one could best describe as a barrack room

lawyer and his favourite topic was politics which he expounded with vigour and some logic. Dark, educated, endowed with a pair of piercing eyes, he was immensely proud to have been chosen for the survey and membership of the expedition.

For several days the team operated in and around Mulanjo village being received with much hospitality and appreciation. Whilst their work was, initially, hampered by the remoteness of the community John was encouraged to go to any lengths to get through the thick bush to them. Warned by the medical authorities of the team's coming a great throng of villagers was awaiting them upon arrival. In spite of some hesitation at first concerning the actual taking of the blood sample the promise of an issue of vitamin tablets and sweets for the children soon overcame serious resistance. Later I was to attend one of these village 'medicals'.

As at Kora my stay at Mulanjo was of brief duration. I was offered a trip to the Nairobi Base House, outward by Landrover and back by bus which occupied much of the week. But a home, wherever it may be and for whatever duration, becomes a place of sacred memories stored away for ever becoming dim with the passage of time and jumbled with the intake of fresher memories. 'What,' we may be asked in years to come, 'were your impressions of Mulanjo?' We shall hesitate a few moments while the computer of our minds delves back into the distant past. No great drama notched a milestone of recollection, but Mulanjo would, in those years to come, spell a serene content, true solitude when the most restless part of a person relaxes and listens in a kind of agreed peace. It will be a place where the full expeditionary team came to live together in a wilderness, but, for me, it was where I learnt the lesson that a man can never truly know another, or be known by another, but that the pleasure of life is in the trying. Mulanjo was a place far from our real homes where we tried to bring the little comforts and courtesies that we know as civilization to a savage acre of a foreign field. Here we entertained the local chieftain to tea searching out the most unchipped mugs in which to serve it. Here we welcomed, like relatives for the weekend, strangers who were not strangers from the planet London. Mulanjo will be a shaft of memory where crocodiles basked on a sandbank just below the camp, a place with an entrance arch and a volley ball court each serving as someone's idea of what makes a home.

From Mulanjo camp onwards, the week-long scientific survey completed, our boats were propelled by a couple of temperamental outboard motors acquired from Nairobi. With one powered vessel towing an engineless one we made a strange procession past Garissa.

The ensuing voyage was uneventful — which is a way of saying that nothing of disastrous proportions occurred. Two small and whimsical engines to four boats do not add up to the perfect ratio for utilising horsepower and inflatables are not designed with sleek streamlining in mind. In spite of this, progress was made; the popular boast being, 'look, no hands'.

The next camp was Korokora characterised by an increase in big game, notably elephant though, alas, many were dead; victims of the poacher's greed. Camp life quickly resumed its pattern with non-scientists undertaking a variety of chores such as water-treatment and the care of body sores made sceptic by the cruel barbs and thorns of a dense undergrowth. The women of the expedition were — and expected to be — treated as men for they were living in a man's world. There is no place for sex and the practising of sexual wiles on an expedition which one of them found out the hard way through rejection.

Korokora provided some exciting night observation prowls into the jungle. On one of these I accompanied Sandy and Mary with, as a specific task, to shoot and bring back a bush baby required by Nairobi Museum. Attractive little animals they are a nocturnal relative of the monkey and are to be found at the top of trees. Their huge eyes glow when the beam of a torch is directed on them and so are easy targets. We had observed them many times on the occasions we had no firearm but this night, equipped with our elderly shotgun, not a single bush baby did we see. Instead, we got very close to an animal that has the distinction of being the first word in the dictionary, the aardvark, or ant-bear. A grotesque, massively-built, short-legged creature as large as a medium-sized pig it has long pointed ears, narrow head and a rounded snout. Being nocturnal they are rarely seen and ours made sure he wasn't seen for long. Following it we got ourselves hopelessly lost which, I suppose, could have been serious but which, for some unaccountable reason, turned out to be rather a novel experience. Distant sounds of lion, leopard and hyena made an eerie background to our own nocturnal meanderings that, eventually, brought us back to the river. Here movement in the thick clinging undergrowth was very difficult while there was also the menace of hippo out of water and in the same undergrowth; in fact we disturbed a herd of them who ran in all directions though, fortunately, not ours. Finding our way back to a worried camp fraternity with the dawn we received a deserved rocket from Nigel.

One factor that these wildlife observation walks began uncovering was that, to varying degrees, game predominated on the further, or east bank of the river but taking into account its size and course changes we were inclined to view the river as a creator of habitats — on both banks — rather than a divider of them.

Korokora to Kipendi was a four-day voyage made erratic by repeated engine failures. As we buzzed like angry wasps down the placid stream the face of the Tana began to change. People were more in evidence on the banks, their faces alive with curiosity and excitement. Children ran, chattering, their shrill voices sounding above the clatter of the engines, while small *manyattas,* the bee-hive-shaped huts covered with hides, mats and foliage, showed amongst occasional patchwork squares of cultivation. The shiny green of banana plantations took over where the forest had been before.

It was opposite one of these villages, nestling in a clearing of bananas, that we camped the first night. Many eyes watched us as we disembarked and struggled up the steep embankment to carry out our well-practised chores. Within half-an-hour we were receiving visitors in the guise of the boldest of the village salesmen who crossed the river in their lean canoes to sell us straw mats of beautiful design.

The site of our encampment was plainly a favourite place for elephant, the sandy plateau, backed by groups of trees being liberally sprinkled with their tell-tale droppings. As we settled down to sleep we heard them crashing around in the undergrowth to send each of us edging surreptitiously nearer the fire. At Korokora we had heard elephant on the *other* side of the river which made all the difference to one's peace of mind.

But what really made that night memorable was a remarkable incident that occurred in the village about midnight. We were awakened from a fitful sleep by a terrific commotion in the river as a herd of hippo thrashed about in the water grunting and gurgling. It seemed to trigger another commotion, this time in the village.

Within seconds scores of fires made an eerie, flickering spectacle against which the villagers could be seen rushing madly about accompanied by a crescendo of shouting and wailing. Gradually the flames died and the hullabaloo subsided into uneasy silence. In the morning we learnt that the two commotions were entirely unconnected. Apparently elephant and buffalo entering the plantation had touched off the alarm of the villagers who, with their bananas the sole means of community's livelihood, had, not unnaturally, reacted dramatically.

Tinned bacon steak made a welcome change of breakfast diet but Tony's early-morning premonition that 'today was going to be one of those days' proved all too true.

A snapped shear-pin in *Charity*'s engine offered the first misfortune hardly had we set off. This is no great problem in itself and we carried spares, but it takes time — especially if you drop the only adjustable spanner into the Tana as Nigel did. Next we experienced another of those hippo turns. Nobody saw him until too late and, apparently, he too had been looking the other way. Panic reigned in all directions as we all caught sight of each other. Smashing towards deep water the great beast loomed over us and we froze, paralysed with fright. Nigel recovered first, made a grab for the warning siren, but it is doubtful if the hippo heard the shrill blast as the waters closed over the great pink-brown body.

Zig-zagging from one side of the river to the other, our flotilla was dogged by misfortune, *Charity*'s shear-pin snapping twice more that morning as we failed to dodge the many logs that lay in wait just beneath the surface. The township of Burra was a preliminary destination for we were to take on petrol supplies there. Informants on the bank, in reply to our numerous 'How far?' enquiries in schoolboy Swahili, invariably offered the standard reply, 'Not far' which, in Africa, can mean any distance at all. Our two Africans were pressed into service to help out with these exchanges and a long conversation in Swahili would ensue. 'What did they say? How far is it?' we would ask at the end of it all. Our Africans look shamefaced. 'Not far', they confirmed.

Burra, so big on the map, hardly measured up to metropolis proportions when, eventually, we did set eyes on it. The usual collection of African hutments was, however, enhanced by a corrugated iron-roofed dispensary, a shop (marked as such on the 1:250,000 map) and a former airstrip. And, to us, unaccustomed to so much urbanity, the place, with its concentration of forever curious bystanders, did arouse notions akin to driving into the centre of Birmingham.

Another night encamped on the Tana's lively banks, steady progress in the morning and the township of Hola was before us. It stood, a strange collection of circular beehive-shaped houses of straw and wattle amongst coconut palms and, new to us, a sprinkling of mango trees.

Every tribe builds its own houses and though often quite simple in structure they serve adequately in a climate which is seldom harsh. Weather-proofing is achieved by the use of materials that come readily to hand: the trees of the forests, the grasses of the savannah and the earth of anthills. To a large extent the shape of a house is dictated by tradition and controlled by what materials are accessible. Generations of experience have resulted in a wide number of distinctive tribal styles. The ones we had seen, and were to see, might have differed in shape and materials, but, more often than not, consisted of a space where food was prepared, a sleeping room containing a low mud bed or straw matting on the floor, and a cooking room from which the smoke escaped through small vents. Sometimes there was a second sleeping room and, occasionally, a pen in which animals — chiefly goats — were kept. Inside the houses, apart from the glowing embers of the fire, it was pitch dark and, because of lack of ventilation, the heat and smoke is all but unbearable for European visitors. But though uncomfortable, these dwellings have the advantage of repelling insects. The cow dung wards off the ticks while the smoke kills the flies.

At the approaches to Hola we had noticed an increase in communication along and across the river by the inevitable dugout canoe. It needs one whole mature tree to make a dugout, the trunk being laboriously chipped out by hand, the job taking perhaps a year or more to complete. Sizes vary and, being a man's prize possession, canoes are handed down from father to son. In every village through which we passed at least one, and often more, of these craft were to be seen under construction amidst a carpet of chippings. A further threat to the trees indeed and the threat increases as the population grows.

Hola is well known for its irrigation scheme started by Mau Mau internees of the local prison and now a flourishing source of rice, cotton and other crops. Subsequently another and even larger scheme was opened near Burra. Unlike Burra, however, Hola is more of a town with identifiable streets and the very beginning of a traffic problem. It is here that a second dam complex was envisaged by the Tana River Development Authority.

We spent a couple of hours in the ramshackle town topping up ourselves with beer and 'coke' and our water cans with what was purported to be pure water from the irrigation scheme. The stuff emerged from a tap in the local garage — if that meant anything at all. There were a number of badly-constructed concrete buildings in Hola plus quite a selection of bars, drapery stores and 'butcheries', the last displaying unattractive carcasses of meat crawling with flies. People were everywhere, drawn from their usual pastime of doing nothing to venture forth to watch us working. They congregated at the 'quayside' where we had drawn up the boats and some of us had to act as a rearguard to keep an eye on the contents and boats. Light-fingered they may have been, but the citizens of Hola made a colourful bunch all chattering away about the queer tribe that had arrived at their town. Staggering along holding, with Mary, a five-gallon drum of water my pride suffered grievously as we lurched by two women each carrying even larger containers of water *on their heads.* And they almost dropped them for laughing, not because their loads were heavier, but at the sight of a man helping a woman!

Another swift dose of urbanity and we were away again, pleased to be out of the stifling concentration of brown mud houses and fly-blown commerce. The countryside became greener; the undergrowth more lush. River birds called thicknees flitted ahead of us then froze on a twig, to speed away once more uttering plaintive cries. Two crocs slid, soundlessly, into the water from the bank. A fish leapt out of the water straight into *Habari* and a weaver streaked, in orange and yellow brilliance, across our bow. Banana plantations, some of their stalks clasping green fingers of fruit and small red tassels, alternated with sentinel ranks of maize to clothe the shore while the perpendicular earthen banks bared their tree-root teeth in eternal grins.

We made our last overnight encampment beneath a copse of mango trees close to the village of Handampia. We never saw the village, but were visited by the head man and his family — including his wife — who bade us welcome. His children helped us carry our provisions ashore and collect firewood so we invited them all back for supper. It was pleasant to be able to entertain an African woman usually left out of such social affairs.

We made good progress again the fourth day in spite of a faulty spark plug in *Charity* and Karen — who had recently joined us from Nairobi — falling out of *Habari,* but it was late afternoon before we passed the village of Wenje, a mile or two above Kipendi.

The open country suddenly contracted and thick jungle closed in to the river's edge. We killed the engines and took to long-neglected paddles, gliding through mirrorglass water. A flight of pelicans sailed, purposefully, towards a dying sun.

We found a campsite virtually besieged by baboons and warthogs; alive with the evocative cry of the fish eagle and the chatter of monkeys. Situated on a double bend of the river, within sight of Kipendi village, the only eyesore — and that only temporary — was the huge bloated carcass of a not-long-dead elephant in midstream upon which hordes of crocodiles feasted.

Even after only four days of being on the move to be, once more, in an organised environment with more or less civilised amenities like earth closets, simple washing facilities and tents pitched in a straight line came as not too unpleasant a shock. For the first time I began sleeping beneath canvas for the sole reason that a tent provides support for the erection of mosquito nets and the Kipendi breed of mosquito was ravenous; our bare legs were devoured by these pests which, if swatted, smeared us with our own blood.

I speak for all members of the expedition when I say that Kipendi will be remembered as the camp, not only of the animals but of the Pokomo people. Even before we arrived the vehicle group had built up a relationship between themselves and the tribal villagers. They came each morning not only to look at us, but help with the camp duties and offer us their simple friendship. We began to know their names, their activities and their prospects. Whenever Richard went into the thickets to build a hide he would be accompanied by a couple of earnest youngsters; when I made a wood-collecting sortie I would find a bevy of children at my heels, and it was sometimes even difficult to go to the lavatory without a hand-maiden.

Morning greetings between our new-found friends and ourselves developed into a ritual, one that was repeated a thousand-

245

fold thereafter on jungle tracks, on river banks and wherever a new contact or re-contact was made. *Jambo!* would come the hearty greeting to evoke an equally cordial reply *Habari!*, and then we were all into a question and answer game concerning each other's health, affairs and destinations. Many of the Berber peoples of the desert have the same custom and it is one I find intensely attractive for, in our modern world, there is little time for such courtesies between strangers — even if there was the inclination.

It was plain that the Tana, and in particular, the state of the Tana, was the chief concern in *their* affairs. That the river was at its lowest ever by virtue of the lack of rain and the action of the dams at Kinderuma proposed a direct threat to their livelihood and, indeed, their lives. This concern is reflected in the songs and dances of the Pokomo, the manner in which they bless their canoes before commencement of a journey as well as their natural affinity to the Tana's waters. Perhaps the answer hid behind a question of priorities or maybe something could be achieved by the harnessing of more streams and tributaries to the river in its upper reaches. However the point of our survey was to lay bare the problems for man and beast, not to solve them.

As well as those of Kipendi we were also to meet the good citizens of Wenje, the district centre. They must have known of our close proximity on their own account, but the fact that John Axford, Sue and Gilbert happened to be 'processing' that village prior to our arrival clinched it. The chief and his son invited themselves to 'dinner' the first evening though they finally arrived in time for breakfast next morning explaining that elephants had barred their path and so had had to turn back. And the excuse was not so lame as it sounds for we too were to discover the scrubland path between the two villages to be liberally inhabited by elephant, buffalo and rhino. Attacks — particularly by buffalo — on lone travellers were not infrequent and a number of Wenje inhabitants had met their end as a result. It was noticeable that, from Wenje onwards, African foot travellers were never to venture far without a spear in their hands.

Fascinating though these contacts with the Pokomo people had been, it was a first contact with big game that gave the edge to Kipendi. Our very first night we were to see some fourteen elephants tiptoe down to their drinking place on the Tana close to where our boats were drawn up. Most of us were asleep, but the two zoologists were as nocturnal as some of their specimens. They woke me up and the word got around so that, before long, some score of human eyes were watching them.

The African elephant is larger than the Indian species. A bull weighs up to six tons and stands twelve feet at the shoulder, yet they can move unbelievably quickly. They are highly intelligent creatures and have a life span — if allowed it — of about sixty years. It is not universally known that when an elephant has lost his last set of teeth or they have grown too worn to chew, a young bull will often keep fierce guard over it. Elephants show a responsibility towards one another that goes far beyond the protection of a cow or calf. And although they normally ignore other animals there have been cases of two bull elephants standing guard over and protecting a blind buffalo or similarly afflicted beast. When he drinks the elephant sucks the water into his trunk and then blows it into his mouth and down his throat. The babies use their mouths, quite often lying on their sides in the water, to do this. All elephants are inordinately fond of water. They bathe every day if they can and are very noisy bathers in contrast to their uncanny silent movement on land. It must be admitted that they are frequently destructive in their eating habits. They will push over small trees, eat a few leaves and wander on.

Another night we were able to observe, by the light of a full moon and through the image intensifier, a herd of forty zebras work their way slowly and with infinite caution down to the river for *their* drink. It was an incredibly wonderful sight, but we had to lie very still for one sound and they would have disappeared in the twinkling of an eye. The zebra is, together with the giraffe, a distant relative of the hippo though, unlike either, they are known to suffer heart attacks if frightened. In East Africa there is the common variety and a species known as Grevy's, slightly taller with larger ears and narrower stripes. As we watched each animal complete its fill they would raise a head, listen and then saunter off so that, for more than half an hour, there was a constant coming and going to the watering place.

I participated in a number of night observation stalks in the dense forest behind the camp. On one we caught a glimpse of an elephant in a thicket and waited, hopefully but in vain, for the animal to emerge. To go in after it would have been dangerous particularly as we had been told that a family of buffaloes lived there. A dozen bushbuck flitting across a clearing rewarded us, however, their beautifully marked bodies with a white underside flowing with a movement that was a joy to behold. Bush babies we saw too, but not for the shooting on this occasion, and a civet, a long-bodied, wiry-coated animal as large as a medium-size dog though looking more like a cat.

Returning to camp we froze at the sound of snapping twigs expecting something of the calibre at least of a black rhinoceros to emerge. Instead a tiny dik-dik, barely a foot high, stood in the middle of the path as though hypnotized, then suddenly raced into the cover of the trees followed by his mate. They never go singly, these dik-dik; perhaps because they are so small and defenceless each acts as sentinel for the other. Richard, accompanying us with his inquisitive camera, managed a fine flash photograph of a nightjar on its ground-floor nest of dead leaves. Mesmerized by our torches the bird simply sat there allowing us to tiptoe right up to it.

We were now in the territory of the Mangabey and Colobus monkey, two primates of the monkey family the observation of which was one of the zoological objectives of the expedition. Another was sighting of the Pels Owl which some of us had optimistically reported as seeing. However, Ken was too fastidious a person to go in for half-measures so a whole night he spent across the river lying up in his tent watching activity in the thick jungle. A single night he found quite enough, returning somewhat white around the gills for it had been an unnerving experience. But he reported the sighting of Mangabey. This crested grey monkey is found only along the Tana river and resembles the long-tailed, more general variety, except for the pointed tuft on the top of the head. It feeds on fruit in the trees or on insects on the ground and alters its social habits accordingly. The Colobus is another somewhat uncommon monkey, or at least the breed that lives along parts of the Tana. They are jet black in colour with a magnificent white mantle, white face and white-tipped bushy tail. All their lives they seldom descend from the trees. However, it was the red variety that is the rarer and was another object of our quest.

Tony too spent much of his time hidden deep in the undergrowth at all hours of the day and night examining snakes and beetles, though once finding himself surrounded by eight elephants with young, his only concern was that of being late for supper. He spoke of crickets as big as a man's fist, but I refused to believe him until I found two of these harmless and non-jumping monsters in my rucksack while repacking it one evening.

For the subsequent leg of the journey three of us chose to walk the eighty-odd miles to the next campsite at Hewani, our special assignment being the location of the two rare brands of monkey as well as the Pels owl all of which were reputed to have haunts close to the Tana's banks. The trio concerned were John Richardson, Sandy and myself. That I was not at my walking best I was aware; one ankle sprained and the other poisoned but a spell away from the boats was an attraction I was unable to resist.

Hardly had we set out, unarmed but laden with bulging rucksacks, when we bumped into a herd of elephants. John, attempting to photograph at close quarters a mother and baby, upset the equilibrium of the mother to the point when we had to beat a very hasty retreat. But it was the moment that our erstwhile companions were lost from view that I cut a new notch in my yardstick of African experiences. Here we were, just the three of us, alone, weaponless, intensely ignorant of the hazards of the African wilds. All around, unseen but undeniably present, was an unbroken frieze of beasts of the jungle, river and bush. Here was the most abundant and varied life still existing on earth; we were surrounded by imminent death; the horns of rhino and buffalo and elephant, the teeth and fangs of crocodiles and snakes, the claws of the great cats. A score of emotions licked the pit of my stomach: excitement, insecurity, alarm and, yes, fear.

It was, however, a day hence before I experienced my own private close encounter with giant beasts. John and Sandy had gone off to spend the evening with a game warden who had materialised out of the forest earlier that day and I volunteered to stay behind and hold the fort, albeit one small bivouac.

Left to my own devices I built up the fire and waited. And never have I felt so alone in my life. Lonely no, alone yes. And there is a difference. Loneliness is a gradual melancholic emotion; being alone in such circumstances can build up into something approaching stark terror. Tripping down to the river to refill a bucket with water I found a monster crocodile leering at me and a quartet of hippos staring fixedly. Before they reluctantly sank out of sight the expressions were a now-there's-only-one-of-you-isn't-there look. I returned, chastened, to the tent and attempted to cheer myself up with the prospect of three tinned treacle puddings for supper and a bottle of lager that John and Sandy might bring back with them later.

Throughout the hot day the elephants had been musing and swaying in some cool recess of the forest, but now they began to rouse themselves and drift to their feeding grounds like great grey shadows, their bodies moving through the undergrowth so gently that the only sound was the faintest whisper of leaves rustled by a tiny breeze.

But if those elephants moved quietly this was not the case with their evening banqueting activites. A herd of them grazed their way in line abreast, like a fleet of battleships, towards me munching raucously and pulling great chunks out of the bushes. On top of this the nocturnal noises of the jungle turned to full volume, each howl, squawk and scream a drumbeat of menace. The hairs on my neck again rose to attention. From the direction of the Tana my riverine companions got into the act with a chorus of belches and farts that defy description.

The trouble was I couldn't *see* anything. I am something of a man of action. Let me see the foe and I'll have a go at him. I searched the night shadows till my eyes ached, but nothing moved. The fire shrank to a glow; to replenish it would mean a lone walk towards those evil noises which was out of the question. Frantically I blew on the dying embers and raised a tiny flame to kindle a spark of courage within my breast. A military maxim from my past came to the rescue with a clarion call to action. *To attack is the best form of defence.* The first of the elephants loomed out of the darkness. I picket up a faggot that had burst into flame, wielded it about my head, uttered a banshee howl last employed in my one and only World War Two bayonet charge, and hurled myself at the oncoming foe. I felt better now. My tormentors were phantoms no longer. I knew where I was going.

The big tusker was too intent upon stuffing his face with trunkfuls of fodder to notice me at first. Then it looked around, perceived a kind of miniature King Kong figure emitting strange sounds fast approaching, opened wide his eyes in disbelief, turned turtle and bolted. A thunder of hooves, a smashing of undergrowth and, what is more, the whole herd was routed. To consolidate my triumph I flung my smouldering faggot at the retreating elephantine rump and had to spend the next hour extinguishing the jungle fire I started.

I would say here and now that my reactions are not to be recommended to anyone in a similar situation. Remaining quite still would have been a wiser course.

John and Sandy's return long after midnight was like the commuting of a death sentence. But what was left of the night was anything but tranquil. We lay, zipped into our tents, listening uneasily to the elephants grazing on palm right up to our guy-ropes. Any moment I expected a great foot to descend through the canvas onto our prostrate bodies which goes to show how little I know about elephants. In the morning we discovered that one of them had sucked dry a whole bucket of water that we had positioned by the tent entrance in readiness for our morning tea. Regrettably it was the treated water, strained and dosed, which meant we had to go through the whole process again. The day before I had covered myself in confusion by accidentally drinking a whole bottleful of the *wrong* water — stuff straight from the disease-ridden Tana — and John envisaged all sorts of horrific results.

We left following a delayed breakfast and a session of first aid and surgery in which John had the odious task of extracting about a pint of pus from my poisoned ankle which hurt abominably. We moved south via an ox-bow, where the river had changed course, with commendable rapidity but still with some caution. Here and there were tiny communities of Pokomo peoples living in stockaded acres of cultivation and *chambas*. In a hollow we came upon the spore of what Sandy took to be a leopard. These animals are very rarely seen, being frequently nocturnal. Their favourite food is baboon and there were plenty of these about, yapping at us at frequent intervals. Another cat we kept our eyes peeled for was the cheetah for these, though elusive and fast, hunt by day. Nearing the village of Baomo a confusion of tracks nearly led us astray, but a charming black lady stoically undertaking a man's job of re-roofing a house directed us with such graceful gesticulation that her rush of Swahili, or whatever, was superfluous.

In spite of steadily eating our way through the tinned rations our packs remained consistently heavy though, on the credit side, we were rarely without the reassuring presence of a tribesman who would appear conveniently in the most unlikely places whenever we were having trouble with our outdated map. From dense jungle to banana plantation, from river bank to bushland we marched making good progress in spite of my lameness. Twice we were

251

provided with an armed escort; a fellow-traveller of the jungle who would insist upon accompanying us carrying his spear at the ready, appalled at our own lack of weaponry. They asked for nothing in return for this service but were very appreciative of the cigarettes or boiled sweets we were able to offer them.

We would have been more than appreciative ourselves for their protective measures one early afternoon when we made the brief acquaintance of a wounded rhino. It happened in a thick-set portion of jungle bordering the Tana. The thicker the undergrowth the more care we applied to our progress and the three of us had dutifully — and to expeditionary instructions — noted our respective climbable trees even as we entered the forbidding gloom. We were walking parallel to the river, but some fifty yards from it, when Sandy, who was leading, raised his arm to bring us to a halt and state of instant readiness. It was I who saw the animal first; its hind quarters appearing from behind a palm clump. 'I think it's an aardvark, I'm not sure,' I said in a voice not my own. John and Sandy were better at the animal recognition game. 'It's a bloody rhino!' they exclaimed in unison. 'Quick. Drop rucksacks and up your tree. Hurry!' This put the wind up me to such an extent that I was unable to disentangle myself from my harness and while struggling to do so we failed to make the silent getaway intended. Like the silver cymbals of a military band the tin mug and mess-tin strapped to various buckles clashed as if for the opening bars of 'The British Grenadiers' and the rhino, not surprisingly, wheeled about with some rapidity. As I finally shook off my rucksack I glimpsed the beast's head lowered for the charge; saw the great horn point at me, turned and ran.

The crackle of undergrowth and low-pitched impatient snorts drove me forward on winged feet. My private tree became the single goal at the further end of a vortex of my life. Heavy breathing came from my left and from my right and, the next instant, the three of us were struggling up the same trunk. I had beaten John to it by a short head to scramble into the slender boughs neck and neck with the agile young Sandy.

From a safe height we looked down to see the bewildered beast hurl a ton of itself beneath us and all saw the spear wound in its flank. The Black Rhinoceros is a solitary animal and a vegetarian, but will charge and overrun anything — even a train — that its poor eyesight is able to make out.

252

The danger passed we descended a little sheepishly and re-shouldered our discarded loads. But hardly had we moved more than a hundred yards when, rounding a bend, we found ourselves cheek by jowl with the same iron-clad bottom. Recognition — by us — was instantaneous and, once more, we took off, this time in all directions. But climbable trees had become scarce and I had to run all the way back to the river before I could find one. Behind us the big rhino could not quite make out what was going on. He remained perfectly still, ears cocked, grotesque head raised, nos-trils wildly dilated as he searched the wind. Uttering a couple of dismissive snorts, looping a stringy tail over its rump, the beast trotted away at a slinging, zig-zag pace through the trees and out of our lives.

In this manner, blundering from one minor disaster to another, we amateur trackers progressed through the riverine jungle. The wonder is that we didn't get lost though this was difficult since we had a wide and visible river to follow. Several times we crossed the Tana by dug-out canoe, an operation that required nerves of steel and an ability to remain absolutely motionless, neither quality of which I possessed, a deficiency that invariably brought about a soaking. Sometimes it was our tent that provided overnight accommodation but more often the local tribespeople would guide us to a village for a more original sojourn in their straw and mud guest-huts. These were not always quite up to Hilton standard but at least they had us feeling more secure from jungle predators.

The two species of monkey we found in plenty and were, duti-fully, photographed but the Pels owl evaded us. At least it did for the duration of the trek though, reunited with the main body of the expedition at Hewani, one of our members, searching the trees above the tents for a mango snack — Alison was *always* hungry — perceived the elusive quarry sleeping peacefully on a top branch.

Hewani camp was not without its shortcomings. Mosquitoes for instance. In spite of elaborate precautions and all manner of Heath Robinson defences their stuka-like attacks struck home. Snakes were another, the only really dangerous one we saw appearing in my tent. And our lavatory beside the Tana. Romantic perhaps, but perilous, too, if you were in a hurry at night and missed the cliff path leading to it.

Hewani was also a clump of mango trees amongst a bristling sea of palms, their trunks grey and straight like factory chimneys, the

253

evening cry of a bird that sounded as though it had swallowed a lawnmower and the morning throb of frogs amongst the dew. Best of all was the prospect of sparse but interesting game and the close proximity of a new Tana tribe — the Orma Galla.

Waterbuck were our first visitors. They took a wrong turning and a small herd of them found themselves amongst the tents. Realising their mistake they leapt the slop pits and vanished. Another, more regular visitor, was a Catholic priest who, on his second visit brought a baboon-ravaged dog that John was persuaded to operate upon. Otherwise our visitors were black and two-legged, emanating from Hewani village, round the bend of the river, and the Orma village, some two miles distant.

The Orma, a part of the Galla tribe, live intermingled among the three Pokomo subtribes. They are tall and slender, with thin faces, long noses, long narrow skulls and narrow shoulders — all vertical dimensions it will be noticed — which description fits, of course, the Masai with whom they are related. Whereas the Pokomo men dress in, basically, Western-style shirt and trousers, or perhaps a more brightly coloured *kikoi* (a cloth wrapped about the waist), Orma men favour gaudy, toga-like apparel, often a strikingly self-coloured blue. In the case of women it is the Pokomo who favour bright cloths (vivid-coloured body wraps called *kanga)* while the beautiful Orma women wear mostly black — embellished, however, by hand-beaten aluminium bangles on the upper arm.

Tribal policy dictates a practice of cattle-owning instead of cultivation. The Orma are less nomadic than formerly; at some places they inhabit separate villages as was the case near Hewani though also they occupy special 'wards' of Pokomo villages.

I was the first member of the expedition to visit the Orma village. I went there by tractor at the invitation of an African plant engineer from Weme who was reinforcing the village well. The community had given up their nomadic habits ten years previously finding the district to their liking, but chose to stick firmly to themselves. The village was an intriguing sight, the houses contrasting strongly with the mud-daub of the Pokomo. These were tall and round, built of grass thatch laid over a series of frames of withy bundles bent over and fixed at either end. They were beautifully made; veritable little cathedrals of straw and the interiors were even more remarkable.

254

Invited into a couple of them I struggled through the doorway slit of the first to behold the intricately woven frame lashed at the joins by thin vines. There is very much more room in these houses than their exteriors suggest and the floor was spotlessly clean. A double bed, raised from the floor and of almost four-poster construction, took up a third of the space and its 'springs' were leaves of the phoenix palm. Animal skins formed the mattress. Various items of 'furniture' and ornaments like raffia gourd holders and shelves containing curling photographs of respected relatives or ancestors gave the house a home-like quality. The second house I saw was similarly fitted though its entry slit was narrower and protected by a curtain of dried grass. I was told that each house lasted for five or six years after which a replacement would be commenced close to the old.

I watched one under construction — by the women of course — and was informed that it was being built for a couple not yet married. My informant gleefully explained that the wretched bride and bridegroom would have to remain indoors until they could produce proof of consummation of the marriage, all food and the necessities of life being passed to them through the doorway in the meantime.

From a group of Orma warriors I purchased a spear to take home for my young son and quickly raised the commercial instincts of the village. Within half an hour of my return to camp the first of the spear and bangle salesmen and saleswomen arrived and, thereafter, there was seldom less than half a dozen Orma around our tents. With everyone short of money we devised a system of barter; spears and bangles for lemonade powder and bars of soap with which we were plentifully endowed. Palm wine was all too easily procurable too. The best 'brew' comes from the phoenix palm, the sap of which is fed into gourds where it is allowed to ferment as a milky fluid. It must be drunk fresh — if drunk at all — for after very few hours the stuff goes sour. Here was another scourge of the forest for, the removal of sap eventually kills the tree, in this case the fine, long-stemmed phoenix so called because it is invariably the first tree to grow following a bush or forest fire.

Being the penultimate base camp of the expedition and the last to be supported by the vehicles with luxuries like laboratories, survey and investigatory work went ahead with renewed vigour. In the zoological field Andrew, Karen, Sandy, Raj and Ken were out in the forests or on the Tana all hours of the day and night. I joined one river night-observation voyage, drifting downstream in silence equipped only with head torches and the image intensifier. A moon, wearing a yashmak of cloud, was only one of many eyes that dolefully gleamed at us from everywhere as we listened for tell-tale noises of the creatures of darkness. Some were spider's eyes, some were crocodile eyes and others we knew not what. Andrew had learnt his lesson in the night when he mistook a crocodile for a spider so treated every little pinpoint of light with respect. Most of the river eyes this night were those of crocodiles, many quite small and, by the end of our nocturnal drift, we had caught five of them. Baby crocodiles have all the attributes of their elders and betters, but scaled down to size. The largest specimen we caught was about two feet long and their snapping ability was considerable as an embarrassing rent in Andrew's trousers was to testify. A few inches to the left and he might have forever lost his manhood. When caught they make evocative little cries which are intended to call their parents to their aid. We allowed three of the objecting offspring to go and held onto only two for further study.

With a great clatter of sound a flock of Haddada Ibis flew out of a bunch of ghostly trees which, in turn, set off a drumbeat of hooves from a hidden herd of buffalo who suffered even more of a fright than we did.

All these sounds were faithfully recorded on tape as were both sights and sounds in all daytime incursions in the forests. A safari was made to Lake Biliso, ten miles to the west, where drinking buffalo were observed and, later, Sandy and Andrew were to come face to face with one at point blank range. Each backed away from the other in a prolonged moment of pure drama. Many hippo were seen and counted near Mziwa on a 'dead' bend of the Tana that still contained water. My dugout capsize disgrace at Mnazini was avenged when John and Robert, between them, upset theirs in much deeper water.

We all had noted the extent of the cropping of vegetation as we proceeded down the Tana, but small mention has been made of more specific botanical tasks that formed part of the general survey. With the help of Samuel Paul Kibua, a bright young Tanzanian from the East African Harbarium in Nairobi who was with the expedition for a period, we continued to identify species

256

of plants and classified the predominant types of trees, bushes and grasses. Even the analysis of hippo dung came into it for the establishment of their food pattern in different regions. At Hewani the vegetation showed a marked difference in texture and type with the influence of the Indian Ocean now making its presence felt.

Bats were either more numerous at Hewani or blinder than elsewhere for our nets caught more. Most flew into captivity at dawn or dusk. Bats are rabies carriers so Sandy and Ken had to take precautions when handling live specimens. Distribution and density of all birds was painstakingly maintained though Hewani was to be the last base camp where Lorio and Joseph were able to mount specimens in the field. This was also the camp of the millipedes and one in particular, a character known as 'Harold' who was as long and as thick as a slow-worm, made himself at home in the 'kitchen' throughout our stay. Charles determinedly continued searching the Tana for differing strains of fish and some unexpectedly interesting species were caught. All were of the smaller variety, the Tana not being a 'big fish' river. Charles obviously was a fish-fancier in more ways than one, frequently having to be restrained from consuming his samples!

It was from Hewani camp that I was able to spend a day with the Tana Pox Team to see how they operated. Their survey had commenced at Garissa and was to end at Garsen, the two largest 'towns' on the Middle and Lower Tana. Garsen was, in fact, just six miles downstream so my investigation of John Axford's activities took place just in time. The district centre of Weme was the location for the day's blood-taking and I was given a lift there, with Sue and Gilbert, on the bonnet of the medical Landrover which was laden with supplies.

One sees the strangest sights in these tiny African communities. Often the most bizarre activities are carried out so naturally that it is not until later that the penny drops, so to speak, and the event is savoured against a European notion of behaviour. Where, in a respectable English village, could you see, for instance, a woman happily extracting *jigga* flea eggs from the big toe nails of her old grandfather sitting in the dust of the roadside? (These fleas are picked up by walking barefoot in sand and the eggs are deposited in the crevices behind toe nails. I was to unearth one from my own foot and Tony ended the expedition with at least half-a-dozen.) And where, in Britain, would you find the local barber shop and beauty parlour installed beneath a tree? Two women, hammering away with a pestle and mortar, were having their hair plaited in rows across their scalps while another young lady — remarkably beautiful, extremely pregnant and wearing a kind of 'shortie' nightie in brilliant orange and pink — was having *her* hair turned into a tight pagoda on the back of her head.

Because of pre-consultation with the district health authorities the team was expected and upward of two hundred souls were awaiting our arrival in the village square. The chief was amongst them and he greeted us gravely. He then announced to his flock — most of whom were no more than onlookers — the sequence of events, the reasons for them and the benefits — including the pot of gold at the end of the rainbow: the issue of a vitamin tablet. A queue was formed and Gilbert took names and particulars of all donors. Between them John and Sue syringed out the blood, applied a plaster, popped a tablet into expectant mouths and the job was done. Most of the donors were children and the snow-white plaster on their bare upper arms became a badge of one-upmanship. Most rural Africans are children at heart and, amongst the adults, I could see expressions of indecision crossing many a face as both men and women wrestled with temptation. Some surrendered to come forward sheepishly for treatment and the pill.

While we packed up the open-air surgery John told me of a few of his earlier experiences. Some of the village dispensaries and clinics were relatively speaking, of a high order. Others were not, but Kenya is progressing fast in the treatment of health in its more backward territories. I have already alluded to types of diseases and afflictions revealed in our survey and the Tana Pox Team spent a lot of time dealing with ailments far removed from Tana Pox. As in all the poorer countries of the world a hard core of prejudice is present that only education can eradicate.

The week was all too short as they all were. Again it was time to go. We were nearing the end of the journey and within very few days were drifting into the mangrove swamps below Ozi. Here among elephants, leopards, hippo, crocodiles and a myriad crabs and mosquitoes, we made our last camp. After three months of living cheek by jowl with the creatures of the wild my earlier terrors had sunk to simple respect. Happily I would lie in or out of my sleeping bag beneath a majestic ceiling of stars listening to the coughing of nearby lions and the eerie cry of bird and beast. Of all animals only the buffalo could strike fear in my heart. It was an animal that would kill without mercy or reason, that had been the scourge of every incursion into the leafy wilderness.

Ozi lay within the sound of the rollers of the Indian Ocean; was affected by tides and lapped by waves and salt water. Disease was rampant in the tiny muddy creeks while persistent rain gave us a picture of yet another side to the Tana's character. The heat was sticky but an occasional sea breeze offered relief.

Nigel and I journeyed down the last miles of the Tana sitting astride bags of rice in a dugout canoe paddled by local tribesmen. An elephant, taking a morning drink, flapped its ears at our approach and withdrew. Two hippos blew jets of water into the air, snorted and submerged. We hardly noticed them. Then the Tana widened to impressive proportions and around the many thousandth bend the coconut palms and thatched roofed houses of Kipini village appeared together with a handful of *dhows* drawn up on a beach that belonged to no river.

We swept into water that slowly turned from rusty brown to a universal grey as the Tana's blood stained this tiny corner of the Indian Ocean and was lost forever.

Appendix
WAYS AND MEANS INFORMATION

Chapter 1
(Trekking a Ghost Highway in Canada's Northwest Territories)

Tour Operators for trekking part of the old Canol Road include:
Rainbow Adventure Tours Ltd,
Box 72,
Dawson City,
Yukon,
Canada, YOB 1GO

Twickenham Travel Ltd,
84 Hampton Road,
Twickenham TW2 5QS
Accommodation at Old Squaw Lodge can be arranged through Mr Sam Miller at Box 2940, Yellowknife, NWT, Canada, XOE 1HO.
Useful Books: Backpacking In North America by Hilary & George Bradt (Bradt Enterprises).
Tourist Offices in London: Canadian High Commission. Commercial Division (Tourism).

Chapter 2
(Travelling by Horse in the Dakotas of the USA)

Historical information about the Medora-Deadwood Stage Line can be obtained from: The South Dakota State Historical Society, Memorial Hall, Pierre, SD, USA.

Applicants wishing to join the annual Fort Seward Wagon Train should contact: Fort Seward Inc, PO Box 244, Jamestown, ND, USA.

General advice about North and South Dakota may be obtained from the US Department of Commerce, US Travel Service, 22 Sackville Street, London W1X 2EA.
Useful Books: Story of the Great American West (Reader's Digest)

Chapter 3
(Desert Travel About the Sahara)

Tour operators arranging Nile felucca voyages include:
    Explore Worldwide Ltd,
    31A High Street,
    Aldersot,
    Hants, GU11 1BH.
Tour operators arranging Atlas Mountain trekking include:
    Explore Worldwide Ltd,
    Sherpa Expeditions,
    131A Heston Road,
    Hounslow,
    Middlesex TW5 0RD.

    Exodus Expeditions,
    All Saints Passage,
    100 Wandsworth High Street,
    London SW18 4LE.
Tour operators arranging Sahara safaris include:
    Encounter Overland,
    271 Old Brompton Road,
    London SW5.
Useful Books:
The Sahara by Jeremy Swift (Time-Life Books)
In Search of The Sahara by Quentin Crewe (Michael Joseph)
Forbidden Sands by Richard Trench (Murray)
The Land of Egypt by Jasper More (Batsford)
Tourist Offices in London:
    Egyptian State Tourist Office,
    168 Piccadilly,
    W1V 9DE

    Moroccan Tourist Office,
    174 Regent Street,
    W1

    Tunisian Tourist Office,
    7A Stafford Street,
    W1

Chapter 4
(Mountain Travel in Morocco, Nepal and South America)

Tour operators arranging treks in the Atlas Mountains include:
   Explore Worldwide Ltd,
   Sherpa Expeditions,
   Exodus Expeditions
Tour operators arranging treks in the Himalayas include:
   Mountain Travel (Pvt) Ltd,
   PO Box 170,
   Kathmandu,
   Nepal.

   Kulu Valley Treks,
   West Himalayan Holidays Ltd,
   66 Hungerford Road,
   London N7 9LP

   Explore Worldwide Ltd,

   Encounter Expeditions,

   Sherpa Expeditions,

   Andrew Brock Ltd,
   10 Barley Mow Passsage,
   Chiswick,
   London W4 4PH.
Useful Books:
Collins Guide to Mountains by John Cleare (Collins)
Mountaineering by John Cleare (Blandford)
The Complete Guide to Hiking & Backpacking by Andrew Carra
(Winchester Press)
The Backpacking & Trekking series by Hilary & George Bradt
(Bradt Enterprises)
The Himalayas by Nigel Nicolson (Time-Life Books)
Kathmandu & The Kingdom of God by Prakash Raj (Lonely
Planet)
A Guide to Trekking in Nepal by Stephen Bezruchka (Sahayogi
Press)

A Trekker's Guide to The Himalayas & Karakoram by Hugh Swift (Hodder & Stoughton)
Tourist Offices in London:
Moroccan Tourist Office,
Peruvian Office of Tourism,
10 Grosvenor Gardens,
SW1.

Chapter 5
(Driving the Historic Highways of Asia and Northern North America)

Tour operators arranging travel/trekking in the Karakorams include:
Exodus Expeditions
Tour operators arranging travel in Sinkiang, China, include:
Study China Travel,
Rose Crescent,
Cambridge, CB2 3LL.

Occidor Ltd,
10 Broomcroft Road,
Bognor Regis,
West Sussex, PO22 7NJ.
Useful Books:
A Trekker's Guide to The Himalayas & Karakorams by Hugh Swift (Hodder & Stoughton)
An Insight & Guide to Pakistan by Christine Osborne (Longmans)
The Gilgit Game by John Keay (Murray)
Where Men & Mountains Meet by John Keay (Murray)
Fodor's Guide to Islamic Asia (Foder/Hodder)
The Silk Road by Jan Myrdal (Gollancz)
Milepost (Alaska Northwest Publishing Co, Box 4 EEE, Anchorage, Alaska, 99509, USA)
Alaska Travel Guide (241 West 1700 South, Salt Lake City, Utah, 84115, USA)
The Canadian Rockies Guide by Brian Patton & Bart Robinson (Devil's Head Press)
Tourist Offices in London:

China Travel Centre,
4 Glentworth Street,
N1.

Canadian High Commission,
Commercial Division (Tourism),
Canada House,
Trafalgar Square, SW1.

US Department of Commerce,
US Travel Service,
22 Sackville Street, W1.

Chapter 6
(Luxury Rail Travel in India's Rajasthan)

Tour operators arranging travel on the Palace on Wheels:
Wings/OSL Ltd,
Travel House,
Broxbourne,
Herts, EN10 7JD.

Speedbird Holidays,
Alta House,
152 King Street,
London W6 0QU.
Central Reservation Office:
Rajasthan Tourism Development Corporation,
Chandralok Building,
36 Janpath,
New Delhi,
India.
Useful Books:
Fodor's Guide to India (Fodor/Hodder)
India by James Elliot (Batsford)
Tourist Office in London:
Government of India Tourist Office,
7 Cork Street,
W1X 2AB.

Chapter 8
(Expeditionary Travel in East Africa)

Enquiries concerning expeditions should be made to:
  The Expedition Advisory Centre,
  Royal Geographical Society,
  1 Kensington Gore,
  London SW7 2AR.
Useful Books:
Expeditions & Exploration by Nigel Gifford (Macmillan)
Tourist Office in London:
  Kenya Tourist Office,
  13 New Burlington Street,
  W1.

General

Useful Books:
The Traveller's Handbook (Future/WEXAS)
Off The Beaten Track (Wilton House/WEXAS)
The Asian Highway by Jack Jackson & Ellen Cramton (Angus & Robertson)